THE
CHAMBERLAINS

THE
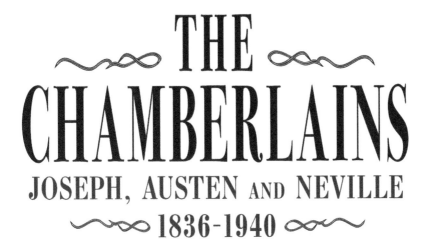
CHAMBERLAINS
JOSEPH, AUSTEN AND NEVILLE
1836-1940

ROGER WARD

FONTHILL

Fonthill Media Limited
Fonthill Media LLC
www.fonthillmedia.com
office@fonthillmedia.com

First published in the United Kingdom and the United States of America 2015

British Library Cataloguing in Publication Data:
A catalogue record for this book is available from the British Library

ISBN 978-1-78155-447-0

Typeset in 10.5pt on 13pt Sabon
Printed and bound by CPI Group (UK) Ltd, Croydon, CR0 4YY

This book is dedicated to the memory of my wife of fifty-one years, Robin Ward, born in Matamata, New Zealand, on 10 August 1939, died in Edgbaston, Birmingham, on 10 April 2014. For their support in the completion of this work, I am grateful to my son and daughter, Mathew and Victoria Ward, and to my friend and neighbour, Anita Shah.

Contents

Preface

Dynasties have long been a feature of British politics and, although less marked than in the past, have continued to the present day. Until well into the twentieth century, such family progressions tended to be based primarily on landed wealth with its concomitant territorial influence. The Chamberlains were an outstanding exception, their wealth and influence urban-based and derived from manufacture and commerce. From the time that Joseph Chamberlain entered Parliament as MP for Birmingham in 1876 until the death of Neville Chamberlain in 1940, there was always one but more usually two Chamberlains in the House of Commons. Moreover, all three Chamberlains operated at or near the apex of British politics, serving in an astonishing range and number of ministerial offices, including the Chancellorship of the Exchequer, the Foreign Secretaryship and finally the Premiership, in the person of Neville—an office which Austen had on several occasions spurned.

The record of the Chamberlains is by any standard remarkable. In contrast to four contemporary Prime Ministers—Balfour, Asquith, MacDonald and Churchill—the Chamberlains never lost a parliamentary election throughout their time in Parliament. For sixty-four consecutive years there was a Chamberlain in the representation of Birmingham, their unique urban citadel. Joe shaped the politics of the city of which he had been a dynamic, modernising mayor, wrenching it from the Liberal left into the Conservative and Unionist camp and establishing what has been widely seen as a 'benevolent despotism'. Upon his demise he bequeathed the leadership of the city to his two sons, but especially to Neville, who replicated his career in a number of respects.

Given the prominent role that Joe and his two sons played in the politics of their era, it would be strange if controversy had not dogged their footsteps. Joe in particular polarised opinion. To Gladstone he was 'the greatest blackguard I have ever come across'; to devoted followers, such as Leo Amery, he was 'the British Bismarck', the Empire's best hope for a secure future. Neville, too, courted intense controversy over his adoption of a policy of appeasement towards the continental dictators, which many have seen as a prime cause of the Second World War. Austen, in many respects the third-string of the Chamberlains, was a less controversial figure, but was not without both detractors and admirers. Consensus concerning the roles of all three remains elusive.

Joseph Chamberlain

Early life and career

Much of Birmingham's economic success in the nineteenth century can be traced to the efforts of enterprising immigrants, drawn to the city by its manufacturing and commercial vibrancy and the skills of its workforce. Prominent among them was John Sutton Nettlefold, manufacturer of wood screws, who moved his business from Holborn, London, to Birmingham in 1843. While visiting the Great Exhibition at the Crystal Palace in 1851, Nettlefold encountered an automatic screw-making machine which had the potential to revolutionise the industry. For a sum of £30,000 he purchased the British rights from its American inventor and, to maximise the machine's potential, set about building a state-of-the-art factory at Heath Street in Smethwick, alongside the canal and the railway and a few miles from the Birmingham town centre. For help to finance this considerable enterprise, Nettlefold turned to the husband of his sister Martha, his brother-in-law, Joseph Chamberlain. Chamberlain was the proprietor of a long-established and solidly successful shoe-making business situated in Milk Street in the City of London. Chamberlain was the sixth member of the family to serve as master of the Cordwainers Company, one the City's ancient guilds, and was an exemplar of the tenacious middle order of society which James Mill described as 'the glory of England'. Both Nettlefold and Chamberlain were Unitarians, and inter-marriage and mutuality in business were common among members of this small and close-knit Nonconformist sect. The rising profits of his cordwaining business encouraged Chamberlain to respond positively to Nettlefold's request and in so doing he transformed the lives and prospects of his family.

Joseph Chamberlain and his wife had eight children: five sons and three daughters. The eldest was, like his father and grandfather before him, named Joseph. He was born in July 1836 in still rural Camberwell south of the Thames, but ten years later the family moved north of the river, to Highbury Place in Islington—hence the name of the great Gothic house Chamberlain was to build on the outskirts of Birmingham in the late 1870s. Joseph had attended University College School in Gower Street, Bloomsbury, which was much favoured by Nonconformist families. There he excelled in Mathematics and French, both of which subjects were to prove invaluable in his business career. Destined to follow in his father's footsteps, Joseph left school at sixteen to work alongside craftsmen at the workbench before moving upstairs to be inducted into the mysteries of management. Such was his father's confidence in his progress that in 1854 he decided to despatch young Joe to Birmingham to represent his investment in his brother-in-law's firm. Shortly after his eighteenth birthday in the autumn of 1854, Joe duly arrived at the freshly opened New Street Station and took a cab to Frederick Street to his new lodgings. Frederick Street was close to Five Ways on the Georgian edge of the Calthorpe Estate in Edgbaston and within easy walking distance of the Broad Street offices of the firm where much of his life in the coming years would be spent. Also joining the firm at this time was his cousin Edward Nettlefold, whose flair for engineering would complement Joe's for marketing and accountancy; together this younger generation would help fulfil all John Sutton Nettlefold's hopes for his new enterprise. The firm's chief accountant commented that 'money was made quickly after Master Joseph came'. Within little more than a decade, Nettlefold and Chamberlain had become the pre-eminent manufacturers of screws and fastenings and one of the Midlands' largest employers, their workforce expanding to over 2,000 workers by the time Joe Chamberlain left the firm in 1874.

The Birmingham in which the young entrepreneur began to make his way stood in marked contrast to the metropolis which he had left behind. The fourth largest in England with a population numbering 233,000 in the 1851 census, this was a town predominantly of workshops, mostly—but by no means exclusively—producing an astonishing range of products in metal. White's directory of 1850 listed no less than 527 distinct occupations. Birmingham's skilled craftsmen commanded relatively high wages by national standards. There were none of the cellar dwellings which disfigured other industrial towns and cities, but there were nevertheless clusters of court-type dwellings—back-to-backs—dating largely from the previous century, where poorer families lived and died in squalor. Although Birmingham society contained a substantial middle-class core, it lacked a corpus of wealthy businessmen such as characterised the mill towns of the north, and this lack was reflected in its urban design and service provision, which generally lagged behind towns such as Manchester. Apart from New Street Station—which boasted the largest glass and iron structure in Europe—its list of notable buildings began and ended with Hansom and Welch's Town Hall, a noble neo-Roman structure which served as both a meeting place and a concert hall and which Chamberlain was later to grace many times over in his career.

When Chamberlain arrived in 1854, the Crimean War was in full swing and the town booming. The Army was hastily expanded and perhaps two-thirds of the guns, plus many thousands of bayonets, swords and numerous other militaria were manufactured in Birmingham. Gunmakers especially prospered and sixteen firms were combining to form what would become one of the most iconic of Birmingham companies, Birmingham Small Arms (BSA), with its ultra-modern factory at Small Heath. The first of a series of battles against the Russians had been fought and won at the Alma in September, a victory commemorated by the naming of no less than eighteen streets and terraces at this time under construction in the town. Birmingham's industry continued to prosper throughout the 1860s and into the early 1870s, attracting new immigrants to the town and enriching many of its entrepreneurs. A remarkable feature of the Birmingham economy was the prominence of families drawn from two of the smallest of the Nonconformist sects, the Quakers and the Unitarians, which according to the religious census of 1851, together constituted less than 5 per cent of the town's church and chapel attenders. Long excluded from the universities, the professions and state employment, Nonconformists had concentrated their energies on commerce and industry to the benefit of themselves and the nation alike.

In a community so dedicated to business, Chamberlain's entrepreneurial talents marked him out as 'a sharp and ready man', in the words of a contemporary journalist and historian, Thomas Anderton.[1] His growing status was reflected by Samuel Timmins' invitation to contribute to his compendium of articles on Birmingham industries, *Birmingham and the Midland Hardware District* (1866). Chamberlain's main theme was less a description of manufacturing wood screws than a manifesto praising the rise of the factory in Birmingham against the still predominant workshop culture. In contrast to the degraded conditions which prevailed in many workshops, Chamberlain claimed that factories provided 'healthier work places, regularity of hours, economy of labour, increased demand, lower prices and at the same time higher wages'. In the case of his own firm,

> [...] the principal works are very large, the shops airy and well lighted. The hours of work are 60 per week and Saturday afternoon is kept as a half-holiday.[2]

Chamberlain stood out among his contemporaries as a spokesman for modern industry—the very model of a modern manufacturer. His rising status in the business community was equally marked by an invitation to become a director of Lloyd's Bank and membership of the Council of the Chamber of Commerce.

By the time Chamberlain made his first foray as an author, he had become well integrated into local society. The Unitarian community included a number of Birmingham's most prominent families—the Nettlefolds, Kenricks, Martineaus, Russells and Oslers—their growing prosperity testified by the replacement of the New Meeting in 1862 by the impressive Church of the Messiah in Broad Street. There, Chamberlain served as Treasurer and taught Sunday School and evening classes. His chief biographer, Peter Marsh, writes disparagingly of his manner as a teacher, which he describes as having 'a nasty edge, sarcastic and sneering'—a style not uncharacteristic of later performances on many a political platform and in the House of Commons.[3] Chamberlain was also active in promoting leisure and educational activities at the firm's works in Smethwick. For his own amusement he joined the Edgbaston Debating Society, which met regularly in the Hen and Chickens Hotel in New Street and whose membership included most of the rising young businessmen and professionals of the town. In 1858 he served as Treasurer, in 1859 and 1860 as Secretary, in 1861 as Vice-President and in 1863 as President—a post to which he was re-elected on an honorary basis in 1896, by which time he was a minister of state at the height of his powers and influence. It was in the Debating Society that he honed his forensic skills, though as a speaker he was initially unimpressive. His early efforts, wrote his official biographer J. L. Garvin, 'reeked of the lamp'.[4] It was at this time that he adopted the trademark monocle, not only compensating for a defect of vision in his right eye but also useful as a kind of theatrical diversion. The orchid button-hole would follow later, a narcissistic touch which paid tribute to his passion for gardening.

In 1861 Chamberlain married Harriet Kenrick, daughter of Archibald Kenrick of Berrow Court, Edgbaston, a hollow-ware manufacturer with premises in Spon Lane, West Bromwich. A wedding gift of £4,000 from Harriet's father enabled the newly-weds to buy a substantial red-brick villa which still stands in the Harborne Road. In the following year their first child Beatrice was born and in October 1863 a son, Austen. When Harriet succumbed to puerperal fever, Chamberlain was left distraught. Fortunately, he had not only the support of the Kenrick family, but also that of his own. In 1863 Joe senior, confident in the progress of Nettlefold and Chamberlain, sold his London business and moved his family to Birmingham, settling in Moor Green Hall close to King's Heath and a few miles from the town centre. Links between the Chamberlain and Kenrick families were reinforced by the marriage of Chamberlain's sister Mary to William Kenrick and of his brother Arthur to Louisa Kenrick. The bereaved children at least had the comfort of growing up surrounded by a cohort of aunts, uncles and cousins. The arrival in Birmingham of the Chamberlain family marked a considerable expansion in its economic involvement. Three of Joe senior's sons initially joined Joe in the firm, but their arrival was ill-received by the firm's patriarch, John Sutton Nettlefold. Joe senior solved the problem by purchasing a brass-manufacturing business, Smith and Chamberlain, which provided an occupation both for himself and his sons. All four—Richard, Arthur, Walter and Herbert—would become successful entrepreneurs and Arthur especially came to be regarded as one of the outstanding professional managers of his day. The business profile of the Chamberlain family loomed large in the history of the Birmingham economy in the late nineteenth and early twentieth century.

Five years after the death of Harriet in June 1868, Chamberlain married her nineteen-year-old cousin, Florence Kenrick. Children came at regular intervals: Neville, born in 1869 was followed by three daughters, Ethel, Hilda and Ida. Tragically, Florence also died in childbirth in February 1875, leaving Chamberlain intensely distressed once more. Her untimely death came during Chamberlain's crucial second year as Mayor of Birmingham and it was only with great difficulty that he was dissuaded from resigning. Shortly after Florence's death, his mother Caroline died only a year after the passing of his father. These devastating blows destroyed what remained of Joe Chamberlain's religious belief. His background and family tradition placed him firmly in the world of Nonconformity and it was in the image of a militant Nonconformist that he first embarked on a political career in the late 1860s; yet this was a familial rather than spiritual connection and he in fact had no sympathy for sectarianism of any variety for its own sake.

In 1874, the Chamberlain family sold their interest in the Nettlefold and Chamberlain partnership for £600,000, of which Joe's share is reckoned to have been £120,000. After twenty industrious and successful years as a 'screw king', he was free to concentrate on the passion that would obsess him for the rest of his life. His interest in politics had so far been slow to ignite and existed only in the margins of his busy career. Given his Unitarian background, his sympathies lay entirely with the Radical Left. The civic disabilities under which Nonconformists had long suffered had inevitably coloured their attitudes to Church, state and aristocracy. During Chamberlain's lifetime these barriers were being steadily demolished, but they left a legacy which persisted. Hostile to the established Church, the landed aristocracy embedded in the House of Lords and, at the

Republican extreme, to the Crown, Nonconformists looked primarily to the radical wing of the Liberal Party to further their political interests. As a commercial community, too, they approved of the political economy of liberalism as exemplified by Gladstone's free trade budgets of the 1860s.

Into politics

Birmingham was comparatively late in acquiring the institutional status that a city of its size and economic importance merited. Not until the passage of the Reform Act of 1832 did it acquire representation in Parliament, its two MPs only increased to three in 1867 and it was only granted a Charter of Incorporation, establishing a mayor and elected council as the principal locus of government in the town, in 1838. The grant of city status, too, was delayed until 1889. Its natural representatives in Parliament were mainly local men who had earned themselves a respectable reputation as businessmen and members of the community. Thomas Attwood, banker; the Scholefields, father and son, merchants; and the Muntz brothers, manufacturers—all had been involved in the Birmingham Political Union's vanguard role in the agitation for the reforms of the 1830s. This sequence was broken upon the death of George Muntz in July 1857. John Bright, recently defeated at Manchester following his courageous opposition to the Crimean War, was immediately canvassed by a committee of leading local Liberals and duly returned to Parliament unopposed. Joe Chamberlain would have been among the enthusiastic audience in October 1858 to hear Bright address his constituents for the first time, pledging himself to campaign for a further instalment of parliamentary reform. Bright, a moral force and inspirational orator, would in spite of his detachment from the life of Birmingham exercise great influence there until his death in 1889. Initial support for Bright was not, however, unanimous. By no means did all Radicals share the Manchester School outlook in matters of foreign policy and Empire. Influential Nonconformist preachers, such as George Dawson and Dr Robert Dale, belonged to a school of thought which looked more to Palmerston than to Cobden and Bright. Expressing strong support for suppressed nationalities such as the Hungarians, Poles and Italians and for revolutionary leaders such as Kossuth—who received a rapturous welcome in Birmingham on the two occasions on which he visited the town—they embraced war against Russia, 'a prison-house of nationalities'. Evidence suggests that the newly-arrived Chamberlain leaned towards the Palmerstonian position. In a two-day debate organised by the Debating Society, he made a speech criticising Bright's opposition to the war and later, at a dinner in George Dixon's house, he challenged

Bright's opinion that Gibraltar should be restored to Spain. In April 1859, when Bright and Scholefield came up for re-election, Chamberlain was one of a number of local men who supported the candidature of Thomas Dyke Acland, former Tory MP for Somersetshire, who was soundly beaten.

Whatever doubts were harboured about Bright's attitude to foreign policy, these paled into insignificance when set against the achievement of parliamentary reform in 1867, for which Bright was popularly regarded as chiefly responsible. As he began to enter more actively into politics at about this time, Chamberlain was too shrewd to set himself against the great tribune of the people.[4] Matters of foreign policy aside, the difference between the politics of Bright and the emerging Chamberlain mainly revolved around the role of the state. Whereas Bright was critical of the encroachment of the state in social and economic matters, Chamberlain recognised its potential power and aspired to harness it in the interests of radical reform. Whereas Bright was hostile to trade unions, Chamberlain was sympathetic to their aspirations and sought to forge relationships with their leaders. Bright's brand of radicalism was old; Chamberlain's was distinctly new.

The Second Reform Act of 1867 brought the issue of education to the forefront of politics. Now that many working men had been enfranchised, it became necessary, as Robert Lowe famously put it, 'to educate our masters'.[6] Over and above political considerations were economic imperatives, namely the need of British industry and commerce for a literate workforce. If Manchester was a pioneer in this field, Birmingham followed close behind. In 1866 George Dixon was elected Mayor of Birmingham and, in a by-election caused by the death of William Scholefield in 1867, he was also returned to Parliament. Much of the rest of Dixon's life would be dedicated, both nationally and locally, to issues of education. In March 1867, he convened a meeting at his home in Augustus Road, Edgbaston, which resulted in the formation of the Birmingham Education Society (BES). Among those present were the Chamberlains, father and son, who both made generous contributions to the society's funds. The objective was to pay the school fees of children whose families were too poor to afford them. Research carried out by Jesse Collings, the Honorary Secretary of the Society and one of Joe Chamberlain's closest friends, revealed how extensive this need was.

Although the BES raised sufficient funds to pay the school fees of some 5,000 children, it quickly dawned on leading members that voluntary effort could not alone solve this problem. In October 1869, with the objective of campaigning for a free, compulsory, rate-aided and non-sectarian system of education, the National Education League was formed (NEL). Once again, Dixon was the principal instigator and he acted as chairman and parliamentary spokesman. Chamberlain was elected to be his deputy. Since much of Dixon's time was taken up with parliamentary affairs, it was Chamberlain who effectively ran the League, which grew rapidly, accruing over 140 branches and twenty affiliated Trades Councils by the autumn of 1870. Until it was disbanded in 1877, the NEL—with its monthly journal, innumerable pamphlets, publications and nationwide public meetings—was one of the most vigorous pressure groups of the century. Unfortunately, and in spite of Dixon's efforts to the contrary, the League became identified with sectarianism and it was as a militant Nonconformist, hostile to the established Church and Anglican predominance in the provision of schools, that Chamberlain became chiefly identified in the public eye. The Gladstone Government's Education Act of 1870, piloted through Parliament by the tough ex-Quaker William Forster, fell well short of the League's demands and generated opposition from the League. Chamberlain demonstrated his fundamental disdain for the Liberal Party by instigating challenges at by-elections. Writing to John Morley, a fellow alumnus of University College School and editor of the *National Review*, Chamberlain declared that he was out 'to smash up this gigantic sham called the Liberal party'.[7] But the Government stood firm and rejected compromise.

Education was the issue which drew Chamberlain into politics, but his appetite inevitably grew and he was drawn deeper into political activity. In preparation for the anticipated franchise reform in 1865, Birmingham Radicals, prompted by the architect and surveyor William Harris, formed the Birmingham Liberal Association (BLA). Dubbed the 'caucus' by Disraeli, the BLA was a pioneering organisation which would be widely imitated in subsequent years. Each of the town's fourteen wards elected a committee, which then sent representatives up the pyramid to an executive committee; this made the BLA a broad-based organisation responsive to leadership, which would for the ensuing two decades, monopolise Birmingham politics. At the annual general meeting of what was initially the '300' and ultimately the '2,000', the agenda for the coming year was set. These were great set-piece occasions, usually graced by the oratory of John Bright. The BLA first demonstrated its effectiveness in the general election of 1868. A principal objective of Disraeli's Reform Act had been to enhance Tory chances in the mainly Radical towns and cities by introducing what his critics denounced as 'fancy franchises'. Birmingham, for example, had been given an additional representative, but each elector was restricted to two votes which could be 'plumped' on a single candidate. In the so-called 'Vote as You're Told' election, the BLA organised the distribution of Liberal votes in such a way as to ensure the return of its three candidates, Bright, Dixon and Muntz, with the two Tories trailing in their wake. If Bright was their chief inspiration in national politics, that role in local politics was filled by George Dawson, one of the most charismatic preachers of his day. His weekly sermons at his non-sectarian Church of the Saviour had an idealistic and highly secular flavour, drawing on his day-to-day observations of the lives of the townspeople. Dawson preached 'the civic gospel', calling on the wealthy and influential people who crowded into his church to tackle the many deficiencies which blighted the town. In the 1860s, Birmingham was still suffering from the aftermath of more than a decade of parsimonious government by the 'Economists', a group of petit bourgeois councillors who, under the leadership of Joseph Allday, had come to dominate the Town Council. The main objective of Allday and his followers had been to keep down the rates, with the unavoidable consequence that public services and amenities were starved of funds. Allday retired from the council in 1859 and in the 1860s, under the cautious leadership of the local scale-maker Thomas Avery, some of the worst of Birmingham's environmental deficiencies began to be tackled. But the pace of improvement by no means satisfied Dawson's disciples. One by one, some of the wealthiest and most prominent men of the town were cajoled into standing for the Town Council, ousting the 'shopocracy' of the Allday era. It was inevitable that, sooner or later, caucus leaders would come knocking on Chamberlain's door. He agreed to stand for election to the council in St Paul's ward, in the heart of the jewellery quarter in November 1869 and was duly returned unopposed. By the time he came up for re-election in 1872, however, he was an established figure in the town and this time came under Tory attack for his alleged irreligious teaching, Republicanism and support for Sunday work. In a close contest he defeated Ellis, a foreman in a local factory, by sixty-two votes. His forthright leadership of the NEL singled him out as the man who could best fulfil Dawson's dreams and in the following year he was elected Mayor, the first of his three successive terms. So began what has frequently been described as the most famous mayoralty in British history. Chamberlain has long been credited with carrying through a transformation of what has generally been characterised as a backward town, environmentally deficient and lacking in social and cultural amenities. There was, of course, more than a hint of propaganda in this appraisal, the chief propagator of which was John Thackray Bunce, editor of the *Birmingham Daily Post* (*BDP*) and a leading literary figure in the town. Bunce was closely integrated into the Liberal elite and one of Chamberlain's inner circle, which met regularly in the library of his house, 'Southbourne', in Augustus Road. In his official *History of the Corporation of Birmingham*, which was commissioned by a small group of councillors including Chamberlain and his brother-in-law William Kenrick, Bunce poured scorn on Allday and the

Economists and contrasted their period of hegemony with Chamberlain's enlightened leadership. His convincing interpretation laid the basis for the identification of Chamberlain as 'the father of modern Birmingham', a perception which has persisted to the present-day.

The famous mayoralty (1873–1876)

Resourceful, headstrong and supremely confident, Chamberlain exploited to the full the executive potential of his office and transformed the mayoralty into something proximate to a dictatorship. Rejecting the rising chorus of Tory complaints of 'caucus despotism', Chamberlain revelled in the powers that the monopoly of elected BLA offices gave him. Writing to Collings in the spring of 1875 following a Liberal clean-sweep in the Board of Guardians election, he exulted: 'This is Liberal tyranny with a vengeance and completes the thing beautifully'.[8] Chamberlain's theory of politics was a simple one: winner takes all. The time was ripe, for behind him stood a remarkable group of dedicated Radicals and with enthusiastic backing from eloquent and influential divines such as Dawson and Dale, the Congregational leader. At this time, too, the economic trends were favourable and ratepayers more inclined to heed Bright's tentative advice that perhaps municipal government might be more 'expensive'.

Although Chamberlain's reforms penetrated into most areas of municipal responsibility over his two and a half years in office, three in particular stood out. The Corporation lacked assets and reform therefore could only be financed by increasing the borough debt and expanding the rate fund. Chamberlain's solution was to municipalise the town's two gas companies. Legislation already existed—of which a number of towns had taken advantage—facilitating the municipalisation of utilities, so resistance on the part of the gas companies was futile. There remained for Chamberlain to negotiate the terms and carry the council with him, which he did by fifty-four votes to two, following a brilliant exposition of the likely financial advantages. The purchase of the gas companies raised the borough debt by £2 million to £2½ million, but within a year the gas supply had been improved, the wages of gas workers increased and a sizeable surplus channelled into the rate fund. With such a triumph behind him there was little opposition to his next initiative, the municipalisation of the water companies. In this instance Chamberlain justified the policy in terms of public health. The existing water supply was both inadequate and insanitary, the source of much of the disease which blighted the lives of the inhabitants of the closed courts and disfigured central districts of the town. Municipalisation was carried through at a cost of £1,350,000 to the ratepayers.

The passage of a set of by-laws regulating building standards was a notable step on the road to improving the urban environment, but Chamberlain's next venture was aimed at rectifying at least some of the ills of the past. In 1875, Tory Home Secretary Richard Cross piloted the Artisans' Dwelling Act through Parliament. The Act gave municipalities powers of compulsory purchase with the object of clearing slums. Chamberlain was consulted by both Cross and Sclater-Booth, head of the Local Government Board, and Birmingham became the first town to formulate a large-scale plan under the terms of the Act. Chamberlain's Improvement Scheme covered some 90 acres of the central districts and entailed the destruction of a large number of insanitary and over-crowded courts. Under the scheme the new and aptly named Corporation Street would be driven through the area from New Street to Aston and would provide developers with the opportunity to acquire leases to build the offices, shops, restaurants and theatres in which the town was deficient. Chamberlain dazzled the council with his vision of Birmingham as the Midland Metropolis. On this occasion, however, he ran into much opposition. The designated area contained not merely slum properties, but soundly-built houses and business premises. Chamberlain stood accused of promoting a grand scheme of property development in the guise of slum clearance. Critics labelled the new street 'Rue Chamberlain', a satirical parallel with the work of Baron Haussmann in the remodelling of Paris. In addition, the scheme met ratepayer resistance. Its estimated cost of £1.5 million necessitated the imposition of a separate rate and, to make matters worse, by the time construction began on the New Street end in the late 1870s, the local economy was sliding into recession and the uptake of leases in Corporation Street slow. Not until the end of the century was the area completely developed, with a new County Court and the Victoria Law Courts helping to fill the remaining spaces. Controversy and criticism rumbled on, especially as the Improvement Committee declined to build municipal houses to replace the 800 houses destroyed, but ultimately approval of Chamberlain's most ambitious undertaking outweighed its censure.

These major schemes by no means represented the sum total of the improvements wrought during the Chamberlain mayoralty, which extended to paving, lighting, sewage disposal and tree planting. In 1874, Chamberlain laid the foundation stone of Yeoville Thomason's new Council House, which at last provided the Town Council with a suitably dignified home. In 1880, at about the same time that John Henry Chamberlain completed the great Gothic house 'Highbury' at King's Heath for the Chamberlain family, his fountain—commemorating above all Chamberlain's achievement in municipalising the water supply—was unveiled in Chamberlain Square, or 'Squirt Square' as the satirists would have it. This was a remarkable monument to a politician not yet fifty, only recently embarked on a new career in national politics. By this time, yet another Chamberlain-led achievement was transforming the Birmingham skyline. The Education Act of 1870 had set up elected school boards; these were supposed to implement the Government's objective of filling up the gaps which voluntary organisations had left in the provision of primary education. From its inception, education policy was heavily politicised, a battle-ground between Tory and Liberal, Anglican and Nonconformist. The Birmingham School Board consisted of fifteen members elected triennially in the same period as municipal elections, each eligible voter having fifteen votes. In the first election in November 1870, the BLA for once over-reached itself, putting up candidates for all fifteen seats. Its opponents concentrated their vote on only eight candidates and as result the 'Bible Eight'—seven Anglicans and one Catholic—gained a majority of one. The Radical minority set out to paralyse the board, using its control of the Town Council to block the necessary supply of rate-aid, an action considered illegal by the Court of Queen's Bench. The banker Sampson Lloyd, an Anglican and leader at this time of the Birmingham Tories, confided to his diary that

> [...] of all the public bodies of which I have ever been a member that Birmingham School Board was the most remarkable for bitterness, unfairness and personalities in debate.[9]

George Dixon alone he exempted from criticism. The consequence was that for three years little was achieved by the school board but, in the election of 1873, the BLA deployed its vote more effectively and secured a Radical majority which promptly elected Chamberlain as its chairman, at the same time as he was also chosen to be Mayor. Subsequent progress was rapid and soon new schools, to the distinctive designs of the Chamberlain and Martin partnership, were rising all over the town. This achievement was by no means the least of Chamberlain's contributions to the welfare of the people of Birmingham. The local historian, Victor Skipp, expressed what many Birmingham people must have been feeling at this time of dramatic development: 'high Victorian Birmingham really did bear some resemblance to a promised land, a holy city'. This sense of pride and satisfaction was reinforced when in 1890 Julian Ralph, a journalist writing for the American publication, *Harper's Magazine*, described Birmingham in a much quoted phrase as 'the best governed city in the world'. Both Chamberlain's mayoralty and his chairmanship of the school board came to an end in 1876. He summed up these three momentous years in a letter to Collings:

I think I have now almost completed my municipal programme and may sing *nunc dimittis*. The Town will be parked, paved, assized, marketed, Gas-and-Watered and *improved*—all as the result of three years' active work.[10]

He remained on the council until 1880 when he resigned following his appointment to Gladstone's Cabinet, yet the business of Birmingham always remained a central concern. His parliamentary influence was at the service of the city when local legislation was required and he was, more than any other single person, responsible for the incorporation and endowment of the University of Birmingham at the turn of the century. Chamberlain was not always immune to criticism and opposition in his adopted city, but his achievements there and rising stature in national politics earned him a priceless dividend—the support of the great majority of the electorate, which would last a lifetime and would even be passed on as a legacy to his sons.

Into national politics

The combined affairs of the NEL and of the Birmingham mayoralty and school board were insufficient to absorb all of Chamberlain's abundant energies. His activities brought him into contact with the world of Westminster, established his national profile and ignited the ambition to attach 'MP' to his name. A visit of the Prince and Princess of Wales to Birmingham in 1874, during which he surprised *The Times* by behaving as a perfect gentleman, destroyed the popular caricature of Chamberlain as the Red Republican. Yet there could be no mistaking his Radicalism. Through his friend John Morley and the *Fortnightly Review*, he proclaimed the following creed: 'Free Church, Free Schools, Free Land, Free Labour'. In Birmingham he fostered links with Labour leaders such as W. J. Davis of the Brassworkers Society, and bid for support by proclaiming his sympathy with trade union aspirations. Like other Birmingham Radicals, notably John Skirrow Wright, Collings and Dixon, he gave material support and encouragement to Joseph Arch's National Agricultural Union. His attempts to build a broad-based Radical movement prompted approaches from various constituencies. In the general election of 1874, a year of Liberal defeat, he accepted an invitation from local Radicals and the Trades Council to stand for Sheffield. Coming third behind two Liberals (Roebuck and Mundella) in a two-member constituency was a great disappointment, but turned out to be a blessing in disguise for both Chamberlain and Birmingham.

With Bright, Dixon and Muntz firmly installed in the Birmingham representation, an early vacancy seemed unlikely. A group of Chamberlain devotees with Bunce in the vanguard, however, put pressure on Dixon to resign and make way for Chamberlain. Dixon, who was worried about the health of his wife, succumbed to this pressure, though he later regretted it and expressed bitterness at the way he had been treated. He would later return to Parliament as MP for Edgbaston, but meanwhile he concentrated his energies on the work of the school board and on educational provision generally in Birmingham, doing great service to the city. In June 1876, Chamberlain was returned to Parliament unopposed, launching thirty-eight years of unbroken tenure which lasted until his death in 1914.

Introduced by John Bright and Joseph Cowan, Radical MP for Newcastle, Chamberlain made his first appearance in the House of Commons on 13 July 1876. Members who had not previously met him were surprised to observe that 'the Brummagem Robespierre' looked every inch a gentleman. His maiden speech a fortnight later on the subject of education, which he considered to be his special field of expertise, made an equally favourable impression. A second and longer speech, advocating municipal control of liquor sales on the Swedish model, followed a month later. Following the recess, all domestic issues were relegated to the margins, as 'the Eastern Question' erupted once again with the Russian declaration of war on Turkey in April 1877. Chamberlain at this time had few formulated opinions on foreign policy and was regarded by many as something of a 'little Englander'. He was content to take a lead from a man fast becoming his closest ally in the House and a boon companion outside it, Sir Charles Dilke, in whose house in Chelsea he frequently lodged before acquiring his own in Prince's Gate, near Hyde Park, in 1883. While Disraeli's Government took a pro-Turkish line, Gladstone, who had retired as leader of the Liberal Party in 1876, roared back into public life, denouncing Turkish atrocities against Balkan Christians. It was clear to Chamberlain that Gladstone and not Lord Hartington was the likely next Liberal Prime Minister and he adjusted his politics accordingly. He was equally aware of how weak and disunited the Radical contingent in the Commons was. With the model of the Birmingham caucus in mind and with the advice of its 'father', William Harris, he wound up the NEL, which had become too sectarian in its public image and set about planning the creation of a Liberal national caucus.

The National Liberal Federation (NFL) was launched at a meeting in Birmingham attended by some 100 delegates, mostly from Midland and Northern towns, on 31 May 1877. A notable *coup* was to persuade Gladstone to anoint it with his blessing. He was given a rapturous welcome upon his arrival in Brum, many workers being given a half-day holiday in his honour. In the evening he addressed an excited and heated audience in an over-crowded Bingley Hall, though it was made clear in his speech that it was the Eastern Question, rather than matters of party organisation, which was uppermost in his mind. He stayed with Chamberlain at Southbourne in Augustus Road, Edgbaston and left with a firm impression of the qualities of his host, who he reported somewhat ambiguously to his friend and colleague Lord Granville was 'a man worth watching'.[11] Even the most cursory examination of the structure of the NLF reveals how dominated it was by Birmingham Radicals. Until he entered the Cabinet in 1880, Chamberlain was President; Harris, Vice-President; and J. S. Wright, Treasurer. Frank Schnadhorst, who had been Secretary of the BLA since 1873, was appointed Secretary to an executive committee which also contained a number of well-known Birmingham Radicals. For the next decade and until he lost control in 1886, the NLF provided Chamberlain with a platform from which he sought to harry the Whigs and shape Liberal policy. The NLF lent plausibility to his claim to be the leading voice of Radicalism.

The remaining years of Disraeli's Government were a frustrating time for Radicals, as public attention focussed almost entirely on foreign and imperial affairs. Disraeli's apparent triumph at the Congress of Berlin in June 1878 was offset by the humiliating defeat of Lord Chelmsford's force at the hands of the Zulus at Isandlwana in January 1879 and by the disastrous entanglement in Afghanistan. While Gladstone railed against 'Beaconsfieldism' from his new electoral base at Midlothian in Scotland, Chamberlain impatiently looked forward to a general election which would surely sweep the Liberals into power. The dissolution of Parliament took place in March 1880 and the election duly followed in April.

For once, the election in Birmingham was hotly contested. With encouragement from the Conservative Central Office (CCO), the Birmingham Conservative Association (BCA) had been making determined efforts to improve its structures and break out of the obscurity imposed upon it by the monopolistic BLA. Lord Randolph Churchill, leader of 'Tory Democracy' and as ambitious a figure in his party as Chamberlain was in his, was taking an interest in Birmingham politics and it was he who recommended the candidature of Frederick Gustavus Burnaby. He was a major in the Blues and Royals—a fashionable regiment of the Household Brigade—adventurer and author of *A Ride to Khiva* (1876). At six foot four and reputed to be the strongest man in the British Army, Burnaby was well equipped to cope with the often violent nature of Birmingham elections. His rumbustious presence made for a lively election, but it was Burnaby's misfortune to be teamed with the Hon. A. C. G. Calthorpe, the shy and self-deprecating heir to the Calthorpe estate in Edgbaston, whose inadequacy courted derision and was savagely lampooned in the satirical press.

The result in Birmingham was never in doubt. In a list of five candidates, Burnaby came fourth and Calthorpe fifth, both trailing well behind the three Liberals, Muntz, Bright and Chamberlain. The latter was not a little disgruntled by his third place behind Philip Muntz, who was frequently a source of complaint within the Chamberlainite clique for his independent views; but such was the price Chamberlain paid for his adversarial style and facility for making enemies. The degree of jingoism that the swashbuckling Burnaby managed to evoke surprised Chamberlain, and opened his eyes to the popular enthusiasm which issues of foreign and imperial policy were capable of arousing. Characteristically, he and Burnaby ended the election on good personal terms, both men respecting the mettle of the other. Burnaby, however, did not live to break another lance with Chamberlain, losing his life at the Battle of Abu Klea in the Sudan in January 1885. His death was commemorated by an impressive obelisk erected in the churchyard of St Philip's Cathedral in central Birmingham, a defiant gesture in stone by local Tories who had at last absorbed something of the Burnaby spirit.

The government minister

The Liberal Party took office with a comfortable working majority over both Tories and Irish Nationalists. The business of Cabinet making was complicated on this occasion, since Lord Hartington was formally the Liberal leader, but expectation in both the country and the party was overwhelmingly in favour of Gladstone resuming the leadership. With great reluctance it was the 'Grand Old Man' that the Queen commissioned to form his second administration. In a bid for a place in the new Cabinet, Chamberlain wrote to *The Times* claiming that the NLF had played a key role in the Liberal victory, seizing sixty of the sixty-seven seats which its members had contested. Gladstone was, however, very reluctant to appoint to the Cabinet men who had not previously served in government, let alone one who had been a member of the Commons for less than four years. It was John Bright, himself a very reluctant recruit as Chancellor of the Duchy of Lancaster, who pressed for Chamberlain's inclusion, confiding to his diary the hope that Chamberlain's coming in would let him out.[12] Chamberlain was offered and accepted the office of President of the Board of Trade but failed to persuade Gladstone to upgrade it to the Ministry of Commerce, a move for which the Associated Chambers of Commerce had been pressing. Chamberlain's *alter ego*, Dilke, was appointed Under-Secretary at the Ministry for Foreign Affairs, but without a seat in Cabinet.

Gladstone's Cabinet was overwhelmingly Whig and aristocratic, seven of its fifteen members sitting in the House of Lords. Chamberlain could look for support only to Bright, but the old Radical detested office and took the first opportunity to resign in July 1882 following the British intervention in Egypt, rebuking Chamberlain for not following his example. The latter was left isolated until joined by Dilke, who was promoted to the office of President of the Local Government Board at the end of the year. Although detested by the Queen for his republicanism, Dilke was *persona grata* in high society in a way that Chamberlain was not. Staying at Dilke's house in Chelsea until he acquired his own, Chamberlain met many high-status figures both British and continental, including the Prince of Wales. He was not, however, seduced by Whiggery and plotted to shift the balance of power in the Liberal Party to the Radicals. The surest way to achieve this was, he believed, to campaign for the enfranchisement of rural labourers on similar terms to those accorded to urban workers in 1867. Such a campaign was firmly in the Birmingham tradition as laid down by Attwood and Bright. Leading Birmingham Radicals such as Wright and Dixon had long been active supporters of Joseph Arch's campaign to create the National Agricultural Union and raise the political consciousness of its members. Enthusiastically supported by Jesse Collings, recently elected MP for Ipswich, Chamberlain coupled advocacy of enfranchisement with a demand that allotments and smallholdings be made available to rural labourers—a policy widely mocked as 'Three Acres and a Cow'. In pursuit of these objectives, Chamberlain mounted a strident attack on the House of Lords. In a speech in Denbigh he declared, 'We have been too long a peer-ridden nation'. Agricultural labourers had been 'robbed of their land ... robbed of their rights in the commons ... robbed of their open spaces' and cheated, too, by the charity commissioners whom he accused of misappropriating endowments intended for the benefit of the rural poor. In the course of a series of speeches, Chamberlain lashed out at 'the insolent pretensions of an hereditary class', wittily comparing the Lords to potatoes whose best part was underground. Lord Salisbury, the Tory leader, was attacked as the spokesman of a class 'who toil not neither do they spin', while a speech in Birmingham at the time of the Bright Jubilee celebrations in June 1883 gave particular offence when he demanded to know, 'what ransom property will pay for the security which it enjoys'. His diatribes against the aristocracy and especially his use of the word 'ransom' provoked complaints from the Queen and magisterial rebukes from the Prime Minister. Chamberlain accepted that 'insurance' would have been a more appropriate term, but remained otherwise unrepentant. The general effect of his campaign was to establish his position as the leading voice of Radicalism, and his contribution to the third Reform Act of 1884, which enfranchised some two million rural labourers, should not be underestimated. One who was inspired by Chamberlain's 'Peers *vs* the People' campaign was an aspiring young Welsh solicitor, David Lloyd George.[13]

As a departmental minister, Chamberlain encountered both success and failure. Successes included an Employers' Liability Act, a modest attempt to provide compensation for workplace injuries; a Bankruptcy Act, which established a network of Official Receivers; and a Patents' Act, which was designed to both protect and encourage inventors. His Electric Lighting Act of 1882, however, has been generally accounted a failure. Reflecting Chamberlain's faith in municipal enterprise, the Act granted powers of compulsory purchase to municipalities but discouraged private investment. In Garvin's opinion, 'The Act retarded electrical development in the United Kingdom for more than a decade'. But the failure that hurt him most was the failure of his Merchant Shipping Bill. Ten years earlier, he had organised a protest meeting in Birmingham in support of the heroic efforts of Samuel Plimsoll, MP for Derby, to improve the lot of merchant seamen, several thousands of whom were lost at sea every year. In this Bill, Chamberlain sought to end abuses such as over-insurance, which enabled ship-owners to profit from the loss of ships and their crews. On the occasion of its second reading on 19 May 1884, he made a speech lasting four hours, a million copies of which were distributed by the NLF. It was to no avail. Like Plimsoll earlier, he met fierce resistance from the powerful shipping interest whose members sat on both sides of the House. In July, he was obliged to withdraw his Bill, though he had managed to pilot through the House minor measures of shipping reform, such as the Grain Cargoes Act. His sense of failure was compounded by the lack of support he had been given by Cabinet colleagues. A personal manifestation of the animus against him, in part due to dislike of his policies but also because of his social origins, was the 'blackballing' of his two brothers Richard and Arthur by the Reform Club, to which most Liberal MPs belonged. Chamberlain was not a man to forgive or forget such slights.

The early 1880s was hardly an auspicious time to be a Minister at the Board of Trade. Both trade and industry were experiencing a downturn and unemployment was on the rise, provoking civil unrest. One consequence was the emergence of interest groups adversely affected by foreign tariffs and bounties which demanded a reconsideration of Britain's commitment to free trade. The most important of these groups was the National Fair Trade League, founded in 1881 with the support of a number of Tory MPs and under the presidency of Sampson Lloyd MP, the Birmingham banker. The permanent officials of the Board of Trade were inveterate free traders and briefed their boss accordingly. There is no reason, however, to believe that Chamberlain at this stage of his career was seriously beset by doubts.

As a result, he made a series of impeccable defences of free trade, arguing that any departures from Britain's established policy would inevitably entail a rise in the cost of living which the working classes could ill afford. When the Birmingham Chamber of Commerce, which had criticised free trade in its evidence to the Royal Commission on the Depression of Trade in 1885, offered him its presidency in 1887, he refused on the grounds that 'I am entirely opposed to Protection in any shape or form'. It would be the some years before his anathema on the Birmingham Chamber of Commerce was lifted as his views shifted. Inevitably, when he himself turned full-circle, his earlier pronouncements would be dusted off and much quoted as evidence of his political inconstancy. It was ironic that Charles Ritchie, the Chancellor of the Exchequer in 1903, who did so much to scupper Chamberlain's plans for imperial preference at that time, was in the 1880s a leading fair trader. From the late 1870s, tariff reform was, in one or other of its guises, rarely off the political agenda. In the words of one historian, it became part of Britain's 'table talk'.[14]

Important as these foreign and imperial issues were, they were eclipsed by the conundrum posed by Anglo-Irish relations, which both perplexed and divided the Cabinet. Anger and discontent in Ireland was boiling over, resulting in an escalation of rural crime and terrorism. In 1880, Charles Stewart Parnell became leader of the Irish Nationalist faction at Westminster and instigated a policy of obstructing business. The Cabinet was torn between coercion and conciliation, the former favoured by the Chief Secretary, 'Buckshot' Forster, and his Whig supporters, the latter by Radicals who argued for remedial legislation. Gladstone wavered between the two alternatives, both of which were attempted without notable success. Chamberlain, recognising the key nature of the Irish problem in British politics, sought to broker an agreement with Parnell, using as intermediary Capt. William O'Shea MP, the husband of Parnell's mistress, Kitty O'Shea. This proved a miscalculation, O'Shea deceiving both men as to the intentions of the other. Gladstone shrewdly preferred to make contact with Parnell through Kitty O'Shea, though he later denounced the liaison once it became public knowledge in the famous divorce case in 1890.

It is amusing that a party which had come to power on the back of a fierce attack on Beaconsfieldism should itself have become embroiled in a series of foreign and imperial misadventures. The crushing of Zulu power encouraged the Transvaal to demand the return of its independence and when Gladstone's Government hesitated, the Boers resorted to force and defeated a small British force at Majuba Hill on 27 February 1881. Gladstone ignored those calling for a punitive expedition and decided on conciliation, a decision in which Chamberlain concurred. Boer independence was restored, but with strings attached by which the British asserted their control over Transvaal foreign policy—an ongoing source of friction which was later to have malign consequences.

If Chamberlain considered himself to be on the side of justice in South Africa, as he told a Birmingham audience, he was more bellicose in the case of Egypt, earning a magisterial rebuke from John Bright. Critics attacked the occupation of Egypt as a bondholders' war, one of the bondholders being Gladstone himself. What was intended as temporary turned into a long-term occupation with serious international repercussions. Relations between Britain and France worsened and British action may well have been the trigger for Bismarck's decision to launch a German bid for colonies in South West Africa in 1883. Egypt became a serious embarrassment for Gladstone's Government, which soon found itself embroiled in the Sudan. In January 1884, Gen. Gordon was despatched to the Sudan with instructions to carry through an orderly withdrawal of Egyptian garrisons. Whether it was because he had no such intention or because he became entangled in the war against the Mahdi, Gordon disregarded his instructions and became beleaguered in Khartoum, where he met his death on 26 January 1885. The Government had been hesitant to act and when a relief expedition under Wolseley was at last despatched up the Nile, it was two days too late to save Gordon. The public outcry was long and loud. Queen Victoria was incandescent and barely refrained from publicly labelling Gladstone, whom she detested and decried, as a murderer.

Parnell, who had been imprisoned in Kilmainham Jail, was released in May 1882 and Forster resigned in protest. Chamberlain was tipped as a likely replacement as Chief Secretary, but instead Gladstone appointed Lord Frederick Cavendish, brother of Lord Hartington and husband of his niece. Cavendish and his secretary Burke were murdered in Phoenix Park, Dublin, on 6 May 1882. The revulsion caused by these murders inevitably provoked a Crimes Bill and a further round of coercion. Chamberlain was not opposed to the concept, but argued that every reasonable concession must first be tried, advocating a further instalment of land reform and of local government and proposing the creation of a system of elected local councils culminating in a Central Board in Dublin, with powers to decide issues particular to Ireland. Contrary to later insinuations, Chamberlain made his opposition to Irish independence crystal clear in his speeches. Reform was not a stage on the way to Home Rule, but the means of rendering it unnecessary. In May, the Cabinet rejected his Central Board scheme, prompting him to resign. However, Gladstone's Government fell when seventy six Liberals failed to support it in the lobbies in the following month. In effect, the split in the Liberal Party had begun. A general election was not possible until completion of the radical changes in constituency boundaries made necessary by the Re-Distribution of Seats Act of 1885, which the Tories had insisted upon as a condition for allowing the Reform Act of 1884 to pass the House of Lords. A minority Government was therefore installed under Lord Salisbury pending a general election in November and December 1885.

While the Liberals, and especially the Radical wing, expected to profit from the enlarged electorate, the Tories anticipated greater support in urban seats as a consequence of the redistribution (which replaced the old list system in all but a minority of cases by individual constituencies). Since most towns and cities were divided on class lines, they could hope to win seats in middle-class areas. Birmingham came well out of the redistribution, thanks in part to the influence of Dilke at the Local Government Board, receiving an additional four seats. The BCA complained, not without justification, that the Town Council gerrymandered the boundaries in an attempt to dilute the middle-class vote. But, in general, the BCA was better organised and more optimistic about its electoral prospects than ever before. A notorious incident which had the effect of galvanising Tory supporters was the so-called Aston Riots. In October 1884, a Tory rally to be addressed by Churchill and Sir Stafford Northcote was held in Aston Park. The gathering was attacked by Liberal supporters, many of whom were in possession of forged tickets, and a series of ugly brawls took place. The BLA claimed not to be implicated, but there was a strong suspicion that Schnadhorst was behind the affair. Lord Randolph Churchill seized the opportunity to rail against the tyranny of the Birmingham caucus and moved a vote of censure against Chamberlain personally in the Commons. It was defeated, but a margin of only thirty-six votes left Chamberlain disgruntled at the lack of support from fellow Liberals. On the surface relations between Chamberlain and Churchill appeared venomous, whereas in fact the two had formed a friendship which, after the storm, was soon resumed. Nevertheless, Churchill was determined to invigorate Conservatism in Birmingham and headed the team of candidates who came forward to contest all of Birmingham's seven constituencies. Chamberlain eagerly anticipated an election in which he expected both Tories and Whigs to lose seats in the counties. In 1885, he published *The Radical Programme*, a compendium of articles by leading Radicals, which had previously appeared in the *Fortnightly Review*. The historian Peter Fraser described this as the first 'campaign handbook' in British politics and at the time it was dubbed by the Whig MP George Goschen as the 'unauthorised programme'.[15] Frequently understood at the time as 'socialism', the programme marked the peak of Chamberlain's reputation as a social reformer before he was inevitably by-passed on the Left by organisations more accurately described as socialist, such as the Socialist Democratic Federation and the Socialist League.

A setback to the Radical cause was the damage done to Dilke's reputation by a salacious and prolonged divorce case involving Donald Crawford MP and his wife Virginia, in which Dilke was named as co-respondent. Rumours that Chamberlain was involved in a conspiracy against Dilke, his one serious challenger as Radical leader, and that he may even himself have been a lover of Virginia Crawford may be safely dismissed. Not before 1892 did Dilke return to the Commons and when he did so it was as a Gladstonian Liberal, bringing to an end their close friendship. By that time, Chamberlain's relationship with John Morley, too, whose election for Newcastle in 1883 he had materially assisted, had also reached its conclusion, and not without recrimination and bitterness. Morley, like Dilke, had been seduced by Gladstone's charisma and became his firmest supporter on the issue of Home Rule for Ireland. Chamberlain often conveyed the impression that he was cold and calculating, even cynical, but this was by no means the whole man. He could be both passionate and emotional; or, as Lord Salisbury once observed, 'as touchy as Juno'. Slights were marked down for revenge but friendships were cherished. The loss of allies of the calibre of Dilke and Morley impoverished Chamberlain intellectually in the later stages of his career. In the next election, the Tories managed to field a candidate in each of Birmingham's seven divisions, all of which to one degree or another declared their support for Fair Trade—a reflection of how deeply this issue had penetrated the Tory Party. Their best chance of achieving victories lay in the Central and Northern divisions with their concentration of middle-class voters and it was there that they put forward their strongest candidates: Lord Randolph Churchill pitted himself against Bright in the Central Division, while Henry Matthews QC, a Catholic and rising barrister who had acted for the prosecution in the Dilke case, opposed William Kenrick in the Northern Division. The Liberals triumphed in both, Bright by 800 and Kenrick by 600 votes. The other five divisions comfortably returned Liberals, enabling the BLA to triumphantly declare, 'We are Seven'. Somewhat bizarrely, Chamberlain's majority of 5,419 in West Birmingham included a woman, Susannah Perks, who had somehow managed to get herself on the electoral register and was allowed to vote by a perplexed returning officer.

The general expectation that the Liberals would win a majority did come to fruition, but the result fell short of Chamberlain's hopes. The Liberals generally performed well in the counties where 'Three Acres and a Cow' had worked its magic. But Chamberlain lamented the absence of an 'urban cow', the promise of free education especially falling on deaf ears. He blamed the appeal of Fair Trade to working men at a time of depression and also Parnell's strategy of throwing the Irish vote behind the Tories. Nevertheless, the Liberals remained the largest party, with 335 seats. Intriguingly, however, the 249 Tories and the eighty-six Irish Nationalists exactly counterbalanced the Liberals. This situation was inherently unstable and gave Parnell plenty of room for manoeuvre. He had thrown his weight behind the Tories, partly because of emollient approaches from leading figures and partly because the Tories enjoyed an enormous preponderance in the House of Lords. It would soon become apparent that hopes of a Tory Home Rule Bill were quixotic, but with the Liberals reluctant to take power, something approaching a stalemate resulted.

Would the Liberals offer more? The Radicals led by Chamberlain held out the offer of reform, but few if any Liberal candidates in the recent election had declared support for Home Rule; Gladstone had not mentioned it and the Whigs were implacably opposed. Chamberlain's own attitude was hardening. On a personal level, he felt that Parnell had played him false and also harboured resentment against Cardinal Manning and the Irish Catholic hierarchy for first appearing to approve of his proposed reforms and then cancelling an invitation to visit Ireland. His suspicions of Gladstone's intentions mounted. While Gladstone denied having contact with Parnell, Labouchère, the Radical MP for Northampton and editor of *Truth,* was telling Chamberlain a different story.

The Irish question and the Liberal split

The political stalemate ended when, on 17 December 1885, Gladstone's son Herbert revealed to the press that his father was prepared to legislate for 'the creation of an Irish Parliament'. This, the so-called 'Hawarden Kite', signalled the fall of Salisbury's Government, which was duly defeated on an amendment to the address on 26 January 1886. Ironically, the amendment, calling for the provision of rural smallholdings, was drafted by Chamberlain and proposed by Jesse Collings. At the age of 76, Gladstone formed his third administration. The split in the party was already palpable. In the vote on the amendment eighteen Liberals had gone into the lobby with the Conservatives, while seventy-six had abstained.

Offered a place in the new Cabinet, Chamberlain could hardly refuse since Gladstone had not yet revealed his hand. The negotiations between them, however, exposed a growing personal antipathy. Absurdly, Gladstone offered Chamberlain the Admiralty and when the latter countered by requesting the Colonial Office, Gladstone made it clear that a Secretaryship of State was above his station. Having settled on a compromise—the Presidency of the Local Government Board—Gladstone further alienated Chamberlain by proposing to reduce the salaries of the two junior Ministers, Jesse Collings and Henry Broadhurst, who Chamberlain brought into office with him. Sir William Harcourt, the new Chancellor of the Exchequer, mediated and Gladstone's demeaning proposal was withdrawn. The dangerous gulf that was opening up between the two men was compounded by the appointment of John Morley as Secretary of State for Ireland. Morley had been an MP for less than three years, yet was appointed to an office withheld from Chamberlain in 1882 and a Secretaryship of State at that. Chamberlain felt both the slight and the severance of a close friendship.

Chamberlain occupied his new office for barely six weeks, his sole achievement being to issue a Circular requesting local authorities to fund public works to provide temporary work for the unemployed at a time of depression. The Circular has been praised as 'a benchmark in public policy', especially by social historians. As soon as it was clear, however, that Gladstone was preparing to concede a separate Parliament in Dublin which would entail the removal of Irish MPs from Westminster, Chamberlain resigned on 26 March together with George Trevelyan. Two weeks later, in a much-admired speech of four hours in the Commons, Gladstone introduced his Irish Home Rule Bill. What had clearly become a personal vendetta was amplified the next day when Chamberlain made his resignation speech, only to be interrupted no less than four times by Gladstone, who denied—falsely—that Chamberlain did not have the Queen's permission to refer to a proposed Land Purchase Bill which had been discussed in Cabinet but not yet presented to Parliament.[16]

In Gladstone's circle, Chamberlain was identified as the main source of the party's disarray. He was, Gladstone told Rosebery, 'the greatest blackguard I ever knew', and to Granville 'the Prince of Opportunists'. A contest now began between the GOM and the young Pretender, who at this stage had no intention of leaving the Liberal Party which, he calculated, would reject Home Rule, force Gladstone's retirement from politics and leave the way open for a new leader. In a letter to his brother Arthur, Chamberlain wrote:

> Either Mr. G. will succeed and get the Irish question out of the way or he will fail. In either case he will retire from politics and I do not suppose the Liberal Party will accept Childers or even John Morley as its permanent leader.[17]

Some Radicals encouraged his hopes of leadership, but believed this could best be achieved by supporting Gladstone's proposals which, as Labouchère put it, 'would clear the nest of these nuisances', the Whigs, 'a consummation that we all want'.

Chamberlain refused to be seduced by such an attractive vision. The die was cast. He had repeatedly declared himself to be against the separation of Ireland from Britain and he deeply distrusted both Gladstone and Parnell. He would do his utmost to destroy the Bill. The risks he ran were considerable. In a struggle for the soul of the party, he soon discovered just how formidable an antagonist Gladstone was. For many Liberals he was their political lodestar and commanded great credibility among the wider electorate. Chamberlain's erstwhile supporters began slipping away, leaving him to marshal a rump of Radical MPs. Nor did he dare to co-operate openly with either Whigs or Tories, though he was soon clandestinely in touch with both and especially with Churchill, whom he found more sympathetic than Hartington, who had many reasons of his own to bear grudges against Chamberlain. Given the drift of support in the party to Gladstone, he dared not openly call for the defeat of the Home Rule Bill. His tactic was to demand revision, his principal objection being to the ending of the Irish presence at Westminster, taken as proof of Gladstone's intention to progress to complete separation. Unfortunately, this held little appeal for many Liberal MPs, for whom the thought of no longer having to tolerate Irish obstructionists was the Bill's most attractive feature. Though he continued to advocate a programme of reforms for Ireland, he was also critical of the Land Purchase Bill on the grounds that it would impose a huge burden on British taxpayers, a criticism which met with greater support.

While Chamberlain struggled to keep his dwindling band of Radical MPs at Westminster up to the mark, he had also to struggle to retain control of his Birmingham citadel, without which his political career would come to an abrupt end. Even on his own turf he could take nothing for granted. The BLA was becoming factionalised and Chamberlain realised that its secretary, Schnadhorst, was working against him. The strength of Chamberlain's kinship network and the loyalty of important allies such as Dr Robert Dale, one of the country's most influential Nonconformists and J. T. Bunce were key assets. Dale spoke for many when he criticised Gladstone's treatment of Chamberlain, whom he felt had been unfairly singled out for abuse. But perhaps his greatest asset was the outspoken opposition to the Bill of John Bright who, unlike Chamberlain, could hardly be accused of unscrupulous ambition. Bright's credibility in Liberal ranks and in wider society, especially among Nonconformists, was comparable to Gladstone's. Throughout his long career he had demonstrated his sympathy for the plight of Ireland, but latterly he had become alienated by the incidence of terrorism and violence and by the obstructionist tactics pursued by Irish MPs at Westminster. He took to calling Parnell's party 'the rebel party' and distrusted Parnell personally, doubting that he would keep to any agreement arrived at. Although Churchill is usually credited with 'playing the Orange card' (mobilising the Protestants of Ulster against Home Rule), Bright was among the first to concern himself with the likely fate of Ulster, coining the phrase 'Home Rule is Rome Rule'. Although Bright refused to become associated with any of the competing factions, his opposition to Home Rule and his criticisms of Gladstone's handling of the issues became widely known and, in the view of some historians, Bright's influence on the course of events was greater than that of Chamberlain. His opposition was a tremendous asset for Chamberlain to exploit, especially in Birmingham where in 1883 the celebrations of Bright's service of a quarter century as a Birmingham MP had been remarkable.

On 21 April 1886, the BLA met in the Birmingham Town Hall to debate the issues. Although there was an overwhelming sentiment in favour of maintaining party unity, Chamberlain was conscious of murmurings of dissent within the ranks, which he came increasingly to associate with Schnadhorst. Defending his position Chamberlain dared not oppose Irish Home Rule in principle; nevertheless, he called for support for the revision of Gladstone's Bill, in particular for the retention of Irish MPs at Westminster as proof that devolution rather than separation was intended. He was also critical in detail of the Land Purchase Bill. Guided by Dale, the BLA expressed support for Chamberlain, but made it clear that Gladstone's leadership was not in question.

While the meeting of the Liberal '2,000' in Birmingham was a modest success, the meeting of the NLF in London on 5 May was a disaster. The mood was highly sympathetic to Gladstone. The leadership of William Kenrick—who had replaced Chamberlain as President in 1880—was repudiated and Chamberlain personally came under muscular attack, labelled 'a traitor' by one delegate to a round of applause. When the vote went overwhelmingly in favour of Gladstone's Bill, the six Birmingham members of the executive committee resigned. Birmingham's leadership of the NLF was at an end and with it Chamberlain's status as the leader and spokesman of Radicalism. The NLF moved its headquarters to London where, under Schnadhorst's guidance, it became a faithful Gladstonian organ. Chamberlain felt a great sense of betrayal but, just as the actions of the NLF had stiffened Gladstone's resolve not to amend his Bill, they did anything but weaken Chamberlain's. He continued to muster what support he could at Westminster, using a letter from Bright to boost the resolve of critics of the Bill at a meeting on 31 May. On the next day, he launched his attack on the Bill upon its second reading in the House of Commons. Several days of the most dramatic and confrontational debate in parliamentary history followed. On 9 June, the vote was called. Gladstone's Home Rule Bill was defeated by 343 to 313, with ninety-three Liberals voting against. Though the majority of these dissidents were supporters of Hartington, perhaps a third were Chamberlainite Radicals whose opposition may have tipped the scales. Parnell certainly thought so, and Chamberlain left the chamber to shouts of 'Traitor' and 'Judas' from the Irish benches. Garvin wrote that the Irish Nationalists hated Chamberlain 'more than they had hated any Englishman in modern times', and this hatred would pursue him for the rest of his political career.[18] Few would disagree that the failure of the British political system to find a solution to the Irish problem and to accommodate the aspirations of the Irish majority was a tragedy which would have malign, long-term consequences on both sides of the Irish Sea. But the blame heaped on Chamberlain was disproportionate. The revolt of the Whigs and the massive Tory majority in the House of Lords would have ensured the defeat of Gladstone's Bill regardless of the actions of the Chamberlainite faction. Nor should Parnell's miscalculations or Gladstone's poor management be left out of the equation.

Into the wilderness: the making of a Liberal Unionist

Gladstone, assured by Schnadhorst of the prospects of electoral victory, dissolved Parliament and the battle shifted to the constituencies. The Liberal Unionists, whether of the Hartington or the Chamberlainite faction, found themselves under enormous pressure from the Liberal caucuses in the constituencies, to which a number succumbed in the next few years. They were, however, materially helped by the decision of the Tory leadership not to oppose their re-election. The salient features of the 1886 election, therefore, were the schisms within the Liberal Party. Essential to Chamberlain's political survival was the maintenance of his hegemonic status in Birmingham:

> In Birmingham and nowhere else his fate would be decided. In that arena would the thumbs be turned up or down. If he lost Birmingham all was lost.[19]

Confronted by the evidence of the emergence of a strong Gladstonian faction in the BLA but anxious to maintain his distance from Hartington, Chamberlain decided to form his own organisation. The National Radical Union (NRU) was convened in the small lecture theatre of the Birmingham and Midland Institute on 18 June 1886. John Bright held himself aloof, refusing to become Vice-President. Rumour has it that a young Welsh

Radical, David Lloyd George, intended to be present but confused dates
and railway timetables. Although little more than 'a friends and family'
pressure group, the NRU was a significant step on the road to a permanent
division, though at this stage Chamberlain had no thought of leaving
the Liberal Party and may still have harboured hopes of the leadership.
Meanwhile, Dr Lawson Tait, a noted surgeon, councillor and chairman
of the Health Committee, had initiated the formation of a Home Rule
Association which was able to attract a large audience to its inaugural
meeting in the Town Hall. Though numerically smaller, the NRU had the
advantage of the support of the most prominent of Birmingham's Liberals.
Five of the seven Birmingham MPs had voted against the Home Rule Bill
while two, William Cook and Henry Broadhurst, had voted in favour. The
dilemma for the Unionists of whether or not to oppose them was eased by
Cook's decision to desert Birmingham for Nottingham, leaving a vacancy in
the Bordesley division. In spite of considerable opposition from supporters
of Schnadhorst, Chamberlain managed to persuade this divisional caucus
by a small majority to nominate his friend and ally, Jesse Collings, for the
vacancy. Collings was duly returned. The five Liberal Unionists benefitted
not only from the benediction of the CCO, but also from the reluctance of
leading Liberals, such as Dr Dale, to split the party and they were returned
unopposed. Only in the East Division was there a contest. Infuriated by
the decisions of the CCO, local Tories demanded a share of Birmingham's
representation and Chamberlain was persuaded by Churchill to support the
candidature of Henry Matthews, a Catholic QC who had been a prosecutor
in the Dilke trial. Cook was a popular Liberal with a distinguished record
of municipal service and the decision to oppose him caused much heart-
searching among members of the BLA. But benefitting from Tory support
and Liberal abstentions, Matthews defeated Cook by a surprising 789
votes, becoming the first Tory to represent Birmingham in Parliament since
Richard Spooner in 1844. Salisbury's decision to appoint Matthews to
the post of Home Secretary, making him the first Catholic to become a
Cabinet Minister, necessitated his re-election but, to Chamberlain's great
relief, his unopposed return was secured. Birmingham, therefore, returned
seven Unionist MPs to Westminster. The forbearance of many Gladstonian
Liberals had been based on the desire not to drive a permanent wedge into
the party. Once it became clear that this was indeed what was happening,
the Gladstonians began to mobilise to challenge Unionist domination.
Chamberlain faced a drawn-out struggle, the result of which could not
be foreseen. A future which had seemed so full of promise had become
precarious and many were keen to write Chamberlain's political obituary.

Chamberlain's intuition that the English electorate was unlikely to
support Irish Home Rule proved correct. In the new House of Commons,

Tories outnumbered Gladstonian Liberals by 316 to 192. In Ireland, Parnell's party swept the board, many of his eighty-six MPs being returned unopposed. In theory, the seventy-nine Liberal Unionists held the balance, but since most were followers of Hartington and were ideologically indistinguishable from Tories, in practice Salisbury had a secure majority and could expect a long tenure. Chamberlain's small band of Radical Unionists found itself in an unenviable position. Committed to reforms in Ireland, opposed to coercion and under pressure to return to the bosom of the Liberal Party, they lacked political leverage and were widely predicted to fade away. They were nonetheless protected by both Chamberlain's obdurate leadership and the sense in the Tory leadership that Chamberlain, both for his Radical credentials outside Parliament and for his effective performances inside, was worth preserving. His main link with the Tory Party was with Lord Randolph Churchill, Chancellor of the Exchequer and 'Tory Democrat'. Churchill's resignation in December 1886 and subsequent erratic course dismayed Chamberlain and put an end to their joint fantasies of creating a new national party. It was Salisbury's nephew, Arthur Balfour, who stepped into the breach and the link was sustained. Perhaps surprisingly, Lord Hartington shared Salisbury's and Balfour's opinion that it was worth keeping the Chamberlain faction on board. Though they would never be close allies let alone friends, it was expedient for both to co-operate; while keeping control of the NRU, Chamberlain quietly joined Hartington's Liberal Unionist Association.

In order to protect his Radical credentials, Chamberlain published *A Unionist Policy for Ireland* and continued to advocate reforms there. His trickiest moment came when Balfour, the new Irish Secretary, proposed a new Crimes Act. Unable to support further coercion, Chamberlain's small band went into the lobby with the Liberals. Chamberlain continued to harbour hopes of Liberal re-union. His olive branch to Morley took the form of a Christmas barrel of oysters and he also kept up a correspondence with Sir William Harcourt, the most sympathetic of the Liberal leaders. The result was the Round Table Conference of January and February 1887, in which both sides met first at Harcourt's house and then at Trevelyan's to seek a compromise. Chamberlain found Gladstone and Morley intransigent. If they expected him to wave the white flag, they had misjudged him.[20] Once he was convinced that no concessions would be made, he kicked over the Round Table by publishing a letter in the *Baptist* which amounted to a blast of defiance. As Garvin commented, 'Even a round table does not help you to square a circle'. The conference was followed by the defection of Trevelyan, leaving Chamberlain more isolated than ever.

Relief from this predicament came in the form of an invitation from Salisbury to head a Fisheries Commission to the US with the task of settling disputes between America and Canada over fishing rights off the Newfoundland coast. Chamberlain accepted with alacrity and was out of the country from October 1887 to March 1888. Although the US Congress eventually failed to ratify the agreement he had brokered, the trip renewed his appetite and enhanced his political credentials. It also re-invigorated his private life. It is hard to resist the conclusion that a subsidiary object was, following the example of a number of British aristocrats, to find himself an American wife. In the course of the visit, he became engaged to Mary Endicott, daughter of the US Secretary of State for War—a woman more than twenty years his junior and approximately the same age as his elder son Austen. They were married in November 1888. Mary was attractive, sociable and supportive of his politics, something which a previous potential partner, Beatrice Webb, had refused to concede. Mary eased his way in elite social circles and, more importantly, brought life and light into a family which had grown gloomy and introspective. If Chamberlain's hunger for politics was indeed renewed, it was high time— for his troubles were far from over.

On his way back from America, Chamberlain was alerted by his brother Arthur to the growing spirit of revolt in the BLA. In the spring meetings of the divisional associations, supporters of the Home Rule Association were winning majorities, which would inevitably culminate in the capture of the '2,000'. The Birmingham Conservative Association (BCA), led by Sir James Sawyer and Joseph Rowlands, was also seething with discontent. Not only were the Tories dissatisfied with their sole parliamentary seat, they demanded a fairer share of representation on the Town (and from 1889 City) Council. Municipal elections had become and would remain occasions of friction, many Liberal Unionists being reluctant to vote Tory when purely municipal issues were at stake. Assured of the support of the Tory hierarchy, Chamberlain's attitude to the BCA was uncompromising. He would dribble out concessions when and where it suited him.

As far as the BLA was concerned, Chamberlain was obliged to recognise that the Gladstonians were gaining ground in the ward associations and would soon be in a position to translate this into control of the '2,000'. Characteristically, his response was to launch the Birmingham Liberal Unionist Association (BLUA) and to call on BLA members to desert the old and join the new. Having lost Schnadhorst to Gladstone, he came to rely more and more on the organisational skills of Joseph Powell Williams, formerly chairman of the Finance Committee of the Town Council and now MP for South Birmingham, who was soon assuring him that things were going swimmingly. Writing to Mary Endicott, Chamberlain displayed a new-found confidence: 'I shall not be satisfied until I have purged the Council of every single Gladstonian'.

The first major test of the relative strength of the contending parties came with the death of John Bright on 27 March 1889, triggering a by-election in Central Birmingham. Predictably, the BCA coveted the seat for Lord Randolph Churchill, their leaders Sawyer and Rowlands claiming that they had Chamberlain's verbal promise of support. Their protestations had more than a ring of truth to them but, from Chamberlain's point of view, the situation had changed radically. Relations between Churchill and his party leaders had deteriorated sharply since his resignation from the Chancellorship and Chamberlain had no intention of handing a Birmingham seat to a political maverick with the potential to complicate his relations with Salisbury and Balfour. Denying that he had made any commitments to Churchill, he instead secured the candidature of Bright's eldest son, John Albert Bright, thus preserving for the Liberal Unionists the magic of the Bright name. Albert Bright comfortably won in a straight fight with a Gladstonian Liberal, Phipson Beale. The Central Birmingham by-election constituted a crucial turning-point. It proved that Liberal Unionism in Birmingham was a reality and, conversely, that the BLA was in decline. Nationally, Central Birmingham ended a sequence of lost Unionist by-elections, demonstrating to the Unionist leaders Chamberlain's value as an electoral asset.

At a meeting of the National Union of Conservative Associations (NUCCA) in Birmingham in November 1891, Chamberlain shared a platform with Salisbury and formally acknowledged what had already become political reality when he declared that 'I neither look for nor desire re-union'. At about the same time, he had the satisfaction of witnessing the end of the Parnell–Gladstone alliance and the factionalisation of the Irish Nationalist Party as a consequence of the divorce case launched by Capt. O'Shea against his wife Kitty (which revealed to the world what politicians had long known). Parnell, a broken man, died in October 1891, aged only 45. There were, of course, those who detected Chamberlain's hand in these events. In Peter Marsh's view, however, the initiative came not from Chamberlain but from O'Shea, Chamberlain merely 'encouraged his disreputable associate to proceed'.[21]

From 1886 to 1895 Chamberlain held no ministerial office. Although his involvement in politics never slackened, he had more time to spend with his family and to develop his Highbury estate, planting trees, creating gardens, constructing terraces and the extensive glasshouses in which his trade-mark orchids were grown. During his lifetime the estate quadrupled in size from its original 25 acres, and Highbury played host to many of the most eminent men and women of the age. It was truly *rus in urbe*. Politically, much of his time and energy was spent on organisational matters, namely the building of a Liberal Unionist Party, which would not be a mere transient phenomenon but a permanency and offered a half-way house to former Liberals for whom a direct transition to Conservatism would have been a step too far. A constant concern was the effort to inject into the Coalition something of the spirit of the Radical tradition to which he belonged and which he believed essential to electoral success. In December 1891, Lord Hartington succeeded his father as Duke of Devonshire and moved to the House of Lords. Chamberlain, insisting on unanimity among Liberal Unionist MPs, succeeded him as leader of the party in the Commons. While the Unionist Coalition benefitted from his organisational skills, his Tory allies had ample reason to appreciate his mettle as a skilled parliamentary tactician and debater. His primacy in the organisation of politics in the counties contiguous with Birmingham, Staffordshire, Warwickshire and Worcestershire—an area which came to be called his Duchy—was acknowledged. In March 1891, the death of George Kynoch, Tory MP for Aston, a constituency neighbouring Birmingham, prompted a by-election. The Tory candidate, Grice-Hutchinson, more than quadrupled Kynoch's 1886 majority, in striking contrast to Unionist fortunes elsewhere as Salisbury's term of office neared its end. As usual, Chamberlain preceded the by-election with an 'unauthorised programme', the centrepiece of which on this occasion was the promise of old age pensions. In preparation he had invited Charles Booth and other social reformers to Highbury and had held consultations with the Friendly Societies. He was by no means the first to advocate OAPs, but he was the first politician of the front rank to do so.

Almost exactly a year later, to his supreme satisfaction, Austen joined him in the House of Commons. His candidature for a vacancy in East Worcestershire was not without drama. The sitting MP had been a Liberal Unionist, George Hastings, and Chamberlain therefore claimed the seat for his party. After a lavish lunch at Highbury, a joint Unionist committee invited Austen to stand. There was strong opposition, however, from the East Worcestershire Conservative Association marshalled by Victor Milward, a needle manufacturer, who had parliamentary ambitions of his own. An attempt was made to force Austen to promise not to support disestablishment, a demand that the Chamberlains rejected. Once again the Conservative leadership was called upon for aid and the East Worcestershire Conservatives were brought into line. Milward was shortly afterwards compensated with a knighthood and Austen was returned unopposed. Flanked by his father and his uncle Richard, MP for Islington, he took his place in the Commons. The regional boss had once again asserted his authority. Ironically, Austen now became Joe's MP, as the East Worcestershire constituency impinged on the Birmingham suburbs in which Highbury was situated.

On 28 June 1892, Parliament was dissolved and a general election called. The Liberal Party was in an optimistic mood. At its Newcastle Conference in 1891, it had drawn up a programme of social reforms to rival Chamberlain's. However, with the 83-year-old Gladstone still at the helm, the principal commitment was, inescapably, to Ireland. The Birmingham results, declared on 7 July, fulfilled all Chamberlain's hopes. They demonstrated conclusively that the Liberal Unionists had become the predominant force in Birmingham, drawing support from across the social spectrum. The Unionist alliance worked reasonably smoothly, the only obvious difference between its two components being the Conservative addiction to tariff reform, firmly rejected by the Liberal Unionists. Unionists won all seven seats with comfortable majorities, the largest being Chamberlain's (4,418 in West Birmingham) and the smallest Matthews' (2,209 in the East Division). Churchill praised these results as 'Napoleonic', while Balfour warmly congratulated Chamberlain: 'You do know how to manage things in Birmingham! I never saw such smashing results'.[22] Unionist success was not confined to Birmingham. Their candidates were comfortably returned in constituencies which bordered Birmingham—Aston, Handsworth and East Worcestershire—while gains were made in a number of others, including Walsall, Wednesbury, West Bromwich and West Wolverhampton. In the whole area of the Duchy, the Unionists won thirty out of thirty-nine seats. Although the majority of those returned were Conservatives, Chamberlain could reasonably claim that the well-organised Liberal Unionist associations had tipped the balance. His reputation as a regional boss, 'the Great Elector', was triumphantly vindicated.

With a majority of just four over the Conservatives, the Liberals would be dependent for their majority on the eighty-one Irish Nationalists. The return of forty-seven Liberal Unionists meant that Gladstone could command at best a majority of *circa* forty. This, the shrewd old campaigner recognised, was too small to intimidate the House of Lords with its huge Unionist majority. Also discouraging was the scant support for Irish Home Rule which had been manifested by English constituencies. Nevertheless, Gladstone remained doggedly determined to make Irish Home Rule the Liberal priority. His efforts to do so and the vehemence of the Opposition made the Parliament of 1893 an epic occasion. Roy Jenkins described Gladstone's performance as,

> [...] a feat of sustained parliamentary resource which has rarely if ever been equalled before or since by any Prime Minister, let alone one aged 83.[23]

His principal opponent was Chamberlain, determined to complete the destruction of Irish hopes for independence. So intense were the emotions aroused that, following one of his speeches on 27 July 1893, an outbreak of fighting occurred on the floor of the House to cries of 'Judas'. The third reading on 1 September resulted in a majority for the Bill of thirty-four. A week later it was thrown out by the Lords, 410 votes to 41. Finding that his party had little stomach for a 'Peers *vs* People' campaign, Gladstone resigned on 1 March 1894. In the remaining fifty months of his life, he did not again appear in the House of Commons. His successor as Prime Minister, Lord Rosebery, was at best a lukewarm Home Ruler. His judgement was that nothing more could be done while the predominant partner, England, was so clearly opposed. It would be fifteen years before the Irish Home Rule issue forced itself back into the forefront of British politics. Parnell was dead, Gladstone retired. Chamberlain had won, but in the judgement of many it would prove to be a pyrrhic victory. Rosebery's unhappy and divided administration limped on for a further year before a minor defeat in the Commons on 20 June 1895 gave him the excuse to bring his Government to a close. Ironically, in spite of personal dislike, Rosebery confessed himself to feeling closer in politics to Chamberlain than any other major figure. A year later, Rosebery, the 'Flying Dutchman' of British politics, resigned the Liberal Party leadership, leaving it in deep disarray.

In spite of his parliamentary success, the struggle over Irish Home Rule had taken its toll on Chamberlain. In April 1895, another constituency dispute had erupted when the Speaker, Arthur Peel, decided to retire, creating a vacancy in Warwick and Leamington. The Liberal Unionists claimed the seat and pressed for the candidature of his son George Peel, a claim that was hotly disputed by the local Conservative Association. Support for its position in the right-wing press broadened into a general assault on Chamberlain, perceived by George Curzon and others as a dangerous and potentially disruptive force. Once again, the Conservative leadership stepped in to support him. Although George Peel was obliged to stand down, he was replaced by the impeccably blue-blooded Liberal Unionist Alfred Lyttleton. Chamberlain's black state of mind was made worse by financial worries. The ill-conceived project to grow sisal in the Bahamas was eating into his capital, while the value of other investments was also declining in the face of the international depression. It is hard to believe, however, that his threats to withdraw from politics were symptomatic of anything more than a passing mood.

That mood was considerably lightened when Salisbury set about forming his third administration and offered the Liberal Unionists a generous four places in the Cabinet. Although offered a choice of either the Home Office or the Exchequer, Chamberlain surprised Salisbury by asking for the Colonial Office and was granted what Gladstone had refused him in 1886. Hitherto a comparatively obscure department, the Colonial Office was headed by a Secretary of State at a salary of £5,000 per annum. Chamberlain was also gratified by the offer of junior ministerial posts to three of his acolytes, Austen (Admiralty), Powell Williams (War Office) and Jesse Collings (Home Office).

Chamberlain's choice of the Colonial Office no doubt reflected the evolution of his political thinking, but was also motivated by the recognition that tenure of a major domestic ministry was likely to bring nothing but frustration in a predominantly Tory Government. While he continued to press for social reforms, he expected to be and was refused in most instances, most damagingly in the case of old age pensions. He did, however, succeed in pressing the Home Secretary, Sir Matthew White Ridley, to promote the Workmen's Compensation Act of 1897, a major piece of industrial legislation. Beyond that he achieved little and it was as an arch-Imperialist rather than a social reformer that he would be chiefly identified for the remainder of his career. The Irish question 'had awakened the slumbering genius of English imperialism,' in the words of Salisbury. Imperial policy became in the 1890s a central political issue which transcended the Anglo-Irish entanglement. The entry of Germany into the scramble for colonies in the previous decade had precipitated a race to divide what was left of the unclaimed regions of Africa and Asia and made war an ever-present threat. His appointment to the Colonial Office would mark a new and final phase of Chamberlain's tempestuous career.

Colonial Secretary and Minister for Empire

Having formed his Government in June 1895, Salisbury called a general election the next month. At the polls a demoralised Liberal Party paid the penalty for Gladstone's obsessiveness and Rosebery's ineffectual leadership: 340 Conservatives were returned together with 71 Liberal Unionists, giving the Unionists a majority of *c.* 150 over the Liberals and Irish Nationalists. In the Duchy, 'the Great Elector' again worked his magic. In Birmingham, the demoralised BLA managed to field only three candidates in the seven divisions, polling a total of less than 6,000 votes. Matthews, regarded as a failure as Home Secretary, was elevated to the Upper House as Lord Llandaff, his place in Birmingham East taken up by Sir J. B. Stone, a glass and paper manufacturer and accomplished amateur photographer. Stone had been knighted in 1892 in acknowledgement of his services to the NUCCA and his emollient role as a leader of the BCA. In spite of the acceptance of Joe's hegemony by BCA leaders such as

Stone, there was once more an outbreak of ill-feeling. Tories in the Central Division adhered obstinately to the belief that they were entitled to its representation and sought to bring forward a well-known naval officer, Lord Charles Beresford, to replace Albert Bright, who was retiring. Once again, Chamberlain remained adamant and called in the Tory big guns in support. Although obliged to alter his original choice of candidate, it was a Liberal Unionist, Ebenezer Parkes, a local manufacturer and President of the BLUA, who was duly elected. The Tories were left to console themselves as best they could with the promise of future gains, one of which duly came three years later in the Edgbaston division upon the retirement of George Dixon. In the meantime, their representation in the City Council was steadily improving and in the new century would eventually exceed both Liberal Unionists and Liberals. In the course of the general election, Chamberlain received strong support from the principal Tory paper, the *Birmingham Daily Gazette* (BDG)—a further indication of how deeply he had penetrated urban Conservatism. In the Duchy as a whole, the Unionists made a further net gain of two seats. Joe had, against many predictions, defied political gravity, not only keeping a small party in being, but managing to enhance its power and influence. He was, as Beatrice Webb rightly put it, 'the man of the moment'.

As Colonial Secretary from 1895 to 1903, Chamberlain was responsible for administering by far the largest of the European empires, a sprawling mass of disparate territories. His office inevitably cast him as a major player in that great 'Age of Imperialism'. As was the case in domestic policy, Chamberlain felt empowered to intervene in matters of diplomacy, creating the possibility of clashes with Salisbury, who combined the office of Foreign Secretary with that of Prime Minister. It is hard to imagine a greater contrast between the pugnacious and thrusting ex-businessman and the astute, pessimistic patrician. Salisbury was at times required to apply tact and restraint as an antidote to Chamberlain's often clumsy attempts to interfere in the relations of the Great Powers towards the end of the decade. Yet, on the whole, the two co-operated surprisingly well.

Although he brought energy and initiative to an office that had previously been lacking in both, Chamberlain failed intellectually to rise above the platitudinous sentiments of the day. His speeches, studded with references to the greatness of the British as a governing race, pandered to crude public opinion. Somewhat grudgingly, when casting about for international support to ease what he believed to be Britain's dangerous isolation, he conceded similar competence to the 'Anglo-Saxon race'—a notion supposed to embrace the US and even Germany. He showed no more appreciation of the national aspirations of Boers and French Canadians than he had of the Irish and he underestimated the strong feeling for independence in the self-governing colonies. Although responsibility for India was outside the remit of the Colonial Office, he never resolved in his mind the place of the largest and most populous of imperial possessions in the grand scheme of things. Like Alfred Milner, whom he appointed to be High Commissioner in South Africa in 1897, Chamberlain can fairly be described as 'a race patriot'; he was passionately concerned with the future of his country, the welfare of which he believed to be intimately bound up with the Empire, its consolidation and where possible its extension.

The mind-set that Chamberlain brought to the Colonial Office was that of an ex-businessman and municipal reformer. The Empire was replete with 'underdeveloped estates' which needed what he had endowed Birmingham with, an improvement scheme. His efforts to promote investment in docks, railways, roads, cables *etc.*, however, found little support in the Treasury, staffed by what Salisbury called 'the Gladstonian garrison'. Although the West Indies and West Africa derived some benefits from Treasury grants, the results fell well short of Chamberlain's hopes. Perhaps his most impressive achievement was the foundation of two Schools of Tropical Medicine, one in Liverpool and one in London, the efforts of which went some way towards ending the reputation of West Africa as a white man's grave.

In contrast to Salisbury, Chamberlain was very sensitive to both popular and commercial opinion and well aware of the resentments generated by the inexorable rise of foreign tariffs—with France and the US particularly egregious offenders. If sponsorship of improved facilities and infrastructure was one response to a tide of complaint, another was to advocate further colonial acquisitions whenever opportunity offered, even if this meant co-operating with unsavoury characters like Cecil Rhodes and incurring protests from missionary societies on behalf of dispossessed native peoples. Protectionist societies were not slow to point out the dishonesty involved in such expansionism. While the British taxpayer would foot the bill for acquisition and governance, foreign traders enjoyed free access to all British markets.

The resulting controversies obliged Chamberlain to re-think his attitude to trade policy and his contacts with the leaders of the self-governing colonies pointed him in the same direction. Pursuing dreams of imperial federation on the basis of imperial free trade, he found colonial statesmen unwilling to abandon their own protectionist policies and to accept the role of producers of food and raw materials in return for British manufactures. In 1897, by the grant of a preference to British goods, Canada nudged him along the only practical path, imperial preference. But Chamberlain was not yet ready to advocate a policy which would logically entail the abandonment of free trade to which so many in Britain still clung to.

Chamberlain *vs* Kruger

With the economy of the West Indies in need of an influx of British capital and West African acquisitions yet to generate profit, Imperialists focussed their hopes on southern Africa as the area most likely to bring rewards. Much of Chamberlain's attention would centre on the complex issues arising in this region. Relations between the British and the Boers had been hostile from the moment that the British had first invaded the Cape and then annexed the region at the end of the Napoleonic wars. To escape British rule, many Afrikaners had trekked north to reclaim their independence, founding the Orange Free State and the South African Republic (the Transvaal). Relations between Boers and the black indigenous people were if anything worse than with the British and it was to protect the bankrupt Transvaal from the wrath of the Zulus that Disraeli's Government annexed the Transvaal in 1877. With Zulu power finally crushed at Isandlwana in 1879, the Boers demanded the restoration of their independence; when the Gladstone Government hesitated, a Boer commando inflicted defeat on Sir George Colley's small force at Majuba Hill in 1881. Independence was then conceded, but not without strings. Anxious to contain the Boer State within its existing frontiers, the Conventions of 1881 and 1884 incorporated a claim by the British to suzerainty, in effect the right to control the Transvaal's external relations. This vague and ill-defined concept was thoroughly resented and it was the constant aim of the Transvaal Parliament, the *Volksrad*, to evade its implications and even deny its validity.

In spite of the show of Boer military strength at Majuba, it was clear that the preponderance of wealth and power in the region lay with the British colonies of Cape Colony and Natal. Rich diamond deposits were discovered in Griqualand West, which was incorporated into Cape Colony in 1880. The situation, however, took another turn when gold was discovered in the Witwatersrand, goldfields lying entirely within the territory of the Transvaal. These deposits were exploited almost entirely by foreign immigrants, with British and German contingents especially prominent. From the Boers' point of view, this influx of *Uitlanders* threatened the stability and racial homogeneity of their state, but it did have the positive effect of transforming the financial status of the Transvaal, as the taxes levied on the profits of the goldfields and such measures as a dynamite monopoly filled the Treasury's coffers. A relatively static *impasse* had become volatile.

It fell to the lot of the new Colonial Secretary to manage these changes. To British Imperialists like Chamberlain, the ideal solution would have been the federation of the whole region under the Union Jack. Such an aspiration could be achieved only by war, the outcome of which could not be taken for granted. Paul Kruger, President of the South African Republic, was the personification of Boer determination to resist hegemony from what Jan Smuts called 'the hated race'. With two Boer Republics in existence and a substantial population of Dutch origin in the British-ruled Cape Colony, Boers could counter the British dream with one of their own—an Afrikaner dominated state of South Africa.

The representative figure of British imperialism in southern Africa was Cecil Rhodes. Rhodes was the founder of the De Beers Company, which controlled much of the diamond-mining industry of Kimberley and through Consolidated Goldfields, he also had substantial interests in the Transvaal. In 1887, he founded the British South Africa Company, which was granted a royal charter in 1889 and in 1890 he became Prime Minister of Cape Colony. Rhodes dreamed of a Cape-to-Cairo railway which would act as the spine of British-dominated Africa and his company thrust into Matabeleland, north of the Transvaal, in what would later be called Rhodesia. Hopes of finding riches comparable to those of the Witwatersrand, however, were dashed. Although to the British Government Rhodes represented imperial expansion on the cheap, to British politicians he was an equivocal figure whose ultimate objectives were shrouded in mystery. He had at one time helped to finance Parnell's Irish Nationalist Party and his wealth enabled him to create a lobby which sought to influence—if not direct—British policy in southern Africa. It was not clear that his aim was a South Africa under the Union flag, rather than one ruled, directly or indirectly, by a Rhodes-dominated network of rich and powerful companies. As the *Uitlander* population of the Transvaal grew, so too did resentment of the treatment meted out to them by the Kruger regime. Their alienation opened up the tempting prospect of an *Uitlander* rising in Johannesburg which, if supported by the company's police force, might overthrow the Boer regime. Rhodes was instrumental in smuggling arms to *Uitlander* groups and in orchestrating their complaints. Military planning was left in the hands of a close associate, Dr Leander Starr Jameson, fresh from the bloody suppression of the Matabele and soon to give his name to one of the most infamous escapades of the Imperialist era. On 29 December 1895, Jameson led a force of 470 mounted men across the Bechuanaland border with the Transvaal and headed for Johannesburg. The raid turned rapidly into a fiasco. There was no rising in Johannesburg and within four days Jameson and the survivors of his force found themselves under lock and key in the Boer capital. The Jameson Raid was to have profound consequences for Anglo–Boer relations and the history of South Africa.

How much Chamberlain knew about the proposed coup would be a matter of speculation for years to come. Like a number of others, he was aware in general terms of what was brewing, but by refusing to receive specific information from Rhodes' agents in London, he was able to deny official knowledge. A number of historians, especially South African, have found this distinction invidious and to confirm Chamberlain's guilt have pointed, for instance, to the ceding of a strip of land in the crown colony of Bechuanaland to Rhodes' Company—ostensibly for the building of a railway, but subsequently used as the jumping-off point for his raid. They have also highlighted the awkward fact that, among Jameson's force of 470 men, were serving British officers seconded to the British South Africa Company. Naturally, the Transvaal Government was convinced that the British Government was intimately involved in this transparently illegal act. What neither Chamberlain nor Rhodes had anticipated was that Jameson would act without clear evidence that a serious uprising was already underway in Johannesburg. His feckless action had put the careers of both in jeopardy.

As the Chamberlain family prepared for the annual servants' ball at Highbury on the evening of 30 December 1895, news of Jameson's filibuster was relayed from the Colonial Office. Chamberlain immediately perceived the implications. 'If this succeeds, it will ruin me,' he told his wife, 'I am going up to London to crush it.'[24] His prompt repudiation of the Jameson Raid may ultimately have saved his career. His political survival was also assisted when Kaiser Wilhelm sent Kruger a telegram of congratulation on repelling the foreign invasion. Public indignation at German interference diverted attention from the role of the Colonial Secretary, who himself moved in the House of Commons for a Select Committee to enquire into the circumstances of the Raid. Bizarrely, he was himself nominated as one of its fifteen members, a clear indication that he was unlikely to be held to account. The report of the Select Committee, published in July 1897, exonerated both Chamberlain and the Colonial Office—a not untypical example of a government whitewash which has aptly been called 'the Lying in State'. Rhodes' involvement in the Jameson Raid obliged him to resign as Cape Premier, but the Charter of his South African Company was not affected. Rhodes' agents in London had done their best to blackmail Chamberlain into exonerating him, threatening to publish the famous 'Missing Telegrams', which, they insinuated, proved Chamberlain's active collusion. Chamberlain's response was unfalteringly characteristic: 'if they put me with my back to the wall they will see some splinters fly'. For all his reservations about Rhodes, Chamberlain had come to the conclusion that he was too valuable an imperial asset to be entirely abandoned and in the parliamentary debate on the Select Committee report he brazenly defended Rhodes as a great servant of Empire, 'a man of honour' who had made, it was true, a gigantic mistake

. By a vote of 304 to 77, the House of Commons endorsed the report, a testimony of just how deeply imperial partisanship had penetrated both parties, Liberal as well as Unionist.

Kruger's Government duly took note. Kruger himself drew the simple conclusion that the British aimed to take his land, a view shared by younger and better educated Boers who might, but for the raid, have led the South African Republic in a more reformist direction. The Jameson Raid had made war between Boer and Briton infinitely more likely. The prospects for a peaceful settlement were lessened still further when, in March 1897, Sir Alfred Milner was appointed British High Commissioner in South Africa and Governor of Cape Colony. A stiff-necked Imperialist who had learned his trade under the pro-consul Lord Cromer in Egypt, Milner had strong personal connections with leading Liberal Imperialists such as Asquith and Sir Edward Grey. His proved a fateful appointment. Charged by Chamberlain to negotiate civil and political rights for the *Uitlanders*, Milner soon concluded that the Boers were intractable and that only by force would they be induced into ceding the rights which public opinion in Britain demanded. While Chamberlain harboured the hope that pressure would ultimately be effective, it was the man on the spot whose view prevailed. Negotiations finally broke down at Bloemfontain in June 1899 and Chamberlain justified British demands for reform by publishing the so-called 'helot' despatch, rehearsing *Uitlander* grievances. The Transvaal Government, meanwhile, had for some years been stockpiling arms bought from Germany—enough to equip not only their own commandos, but also their fellow Afrikaners in the Orange Free State and Cape Colony. When the British showed signs of reinforcing their own, inadequate forces, the Kruger Government issued an ultimatum on 10 October 1899, swiftly followed by the invasion of Natal and Bechuanaland. It was the beginning of a long, bitter and costly struggle which Salisbury characterised as 'Joe's War', an impression widely replicated in public opinion.[25] Although Chamberlain undeniably bore a major responsibility for what had occurred and, as the strongest and most forthright member of the Cabinet, would occupy centre stage throughout the war, this was nevertheless an unfair attribution. The Boer War was the work of many authors besides Joe—Kruger, Milner, Salisbury himself. At its root was the refusal of the British Government to abandon its claim to suzerainty over the Boer states and the equal determination of the Afrikaners to evade its implications. It was also a clash of cultures and even of two competing forms of imperialism. Neither side took much account of the interests of the majority population, the black natives and immigrants, mostly of Indian origin. Far more than the *Uitlander*, it was they who were the true 'helots' of South Africa.

The Boer War and its aftermath

The Boer commandos made full use of their temporary superiority in numbers, armament and knowledge of the terrain, inflicting a series of humiliating defeats on British forces. They besieged important centres such as Ladysmith, Mafeking and Kimberley, where Cecil Rhodes was among the beleaguered. In the course of a single week in December 1899, 'Black Week', British forces suffered three major defeats and in January 1900 they suffered heavy casualties on Spion Kop in Natal. It was time to supersede the bungling commander-in-chief, Redvers Buller ('Sir Reverse') and to replace him with Generals Roberts and Kitchener, who arrived at Cape Town in January with 40,000 reinforcements. Volunteers from the self-governing colonies also began to arrive in numbers. The surrender of Piet Kronje's force at Paardeburg on 27 February marked the turning of the tide. On 13 March, Roberts occupied Bloemfontain, the capital of the Orange Free State, in May Johannesburg and in June, Pretoria, capital of the Transvaal. On 17 May, Mafeking, a scruffy border town on the frontier of Cape Colony which had been stoutly defended by Maj. Baden-Powell for 217 days, was relieved, triggering scenes of hysterical rejoicing in British towns and cities, or 'mafficking'. With both Boer states annexed to the British crown, it seemed that the war was over. This was to be an illusion. Substantial Boer forces, 'the Bitter-Enders', determined to fight on. They were to write a new chapter in the history of guerrilla warfare, leading British forces in a far from merry dance until they were ultimately forced to the negotiating table at Vereeniging in May 1902.

Those two years inflicted large-scale casualties on both sides and imposed a cost of over £200 million on the British Exchequer. Among the worst sufferers were Boer civilians, ejected from their farms and confined to camps where many died of disease and starvation. This brought great discredit on the British Government, which was accused of initiating the first 'concentration camps'. The jingoism of the 1890s was stifled, giving way to a far more sober estimation of the pros and cons of imperialism.

Although Parliament had two more years to run, the formal annexation of the Transvaal in September 1900 offered the Unionists a golden opportunity to dissolve it and stage a general election. Chamberlain was instrumental in this decision and became the central figure in the campaign that followed. 'The war may not have been Chamberlain's war, as many claimed,' comments his biographer Richard Jay, 'but the election was certainly his election'.[26] The 'khaki election', as it became known, was one of the most scurrilous of recent political history. Chamberlain, as Beatrice Webb alleged, 'played it low'. Ignoring the fact that many Liberals had supported the war, he lumped all Liberals together as pro-Boers. Publishing letters from Radical MPs to Boer leaders captured in Bloemfontain, which appeared to encourage them in their resistance, he campaigned under the slogan 'Every seat lost to the Government was a seat gained by the Boers'. His opponents naturally hit back, with the young Welsh Radical MP, David Lloyd George, in the vanguard. By trawling through the records at Somerset House, he exposed all the business connections of the Chamberlain family, insinuating that Joe had provoked the war for the financial benefit of his numerous clan. Lloyd George's campaign was wittily summarised by *Punch* thus: 'the more the Empire expands, the more these Chamberlains contract'. The campaign against his family incensed Joe and triggered law suits, but a more sinister sequel was the infamous attack on Lloyd George on 18 December 1901, when a riot prevented the latter from speaking in the Birmingham Town Hall and obliged him to flee disguised in the over-large uniform of a police constable.

In the course of the election campaign from 28 September to 24 October 1900, Chamberlain largely confined his efforts to the Duchy, making one of his few excursions to Oldham to speak on behalf of Winston Churchill, son of Lord Randolph, a favour that would prove ill-requited. The result in Birmingham was never for a moment in doubt. A demoralised BLA contested only one of seven divisions, concentrating on the industrialised Eastern Division where Sir Benjamin Stone defeated a trade union leader standing as a 'Lib-Lab', J. V. Stevens, by over 2,000 votes. The *status quo* was maintained in the Duchy, while overall the Unionists returned to Westminster with a small net gain of 3 seats. It would have seemed inconceivable to even the most clairvoyant of political observers that this would be the last Unionist electoral success for over twenty years.

The opening of the year 1901 was marked by the death of Queen Victoria and the accession of King Edward VII, with whom Chamberlain had once played baccarat. It was the end of an era in other ways. An increasingly deaf and feeble Lord Salisbury retired in July 1902, accompanied by his venerable Chancellor of the Exchequer, Sir Michael Hicks-Beach. In a move typical of the 'Hotel Cecil', Arthur Balfour succeeded his uncle as Prime Minister, while Charles Ritchie was appointed to the Chancellorship. The Government of which Balfour assumed the leadership was already in steep decline. The victory secured in 1900 had proved chimerical and the prolongation of the war had drained the Exchequer and cost some 20,000 lives. The Liberal Party was beginning to gain a measure of unity under Sir Henry Campbell-Bannerman, who denounced the measures taken to subdue the Boers as 'methods of barbarism'. Britain's reputation abroad was at a nadir, while in Britain itself critical analysis of imperialism by J. A. Hobson and others denounced it as a policy for the enrichment of special interest groups.

Chamberlain attempted to stem the tide of public opinion by publicising the assistance rendered in the South African campaign by contingents from the self-governing colonies but, upon meeting the colonial Premiers at the Colonial Conference in 1902, he found them no more inclined to adopt measures of closer co-operation than they had been in 1897 and certainly not imperial free trade. He emerged from the meetings clear in his mind that the only viable route to the federation of which he dreamed was imperial preference.

In spite of his central role in government, Chamberlain had largely escaped the obloquy which was directed at fellow ministers widely judged incompetent, although *The Times* was surely indulging in hyperbole in describing him as 'the most popular and trusted man' in England. He was depressed, not only by the decline of the Unionist Government, but by the sense that his own position within in it was deteriorating. When Balfour succeeded Salisbury in July 1902, Joe was at Highbury recuperating from a nasty cab accident in the Mall. It is most unlikely that he harboured expectations of the succession—although it must certainly have occurred to him—but he nevertheless felt slighted by the failure to consult, believing himself to occupy a special position in government. The Cecils ought to have been aware of how dangerous it was to take Chamberlain for granted. He had other causes for grievance too. Balfour, fully supported in the Lords by the Duke of Devonshire, sponsored an Education Bill in early 1902, intended to put secondary education on a firm footing. It was a much needed reform, yet became highly contentious and once again education played host to the battle between the sects. Nonconformists perceived the Bill as consolidating Anglican supremacy in the provision of schools and were particularly incensed by the proposed abolition of school boards in favour of control by local authorities. Resistance was especially ferocious in Wales, where protests including the withholding of rates were orchestrated by Lloyd George. While alert to the need for educational reform, Chamberlain was sensitive to its likely damage to the Liberal Unionist Party, many of whose members were Nonconformists. A substantial wave of protest on his home patch was led by George Titterton, an activist in his West Birmingham constituency and one of his former evening class pupils at the Church of the Messiah. Chamberlain pressed the Cabinet for amendments to the Bill, but these were swept away in its passage through Parliament. His mood that autumn was savage. A letter to the Duke of Devonshire, a strong proponent of the Bill, in September 1902, reveals the depth of his resentment:

> The political future seems to me—an optimist by profession—most gloomy. I told you that your Education Bill would destroy your own party. It has done so. Our best friends are leaving us by the score and hundreds and they will not come back.[27]

Chamberlain was pessimistic about the future prospects of the Unionist Party, conscious of his own slipping influence in Cabinet and fearful that public enthusiasm for imperialism was waning under the impact of the revelations of incompetence and worse in South Africa and the intellectual assault from the Left. Mentally and physically jaded, he needed a new inspiration and decided to seek it on 'the illimitable veldt'.

On 25 November 1902, Chamberlain and his wife Mary set sail for South Africa aboard the *Good Hope*, the newest cruiser in the British fleet. His purpose was to investigate the South African situation for himself and to confront the Boer leaders, who were by no means reconciled to the peace terms agreed in May. This was a remarkable initiative which demonstrated physical as well as political courage. In order to reach remoter parts of the region, the Chamberlains were sometimes required to travel in covered wagons drawn by mules and to sleep under canvas. At every stop Chamberlain addressed meetings, received deputations and visited sites associated with the recent conflict. Risking assassination at the hands of vengeful 'Bitter-Enders', he responded to Boer discontent with his usual frankness, seeking to convince them of the essential fairness of the terms granted at Vereeniging and of the many advantages that would accrue through their inclusion in the British Empire. The journey, though arduous and wearing, renewed his enthusiasm for the cause and his hopes that, following the federation of Australia in 1900 and the uniting of South Africa under the British flag, the movement for closer imperial unity would achieve greater impetus. He arrived home, however, to be quickly disillusioned.

In his final budget in 1902, Hicks-Beach had introduced a small tax on imported corn and flour. The Canadian Government promptly demanded exemption from the duty in return for the preference given unilaterally to British goods. Before he had left England, Chamberlain believed that he had secured the agreement of Cabinet to respond positively to the Canadian request and thus make a small but relatively uncontroversial start on introducing imperial preference. However, the new Chancellor, Charles Ritchie, strongly influenced by the permanent officials of the Treasury, was determined to abolish the corn tax in his spring budget. The Cabinet, unwilling to lose a Chancellor so recently appointed, acquiesced. This has been recognised by historians as a vital turning point in the fortunes of Unionism. Should Balfour have overruled Ritchie and perhaps appointed Chamberlain in his place? Should Chamberlain have pressed Balfour harder? To Chamberlain, this was a further revelation of the decline of his influence in Cabinet and he was left with a strong sense of betrayal, especially by Balfour and by his nominal leader, the Duke of Devonshire.

Chamberlain's last 'unauthorised programme'

Never a man to take defeat lightly, Chamberlain contemplated his next step. Through his many contacts in West Midlands industry he knew that a renewed wave of fear and resentment at foreign protectionism was sweeping through the region. He ordered his agent in Birmingham, Charles Vince, to take soundings about the likely degree of support for a Fair Trade policy. Vince's answer was positive. On 15 May 1903, Chamberlain made one of the most portentous speeches of his life and of the century. Delivered to a packed and excited audience in the Birmingham Town Hall, it was a frank revelation of the disarray in which he had found the Government upon his return from South Africa. He reiterated his belief in the absolute necessity of Empire for Britain's wellbeing in the twentieth century and the need for closer relations with the self-governing colonies. The Government had received an offer from Canada, but adherence to free trade, which he believed to be incompatible with Empire, stood in the way. Britain needed to recover her freedom of action to grant preference to her colonies and, if necessary, to take action against foreign tariffs. 'You have an opportunity', he declared, 'You will never have it again'. He ended with a call for a national debate.

Although there was little in Chamberlain's speech that he had not advanced on previous occasions, in the political context of the moment, it was widely recognised that the speech heralded a new departure, the launch of a new 'unauthorised programme'. It was for this reason that imperial zealots like L. S. Amery and J. L. Garvin were so excited, while free traders in the ranks of Unionism were correspondingly dismayed. Liberals meanwhile, already energised by the education controversy, sensed a further opportunity for revival. Chamberlain's call for a fiscal enquiry was deceptive, as it was soon apparent that his mind was already made up. In the House of Commons on 22 May, he was goaded by Lloyd George into linking the financing of old age pensions with tariffs. On 28 May, he voiced the concerns of British manufacturers struggling to compete with American trust-based competition. One by one the elements of a social imperial package were being revealed, though it was not until October that, in a speech in Glasgow, he unveiled his master plan. This turned out to be virtually identical to the programme of Sampson Lloyd's National Fair Trade League, which he had combatted in the 1880s while President of the Board of Trade. Chamberlain proposed a tax of two shillings a quarter on foreign wheat, a corresponding tax on imported flour and a duty of 5 per cent on foreign meat and dairy products—all subject to imperial preference. In addition, he proposed a duty of 10 per cent *ad valorem* on foreign manufactured imports, subject to reciprocal negotiations. 'There is the murder,' he told his Glasgow audience, 'the murder is out'.

By the time he had set out his programme, Chamberlain was free of Cabinet responsibilities. He had resigned in September in order to pursue the cause which now completely engrossed him and to which he would devote the remainder of his life. Since the Birmingham speech in May, the political scene had changed. While the Imperialists in the Unionist Party had responded enthusiastically to Chamberlain's crusade, a minority was deeply hostile. In July, a Free Food League supported by about sixty Unionist MPs had been formed and three members of the Cabinet had resigned, followed after some hesitation by the Duke of Devonshire. In the same month, Chamberlain formed the Tariff Reform League, which attracted widespread support from manufacturers. The League, well financed and able to distribute its views on a vast scale, has been described by Richard Jay as 'the most powerful propaganda machine that British peacetime history has seen'.[28] As always, Chamberlain paid special attention to Birmingham and the Duchy, retaining control of a related but separate organisation there under Charles Vince's direction, the Imperial Tariff Committee.

The factionalisation of the Unionist Party posed acute problems for Arthur Balfour. Without any firm convictions on fiscal questions himself, his overriding concern was to retain the unity of the party and not to replay the role of Robert Peel in the 1840s. His *Insular Notes on Free Trade* was an attempt at a *via media*. Amounting to an advocacy of reciprocity in trade relations, it satisfied neither tariff reformers nor free traders. Many suspected that Balfour and Chamberlain had arrived at a private understanding by which the former would prepare the way for the latter. The truth was otherwise.

Anxious not to wreak the havoc on his party which a repudiation of Chamberlain would cause, he was in his heart deeply hostile and resentful of Joe's 'mafficking'. His feelings were shared by the aristocratic and traditionalist wing of the party, which had always regarded this upstart ex-manufacturer with intense suspicion. Lord Derby spoke for this segment of the party when he expostulated, 'Damn these Chamberlains. They are the curse of our party and of our country!' Chamberlain offered no quarter to his critics. With his usual mastery of organisational politics he succeeded in forcing out the Duke and taking control of the Liberal Unionist Party. Meanwhile, a group of Tory supporters sought to undermine his critics in their constituencies. He stopped short of ousting Balfour from the leadership, reluctantly recognising that, for many Tories, he himself was unacceptable as leader.

At the extreme, a number of Unionist free traders gravitated towards the Liberal Party, which was rejuvenated by these events. Their own internal divisions were healed and the leadership of Campbell-Bannerman consolidated. Even the Liberal Imperialists came out against tariff reform and Henry Asquith became the most effective of Chamberlain's opponents, pursuing him round the country and forensically exposing weaknesses in his arguments which, in spite of the advice of W. J. Ashley, the first Professor of Commerce at the University of Birmingham, and Professor W. A. S. Hewins of the LSE, were not always adequately prepared. The anti-tariff reform position was importantly reinforced by the decision of both the Labour Representation Committee, the nascent Labour Party and the Trades Union Congress (TUC) to reject Chamberlain's programme, a serious setback which Joe tried to offset by forming the Trade Union Tariff Reform Association. As the campaign proceeded, it became more and more apparent that its Achilles heel was the food tax proposals, which even those sympathetic to the cause recognised would be a liability at the ballot box. Yet without food taxes, there could be no imperial preference, the cause on which Chamberlain had set his heart and for which he had 'taken off his coat'.

Chamberlain's efforts were nothing short of heroic. In the course of 1903 and 1904, he embarked on extensive speaking tours, addressing large and excited audiences and scattering warnings of impending peril like a modern-day Cassandra. Decline, he declared, was an inevitability if Britain failed to develop and consolidate its Empire. He warned, too, of the dangers of industrial weakening and the threat to employment posed by tariff-protected foreign competition.

For a time it appeared that the campaign, well supported in the press and well financed by industrial interests, was bearing fruit. Tariff reform had diverted public attention from the failings of the Unionist Government and a sequence of by-election victories reversed the pattern of losses. Had Balfour dissolved Parliament in 1904, the Unionist Party might at worst have suffered a limited defeat. This he stubbornly refused to do, effectively nailing Chamberlain to the cross of continued and intensive electioneering. As the initial impetus petered out, the tide began to turn strongly against the tariff reform cause, ensuring that defeat, when it came, would be all the more severe.

One by-election took place in February 1904 as a result of the death of Joseph Powell Williams, who died two days after suffering a stroke on the floor of the House of Commons. The loss hit Chamberlain hard. He had come to rely heavily on this dependable and hard-working colleague and blamed himself for the heavy workload Powell Williams had willingly borne. Attention turned to the by-election in South Birmingham, the first test of opinion in the city since the launch of tariff reform.

It was easy to assume, as contemporaries and subsequent historians did, that Chamberlain's grip over Birmingham was absolute. But this ignored currents of resistance which Chamberlain determined to stamp out.

The *Post* was hostile to tariff reform from the outset and it was not until Chamberlain was able to force a change of editorship in 1905 that it changed its tune. To the great delight of free traders, his brother Arthur emerged as a trenchant and outspoken critic of tariff reform, publishing a critique in the form of a letter to his workpeople at Kynochs, warning them of the likely disastrous consequences. The hitherto excellent relations between the brothers, neighbours in King's Heath, were abruptly put on ice, as Neville Chamberlain's diary revealed. Arthur's son-in-law and Joe's nephew, John Sutton Nettlefold, shared his father-in-law's view and, as treasurer of the Midland Liberal Unionist Association, refused to sign cheques which he deemed were being used for tariff reform rather than party purposes. Like Pountney, editor of the *Post*, Nettlefold was removed from office to be replaced by his cousin Neville. He went on to found a Free Trade Association in Edgbaston, which attracted a nucleus of Unionist dissidents. The issue also re-ignited anti-Chamberlain stirrings in the BCA, where a faction led by Joseph Moore Bayley, President of the Central Birmingham Division, supported the Balfour compromise rather than 'the whole hog'. In November 1903, he invited two Unionist free traders, Lord Hugh Cecil and Winston Churchill, to put their case in the Birmingham Town Hall. It was widely anticipated that the pair would suffer much the same fate as Lloyd George two years earlier, but to general astonishment the event passed off peacefully. The by-election in South Birmingham provided a test of the temperature. Chamberlain's nominee was Lord Morpeth, son of the Earl of Carlisle and Austen's former fag at Rugby, who had served in South Africa. His opponent was Hirst Hollowell, Secretary of the Northern Counties Education League, who made the Tory Education Act his main point of attack. The *Post* commented on the evidence of Liberal revival in Birmingham but, to Joe's relief, Morpeth won a comfortable victory, with a majority of over 3,000 on a low poll of only 60 per cent. This victory marked the end of effective resistance to tariff reform in Birmingham, the baffled Liberals reduced to comparing Chamberlain to the city-state despots of ancient Greece.

Nemesis

Behind the façade of collusion, Balfour was undermining the tariff reform campaign and bringing Joe to the point of exhaustion. By-elections resumed the trend of Unionist defeat. At last, in December 1905, Balfour resigned on behalf of his Government, in the vain hope that remaining divisions in the Liberal ranks would prevent Campbell-Bannerman from forming a government. This was in vain. Having successfully formed his administration, Campbell-Bannerman dissolved Parliament and a general election was set for January 1906. It resulted in a landslide victory for the Liberal Party and represented a decisive rejection of tariff reform, which—although other issues such as the Education Act and the importation of Chinese labour into South Africa also told against the Unionists—was the central feature of the election. It was clear that the working-class vote had gone heavily against the Unionists and that a large proportion of the middle class feared to embark on the uncharted waters implied in the ditching of free trade, belief in which remained deeply embedded in public consciousness. Against 377 Liberals, 83 Irish Nationalists and 54 Labour MPs, only 157 Unionists returned to Westminster, perhaps three quarters of whom were 'Whole-Hoggers' rather than Balfourites. Balfour himself suffered defeat in Manchester, but returned in March as MP for a City of London constituency. Balfour's eclipse offered Chamberlain what proved to be his final opportunity to snatch the leadership of the party, but again he refrained from doing so and continued to pursue the course of pinning the elusive Balfour to the support of his programme.

In contrast to Balfour's abject performance, Joe emerged triumphantly from the election. All seven Birmingham seats were won by his supporters. Only in East Birmingham was there anything approaching a contest, with Sir Benjamin Stone emerging the victor over his opponent, James Holmes of the Amalgamated Society of Railway Servants, by 585 votes. Seats adjacent to Birmingham also resisted the rising tide—with the exception of North Worcestershire, where 'the Cadbury effect' prevailed and a renegade Liberal Unionist, J. W. Wilson, who had crossed the floor of the House of Commons on the education issue, was re-elected. Seats were also lost in the Black Country, though the swing to the Liberals was less than in other regions. While Chamberlain could extract some satisfaction from this regional response, it stood in stark contrast to the verdict of the country as a whole. There was little for it but to wait for a reversal in public opinion which, as it happened, would not occur in Chamberlain's lifetime.

Yet, Chamberlain had no intention of giving up the fight. His immediate objective was to persuade Balfour to endorse tariff reform as the official programme of the Unionist Party. Balfour proved as evasive as ever, but was obliged by the weight of opinion in the party to move closer to Chamberlain's position. There was little that could be done except to continue the flow of propaganda and to await the swing of the pendulum. To some extent this came in 1910, a year of two general elections. The Unionists regained much of their lost ground, but not enough to unseat the Liberal Government led by Asquith, who had succeeded Campbell-Bannerman in 1908. Tragically, by that time Joe was no longer fit to lead the campaign and could do little but seek to influence the direction of events from the sidelines.

In July 1906, impressive celebrations were held in Birmingham both to mark Joe's seventieth birthday and to celebrate his thirty years of service as a Birmingham MP. For several days factories were closed, special trains ferried people from all over the region into the city, commemorative medals were distributed to school children, firework displays were mounted in local parks and there was the inevitable civic banquet and speech-making. Following a meeting in Bingley Hall at which Chamberlain spoke movingly of his dedication to the people and the interests of Birmingham, he was escorted home to Highbury by a cavalcade of torchbearers. The festivities were a remarkable exhibition of the relationship between the man and his adopted city, as well as of Birmingham's defiance of national consensus, which had so recently rejected the nostrums of the local hero. Two days later, having returned to his house in Prince's Gate in London, Joe suffered a crippling stroke. The family did its utmost to hide the extent of the damage and his friends and followers lived in hope of a recovery that never came. For the last eight years of his life, Joe was consigned to a bathchair, able to do little more than transmit advice and directives to his followers via Austen. He was returned unopposed for West Birmingham in 1910, but thereafter stated his intention to stand down at the next election. He continued to reflect on the issues of the day, to offer advice to his supporters and to despatch frequent letters to the press. With typical pugnacity he sided with the 'Ditchers', those members of the House of Lords who opposed the Parliament Act of 1911 and he also advised Bonar Law and Edward Carson to resist Irish Home Rule, which had become a central issue once again with the Liberals dependent on the Irish Nationalist vote, even at the risk of civil war. If Joe could still be defined as a Radical, it was as a Radical firmly on the Right. His critics perceived this as the final, ironic chapter of a career marked by inconsistency: the man who had entered politics as an advanced Radical ended it by defending the privileges of the House of Lords. As Lloyd George jibed, 'Three Acres and a Cow' had become 'Three Dukes and a Pig'. These were years of physical and mental torment for Joe, as one lost cause succeeded another. Perhaps the worst of his disappointments was Austen's failure to grasp the leadership of the Unionist Party in 1911, when Balfour had finally been forced to resign. The son whom he had groomed to seize the glittering prize which had eluded his father had in fact inherited little of the old wolf's temperament.

Joe Chamberlain died in July 1914, two weeks short of his seventy-eighth birthday and on the eve of the outbreak of the Great War. Birmingham aside, his legacy is ambiguous and far from easy to define. To those who contrasted his political stance in the Liberal phase of his career with the Unionist phase, Joe would have replied that the world had changed and he with it. Against the charge of inconsistency, some have sought consistency less in terms of programmes and political allegiance, but more in terms of political method. He was the most professional politician of the day, an inveterate organiser with a well advanced political method. Profoundly ambitious and self-confident, he sought to shape and control the parties with whom he associated himself and to underpin their popular base in an increasingly democratic age. Ironically, he helped to undermine first the Liberal Party and subsequently the Unionist Party, whose troubles, according to a recent historian of the Unionist Party, already in the doldrums, grew much worse as a result of Joe's speech in the Town Hall on 15 May 1903.[29] In his career as a Unionist, he made himself the arch-exponent of imperialism in the Age of Empires. Again, the role is shrouded in ambiguity. Was his imperialism a valid formula for the future, as his passionate and devoted followers believed, or was it already becoming anachronistic? Whatever the verdicts, it was a truly remarkable and compelling career. A man who never occupied any of the highest offices of state and left little that was substantial in legislative terms had nevertheless made himself a major factor in most of the political decision-making of his generation. From commercial and middle-class origins, he had also succeeded in founding a dynasty to rival that of gilded aristocratic families such as the Cecils, Stanleys and Cavendishes.

Joseph Austen Chamberlain

Introduction

Addressing the House of Commons in October 1922, Lloyd George launched an attack on Lord Gladstone, son of the great William Gladstone. He was, declared Lloyd George, the best living embodiment of the Liberal doctrine that quality is not hereditary.... There is no more ridiculous spectacle on the stage than a dwarf strutting before the footlights in garments he has inherited from a giant.[1]

Stripped of the vituperation of which Lloyd George was a master, the same thought could have been applied to Austen Chamberlain. Being the son of a figure with such clout conferred huge advantages in terms of access to power and promotion but it also had a downside. For much of his career, Austen would be compared to his formidable father, usually adversely. Many of Joe's disciples were disappointed that the son showed few of the steely characteristics which had made him so influential. Austen himself was morbidly conscious of the ways in which he fell short of his father's and family's hopes. Perversely, he invited such comparison with his appearance and the manner of his dress: dapper, clean-shaven, adorned with the trademark orchid and monocle—all gifts gratefully received by the satirists. Throughout his career he made his father his constant reference point. More carefully groomed for high office than any politician since William Pitt, Austen lived in his father's shadow and under his roofs until he was past forty. As George Dangerfield put it, he was 'father haunted'.[2]

And yet the reality was that Austen was unlike his father in many ways. Though a competent speaker and debater, he was incapable of dominating the House of Commons as his father had once done. He was less sensitive to the social context of politics and had little of Joe's appetite and flair for campaigning. A conciliator where Joe had been abrasive, Austen was a natural Conservative, uncomfortable in the role into which he was thrust following Joe's stroke in 1906. Unlike Joe, he was not a political obsessive and confessed that his ideal life would have been that of a country gentleman, cultivating his alpine garden. He lacked his father's physical resilience and was quickly worn down by the toils of office, suffering frequent and sometimes severe bouts of ill-health. Contemporaries expected more from Joe's son and were quick to point to his failings, their criticisms carefully logged by his principal biographers, Peter Dutton and Robert Self. Balfour, the man Austen admired most in politics other than his father, deemed him 'rather a bore'. Leo Amery, fellow Birmingham MP and Joe's passionate disciple, 'a self-satisfied ass'. A number of those with whom he sat in Cabinet found him unimaginative and unconstructive— in Lord Halifax's description, 'a log'.[3] There were too many references to his 'aloofness' and lack of rapport with rank-and-file MPs for this to have been mere tittle-tattle. Fellow politicians found his obsession with his honour puzzling and inevitably conceived the thought that it was a reaction to his father's defects in this regard. Above all, his failure to grasp the premiership on the several occasions on which the prize was within his reach made him an enigma. His diffidence could not be explained by any sense of inferiority or unfitness. 'The trouble with Austen was not undue humility or diffidence on his part,' Amery commented. 'He had quite a good opinion of himself,' as Austen's many letters to his sisters confirmed.[4] While he acknowledged that Balfour and Lloyd George were greater men than himself, he certainly did not feel the same about Bonar Law and Baldwin, both of whom he came to despise. Explanations of his self-denial have included concerns about his health and worries about his financial situation, but the truth seems more likely to have been rooted in his over-scrupulousness, his overwhelming desire not to be seen as pushy or anything other than correct, open and loyal in his dealings. Austen lacked that streak of steely ambition that characterised both Bonar Law and Baldwin, arguably less able men than himself.

Though criticism of Austen's failings echoes down the years, it should not be allowed to obscure the fact that his was a remarkable and distinguished career. If never number one, Austen was a perennial number two. For much of his career he sat at the top table of British politics, for half of it in Cabinet office itself. No Tory or Coalition Cabinet seemed complete without him. When a gap opened or a crisis occurred, 'Send for Austen' was for many Conservatives a standard cry. Not only had he an unblemished reputation for honesty and fair dealing, but he commanded respect as an administrator, a safe pair of hands and as such was more appreciated by his civil servants than by many of his political colleagues. Austen was, *par excellence*, a 'Man of State'. As Joe dryly remarked in his later years, Austen was 'born in a red box and would die in one'.[5] Not quite.

Out of office for the last six years of his life he may have been, but this was a time in which, in Peter Dutton's opinion, he exercised more influence than ever before. His experience and his wisdom were appreciated especially by younger Tories such as Antony Eden and Harold Macmillan. For Macmillan, he was 'a trusted statesman' notable for his 'courtesy and his sweetness of character as well as his high sense of honour'.[6] However much he may have fallen short of his father's capabilities, as a man he was, in Roy Jenkins' opinion, 'immensely his father's superior in both decency and loyalty'. Austen Chamberlain was a credit to his family and to his native city, though 'there was not really much of Birmingham about him,' Macmillan later conceded.

Early life

Joseph Austen Chamberlain was born on 16 October 1863, the second child of Joe and Harriet. His birth was followed a few days later by the death of his mother. Joe sought refuge with his Kenrick in-laws at Berrow Court in Edgbaston, where Austen spent the first five years of his life. Joe's second marriage to Harriet's younger cousin, Florence Kenrick, provided the two children with a step-mother and four additions to the family—Neville, Ida, Hilda and Ethel—all six treated with the same love and care. Florence's premature death in 1875 once again threw the family into turmoil and Joe fell back on the support of his sisters, Mary and Clara. The near presence of a legion of aunts, uncles and cousins was a great solace to Joe's children. Austen, however, was old enough to be despatched to a preparatory school at Brighton, a far from happy experience. Aged nearly fifteen, however, he was sent to Rugby School, where he flourished both academically and socially, becoming Head of House and a firm friend of his housemaster Lee Warner. If Rugby was a somewhat surprising choice of school, it was evidence of Joe's determination that Austen should join the gentlemen of England and suffer neither the handicaps of a background in trade nor the social condescension of which he himself and his brothers were conscious. Later in life, Austen would become chairman of the governors of his old school.

Austen's grooming continued when he left Rugby for Trinity College, Cambridge—considered to be a nursery of statesmen—where he studied history. There he became politically active, an echo of his father's Radical ideas and was elected Vice-President of the Union—a number two position, an omen for his political future. After graduation in 1885, he was despatched to the continent to learn languages and expand his understanding of European politics. Following in the wake of his older sister Beatrice, who had attended school there, he arrived in Paris in September to lodge with a French family and study at the École des Sciences Politiques. The reputation of his father opened many doors for Austen and among those offering him hospitality were leading French politicians such as Clémenceau, Cambon, Ferry and even the President, Grevy. Nor did Austen neglect the artistic and literary dimensions of Paris society. It was altogether an intoxicating time for him, of which he wrote nostalgically in his memoirs, *Down the Years*, in 1935. The seeds were sown of a lifelong love of France which would greatly influence his future politics.

Returning to England in May 1886, Austen found his father embattled in the struggle with Gladstone and Parnell over Irish Home Rule, but his continental education was not yet complete and in February 1887 he was sent back, this time to spend best part of a year in Germany. This proved to be a much less congenial experience. Lacking fluency in German, he struggled hard to be an effective communicator. Once again, his father's growing reputation opened doors, the highlight being an invitation to dine with the German Chancellor, the great Count Otto von Bismarck. Asked later by Sir Charles Dilke for his impressions of Austen, Bismarck is reputed to have remarked laconically, 'Nice boy that Chamberlain but not much of a drinker'. Austen found little in either German political or social life that was sympathetic and was particularly alarmed by the nationalistic tone of lectures he attended at the University of Berlin, especially those given by the historian von Treitscke, which he judged to be 'narrow-minded, proud and intolerant Prussian chauvinism'. Treitscke's was 'not a comfortable classroom for an Englishman'. Austen's francophilia was confirmed, and his Berlin experiences made him aware of the German danger in the years before 1914.[8]

It is difficult to reconcile the widespread characterisation of Austen in later life as aloof, reserved and rather prickly with impressions of him in his youth and early manhood. Even the waspish Beatrice Webb, on a visit to Highbury in 1884, found him to be 'amiable', describing him as 'a big fair-haired youth of handsome feature and open countenance and sunny sympathetic temperament'.[9] A social asset to his father at the many gatherings at Highbury, he was also a welcome guest at a number of aristocratic houses, more so as his father became closely allied to the Whigs and Conservatives. One such salon was that presided over by Lady Desborough, the locale of a group known as the 'Souls' of which Arthur Balfour was the most distinguished member. Ettie Desborough's biographer, Richard Davenport-Hines, relates an incident in which Austen was left in charge of her four-year-old son, Ivo. He took him for a walk, fed him with hot-house grapes and allowed him to puff on his pipe. Clearly, his experience of his many siblings and relations in Birmingham had made him adept at handling children, however incorrectly! In time

Austen would become a devoted husband and father. Davenport-Hines comments that Ettie 'always retained an affectionate respect for that most diligent, dutiful and upright of men'.[10]

Returning to the bosom of his family in 1887, Austen became re-acquainted with his siblings from whom he had been so often separated and entered into the life of Highbury. Joe was steadily developing and expanding the estate and Austen's task was to take charge of a herd of cows which supplied the house with its milk and butter. He also absorbed his father's love of gardening, though where Joe favoured orchids, Austen preferred alpines. Although his father's most favoured offspring, relations between the two cannot have been easy, whereas relations between Joe and his children were immensely improved following his third marriage to Mary Endicott in 1888. Mary was welcomed into the family, not least by Austen, and the emotional gulf between Joe and his children bridged. Mary and Austen were close in age and both of a conservative disposition and became firm friends. Mary would become the intermediary between Joe and Austen after the former's stroke in 1906, their letters published many years later in *Down the Years*. The friendship cooled following Mary's marriage to Canon Carnegie in 1916, but Austen's and Neville's children remembered her fondly as a loving grandmother.

Into politics

His continental sojourn behind him, it was time for Austen to become ADC to his father and to learn the dark arts of party management. Joe was anxious to bring him into Parliament as early as possible and in 1888 secured his adoption as candidate for the Scottish constituency of Border Boroughs. With no parliamentary election immediately on the horizon, it seemed sensible to gain experience of local government and to this end Austen became a Liberal Unionist candidate for St Thomas's Ward in the municipal elections of November 1889. He was opposed by John (later Sir John) Stevens, leader of the Tinplate Workers' Society, who stood with the backing of the Birmingham Liberal Association. It was, of course, a time of agitation in Birmingham politics. The Birmingham Liberal Unionist Association had shown its new-found strength in the by-election in April following the death of John Bright, but was still dependent on Tory votes. Conservative leaders, believing themselves to have been cheated out of the representation of Central Birmingham, were still smarting and the Tories now retaliated, abstaining in large numbers. 'The lad' was beaten by eleven votes, the only electoral setback suffered by the Chamberlains in all their sixty-four years of campaigning.

Austen's biographers have largely ignored this episode, its significance unappreciated. Most Birmingham MPs at this time had cut their political teeth in municipal politics: Joe, of course, and later Neville served as mayors, as did Richard Chamberlain (MP for Islington), Jesse Collings and George Dixon. Powell Williams and William Kenrick had also done notable municipal service. All gained valuable experience of local affairs and cemented their relationships with the Birmingham electorate. Not serving on the council left a significant gap in Austen's career, which was destined instead for 'High Politics'. Had he had more experience of the lives and problems of common citizens, his career might have taken a different turn. Neville deemed him unprogressive and, tellingly, he turned down the offer of the Home Secretaryship in 1918 on the grounds that it was beyond his field of experience and interest. Although he recognised his dependence on Birmingham, he was detached from it from the time he became Chancellor of the Exchequer in 1903, never again living in the city or maintaining a residence there. The loyalty of Birmingham voters was to Joe and the memory of Joe, not Austen.

Into Parliament

Border Boroughs was never the most convenient of constituencies and, as the general election of 1892 loomed, a more alluring prospect presented itself. The sitting Liberal Unionist member for East Worcestershire, G. W. Hastings, was found guilty of embezzling trust funds and fled the country to avoid imprisonment. The constituency impinged on the southern suburbs of Birmingham, ironically including Highbury. Nothing could have been more convenient other than a Birmingham division and Joe promptly claimed the seat for his son. The Tories of the East Worcestershire Association, however, had no desire to be drawn into the Birmingham orbit and their protests were headed by the needle manufacturer, Victor Milward, who coveted the seat for himself. As in the case of Central Birmingham in 1889, Joe called on the Tory heavy brigade to put pressure on local representatives to withdraw their opposition. A final attempt to extract a pledge that Austen would not vote for the disestablishment of the Anglican Church met with a firm rejection from Highbury, after which they gave way. Milward was later compensated with a knighthood. Austen was duly elected unopposed on 30 March 1892. Flanked by his father and his uncle Richard, Austen took the oath and signed the Register with shaking hands. It was an emotional moment for the Chamberlains and the beginning of Austen's unbroken forty-five years as a member of the House of Commons, a place he came to revere. The general election followed in July and Austen duly saw off the challenge of Oscar Browning, a Cambridge historian, with a majority of 2,594. One of 47 Liberal Unionist MPs, he was appointed Junior Whip, acting closely with his father in what turned out to be a dramatic Parliament.

Dependent on the Irish Nationalist MPs for his majority, Gladstone was well aware of the weakness of his position, yet perished heroically with his attempts to pass the Irish Home Rule Bill, which he introduced on 13 February 1893 in a two-and-a-half-hour speech. While Gladstone pleaded for justice for Ireland, 'Chamberlain stood forth as the unequivocal voice of British patriotism'.[11] The struggle became heated and emotional, and included an outbreak of fisticuffs in July. In September the Bill was passed by a majority of 34, only to be summarily dismissed in the House of Lords by 419 votes to 41.

Finding his Cabinet had no stomach for a 'Peers *vs* People' crusade, Gladstone resigned the Premiership on 3 March 1894, to be replaced by Lord Rosebery. In the course of the heated debates, Austen made his maiden speech on 18 April 1893, Gladstone reporting to the Queen, praised his contribution and three days later in the House complimented Austen on 'a speech which must have been dear and refreshing to a father's heart'.[12] In a rare display of emotion, Joe rose from his place and bowed to the PM. For a year Rosebery, at best a highly reluctant Home Ruler, presided over a divided and confused party. He was grateful to resign in June 1895, triggering a general election which returned a Unionist majority of 152 and laid the basis for ten years of Unionist hegemony.

Into office

Joe had amply proved his value to the Unionist alliance and was accorded a generous share of the spoils. He became Colonial Secretary, the post Gladstone had refused him in 1885. Jesse Collings and Powell Williams became junior ministers in the Home Office and War Ministry respectively and Austen was appointed a Civil Lord of the Admiralty, with the experienced George Goschen as his superior. These were halcyon days: Joe was reaching the height of his power and influence, brushing aside the backlash from the Jameson Raid, while Austen was enjoying a post which he found congenial and gave him access to the highest in the land. Their ministerial salaries were also welcome after a decade in which Joe had been out of office and living off capital.

This was but a period of calm before the storm. At the end of the 1890s, Britain was plunged into war against the Boers in South Africa, with Joe once again in the spotlight. It was largely under pressure from him that

Salisbury dissolved Parliament and called a general election in September 1900, an acrimonious affair in which low blows were exchanged on both sides. On the part of the Liberals, David Lloyd George followed Labouchère's advice to 'go for Joe', combing the records of Somerset House to unearth the links between the Chamberlain family and Government arms contracts. The main issue concerned Kynochs, of which Joe's brother Arthur was chairman, and in which the family held shares in a trust. In Austen's case, Lloyd George accused him of holding shares in Hoskins, managed by Neville, and contracting with the Admiralty for ships' berths. Joe was embittered by this 'petty flow of malignity' and marked down for retaliation those who had defamed him. He received full support from Arthur Balfour, but less so from the rank-and-file of the Unionist Party. Lloyd George was protected from legal action by parliamentary immunity, but Neville and his uncle Arthur successfully sued newspapers which had taken up the cry.[13]

The Unionists retained power with a slightly augmented majority in the House of Commons. Joe had once again proved himself to be the most effective electioneer of his generation. Austen was again returned unopposed for East Worcestershire. In November he was promoted to the post of Financial Secretary to the Treasury, serving a valuable apprenticeship under 'Black Michael', Sir Michael Hicks-Beach, Unionist Chancellor since 1895. He was steadily building a reputation as a competent administrator and when Lord Salisbury retired in July 1902 and Balfour reconstructed his ministry, Austen gained a further promotion, becoming Postmaster General with a seat in the Cabinet and a salary of £2,000 per annum. He now enjoyed the considerable satisfaction of sitting alongside his father in Cabinet. This was regarded by many Liberals as a case of nepotism, though dwarfed in this regard by the Cecils. Joe's gratification was somewhat muted when the Government dropped his old friend and ally, Jesse Collings, an indication that Balfour was taking Joe's loyalty for granted. This became more apparent as Balfour and Devonshire, leader of the Liberal Unionist Party in the Lords and Lord President of the Council, ignored Chamberlain's concerns over the Education Act and failed to respond to his demands for amendments. Joe's alienation was complete when the Chancellor of the Exchequer, Charles Ritchie, abolished the corn tax which Chamberlain wanted to become the starting-point for imperial preference, a policy for which he believed he had the acquiescence of the Cabinet. Joe's riposte to Ritchie took the form of his famous speech on 15 May 1903 in Birmingham, the start of his last 'unauthorised programme', the tariff reform campaign. The Unionist Party was thrown into disarray. Austen's sedate and largely untroubled political career came to an abrupt end. As the party divided into factions, he had little choice but to declare his support for his father, which he did in a speech in the Commons in

June 1903. But his heart was not in it. He had been comfortable with the cautious Conservatism of Salisbury and Balfour, his respect for the latter amounting almost to reverence, as he would later count him among 'our great Prime Ministers'. To Austen, 'he was always the kindest of friends and most helpful and encouraging of chiefs and colleagues'.[14] This fond reminiscence seems almost bizarre in light of the events of these years. Balfour's subtle antagonism to Joe Chamberlain did much to thwart the tariff reform campaign and to break Joe physically. Filial loyalty obliged Austen to follow his father, but the strain of these years helps to account for the personality changes perceived by contemporaries—from the open and amiable man of his youth to the aloof, reserved, and prickly statesman of later years. Never a Radical like his father, nor inclined to antagonism or vengeance, Austen was by nature a conciliator.

Such qualities were in short supply in the Edwardian Unionist Party. Split loyalties and in-fighting affected Austen badly, but paradoxically brought him an important promotion. In September, believing that he had cut a deal with Balfour, Joe Chamberlain resigned in order to devote all his time and energy to tariff reform. Balfour cleared out of his Cabinet those adamantly opposed to any changes in fiscal policy, including the Chancellor of the Exchequer, Charles Ritchie. In October 1903, Austen took his place, which was taken as a sign that Balfour and Chamberlain were working in tandem—an astute move on Balfour's part. Austen had become something of a hostage, Joe's growing irritation with Balfour muted by his reluctance to undermine his son's position. Gratified by the promotion and by the salary of £5,000, Austen was nevertheless in an uncomfortable position—pull devil, pull baker.

Chancellor of the Exchequer

Promotion to the Chancellorship was a life-changing event for Austen. No longer living under his father's roofs or in the bosom of his family, he took up residence at No. 11 Downing Street. On his very first evening there, he poured out his feelings of love and respect for his father in a letter, concluding:

> It is at once a great encouragement and a great responsibility to be heir
> to so fine a tradition of private honour and public duty and I will do my
> best to be not unworthy of the name.[15]

On the whole Austen performed creditably in his new role. Understandably, he made a rather nervous start. In February 1904, he was called upon to deputise for a sick Balfour at the opening of Parliament and was considered to have floundered badly, thrown off his stride by spilling a bottle of ink down his trousers. Never an outstanding orator, he performed best in less formal situations. However, his presentation of two budgets in 1904 and 1905 demonstrated a growing confidence. Conditions were hardly favourable, the national debt having been considerably increased by the exorbitant cost of the Boer War but Austen was considered to have made the best of a bad job, no doubt heavily guided by the mandarinate at the Treasury. Though cautious and conventional, his budgets were, in Roy Jenkins' opinion, 'taut and competent'.[16] In the first, in April 1904, he increased income tax by one penny in the pound, added twopence to the duty on tea, and increased tobacco duties. By 1905 the economy was more buoyant and he was able to reverse the tax on tea and set aside a small sum for debt reduction. His speech, lasting less than two hours, was less than half as long as Gladstone's had been a generation earlier, as well as one of the shortest on record. His stint as Chancellor consolidated Austen's position in the Unionist hierarchy, ex-Chancellors enjoying a status second only to ex-Prime Ministers.

Although gratified by his enhanced political role, Austen nevertheless found his position between Balfour and his imperious father stressful. Expected to uphold the tariff reform cause in Cabinet, he struggled manfully to bridge the growing gap between the two. In a letter in August 1904, he explicitly accused Balfour of letting his father down.

> You encouraged my father to go out as a 'pioneer'; you gave your blessing to his efforts for closer union with the colonies.[17]

But he had failed to give the party a lead, leaving it mired in 'perpetual controversy and parliamentary impotence'. What the Chamberlains wanted was an early dissolution of Parliament to capitalise on the initial impact of tariff reform. But, after a brief flurry of by-election victories, a depressing sequence of defeats followed and it became increasingly clear that the public response was unfavourable. The Chamberlains had to come to terms with the near certainty of defeat at the next general election, but reached the conclusion that the longer the delay, the worse the likely result.

'Beaten we shall be in any case,' Austen wrote to Balfour, 'I think we are on the brink of disaster'. The family was increasingly concerned about Joe's health, severely threatened as it was by his extended campaigning. But Balfour, supported by his party managers, Jack Sandars and Acland Hood, refused to budge. In his replies to Austen's entreaties, he blithely argued that his own Sheffield policy—reciprocity but no taxes on food—was 'logical and self-contained'. He acknowledged that protectionism had a long history in the Conservative Party but that it should 'remain what it had long been, a doctrine largely held by the Party, but with no place in its official creed'. In a speech in Edinburgh in October 1904, Balfour further infuriated the Chamberlains by putting forward his 'two-election' proposal. Should the party win the next election, it would consult with the colonial Premiers and then put any resulting proposals before the electorate in a further general election. This was rightly seen by the tariff reformers as kicking imperial preference into the long grass. Balfour's hostility to the tariff reform programme was becoming more and more apparent.[18]

The attempts of the Chamberlains to tie Balfour down and the latter's slippery evasions continued until Parliament was finally dissolved in December 1905. The general election of January 1906 proved a greater disaster than even Austen had predicted. The strain of events had undermined Austen's health. He was wracked with sciatica and described by sister Ida as 'a total wreck'. While his indefatigable father rampaged across the country, Austen was unable to join the campaign until its latter stages, whereupon he was confined to his own constituency in East Worcestershire. A mere 157 Unionist MPs were returned, the majority 'Whole-Hoggers'—full supporters of the tariff reform programme. Only in Birmingham and its periphery was there whole-hearted endorsement. Joe Chamberlain's majority in West Birmingham exceeded 5,000, while Austen's was by a creditable 4,366. Among the legions of the rejected was Arthur Balfour. Defeated in Manchester, a seat was shortly found for him in the City of London. The temptation for Joe to seize the leadership of the party was resisted and the attempt to pin down Balfour continued. A three-week negotiation resulted in an exchange of letters, largely drafted by Austen and dubbed the Valentine Compact, in which Balfour appeared to endorse 'the Birmingham programme'- 'Fiscal Reform is and must remain the first constructive work of the Unionist party'. If the Chamberlains considered this agreement to have ended the era of ambiguity, they were soon to be sadly disillusioned.

A decade on the back benches

It was nearly a decade and two more lost elections before Austen once again became a government minister. With Joe also out of office, the Chamberlains faced straitened financial circumstances, increasingly reliant on Neville's financial acumen to maintain their customary lavish level of expenditure. Austen's health was causing the family concern, Neville complaining alarmingly to his sisters that he was 'becoming a chronic invalid'. An extensive period of rest and recuperation was called for and as soon as the parliamentary session ended, Austen headed for Algiers with his friend Leverton Harris. His recovery was due less to the North African sun than to his encounter with Ivy Dundas, with whom he very quickly fell in love, announcing their engagement to his delighted family in May. Ivy was twenty-seven years old, the daughter of a serving soldier, Col. Dundas, and from a family whose male members had traditionally been soldiers and Anglican clergymen. She knew nothing of politics, which may well have been part of her attraction, but for all thirty-one years of their marriage she proved supportive of Austen's career. The pair were married on 21 July 1906 at St Margaret's in Westminster, in one of the most publicised society weddings of the year. The 12,000 guests included all members of the Tory front-bench and more than a few Liberals. Neville acted as best-man, while Ivy was tended by eight bridesmaids and two train-bearers. Her dress was made by Mary's dressmaker, Worth of Paris. Austen's present to her was a diamond tiara and among the many presents was a silver inkstand from the King and a diamond pin from the Queen. Truly, the Chamberlains had arrived. Following their honeymoon, Austen and Ivy moved into their own house for the first time, 29 Egerton Place, off the Old Brompton Road. The marriage was a very happy one, giving Austen an emotional stability he had previously lacked. He proved to be a devoted husband and father to their three children.

There was one conspicuous absentee among the families and friends at the wedding: Joe Chamberlain, who had suffered a stroke a fortnight before. Mary was doing her best to hide the full extent of the damage, desperately hoping for a rapid recovery. Among the interested parties anxious to learn the full extent of Joe's disablement was Arthur Balfour, whose spies reported accurately that he had suffered a severe stroke and was unlikely to recover his full powers.

Austen was now charged by his father to take over the leadership of the tariff reform movement and to continue the pressure on Balfour. Although this went against the grain, Austen strived to comply. Ironically, his harrying of Balfour earned him a similar reputation in the eyes of a hostile squirearchy to that of his father. That most honourable of men stood indicted for disloyalty to his leader. 'By nature a congenial man,' wrote Peter Marsh, 'Austen had to become a gang leader'. The arrival in Parliament of over fifty Labour MPs and the radical social reform programme advanced by the Liberal Government obliged the tariff reformers to adjust their ideas and put greater emphasis on the social dimensions of 'Imperialism and Social Reform'. Austen's letters to Balfour in this period show him advocating commitment to old age pensions, land reform, measures to outlaw sweated labour and other proposals emanating from the Unionist Social Reform Committee. All his dealings with Balfour were faithfully reported to Joe via Mary, published in *Politics from Inside* in 1936.

Austen's advocacy of social reform was an affair of the head rather than the heart. His natural conservatism was nowhere better revealed than in his strong opposition to the emerging Suffragette movement, aligning himself with Lord Curzon and other 'diehards'. Sharing a confidence with a Palace yard policeman in March 1907, Austen exclaimed, 'Drat the Women! I wish the Magistrate would give the leaders a good heavy sentence'. His attitude was shared by his father and even the women of the Chamberlain household. In a letter to Joe and Mary in March 1909, on the eve of a speech in which he attacked the Suffragettes, he expressed his distaste for

> [...] their whole movement and all it means in politics and social life. The more I think of it, the more my whole soul revolts against it....

The notion of admitting women to the cosy, male-dominated world of politics let alone to the hallowed halls of Westminster was anathema to him. To his credit, he later regretted this stance, and admitted that he had been wrong.[19]

Although some of the more committed tariff reformers—such as Leo Amery and Alfred Milner—were critical of Austen's leadership, he did his utmost to fulfil his father's expectations and harass Balfour into commitment to the cause. At the NUCCA Conference in Birmingham's Bingley Hall in September of 1907, Balfour made a speech which seemed to commit him to 'the Birmingham programme,' afterwards visiting Joe at Highbury. But this was easier to do now that Joe was side-lined and there was no immediate prospect of a Unionist Government. He and his advisers remained convinced that any advocacy of food taxes would once again court electoral disaster. However, in 1909, Balfour's subtle hostility was complemented by the frontal blow delivered to tariff reform by Lloyd George's famous 'People's Budget', in which he proposed a raft of new taxes to pay both for old age pensions and for 'Dreadnoughts'. His proposals entailed 'a complete reconstruction of the methods of evaluating property'. The necessary money could be raised, therefore, without recourse to tariffs.

Lloyd George's budget speech in April was by no means his finest hour, or rather four and a half hours. At times his voice failed him, so much so that Balfour suggested a half-hour adjournment, during which, Megan Lloyd George reported, 'Mr Balfour gave daddy a beef tea when he was tired'. Austen was highly critical of the Chancellor's speech in his report to Joe, no doubt recalling how Lloyd George and Winston Churchill had harried him when he had delivered his first budget speech in 1904 (irked by what they considered Austen's pomposity, they had extended the debate far into the night).

[Lloyd George] was fagged before he began ... much of the speech was read and badly read. He stumbled over sentences, rushed past full stops, paused at the commas and altogether gave the impression that at these points he did not understand what he was saying.

Perhaps because of the Budget's complexity, Austen was slow to recognise its implications. Replying for the Opposition as their only ex-Chancellor in the Commons, his criticisms tended to be mild and technocratic, at some points even approving. But the penny eventually dropped. 'This Budget is Socialism,' he declared, 'the alternative is Tariff Reform'.[20] Recognising that Lloyd George's proposals constituted a refutation of their fiscal arguments, the Unionist tariff reformers—led by Austen— fought the budget clause by clause. Landowners were equally appalled by the proposed new taxes on land and other assaults on wealth and on 30 November the Lords threw out the budget, in defiance of the convention that they should not reject money Bills. Whether or not Lloyd George had deliberately set a trap is debateable, but he reacted gleefully. Here was the opportunity for Liberals to extract revenge for many earlier defeats. Asquith dissolved Parliament and the 'Peers *vs* People' election was underway. 'Peers *vs.* People' joined 'Socialism *vs.* Tariff Reform' among the issues in the election. Joe Chamberlain, always anticipating that public acceptance of tariff reform would require more than one election, was optimistic—Austen, less so. Joe was the first candidate from Birmingham returned to Parliament, unopposed in West Birmingham, as Austen was in East Worcestershire. The response in the Duchy was positive, all Birmingham seats returning Unionist candidates and several other seats returning to their pre-1906 allegiance. But the general election nationally disappointed. The pendulum certainly swung, for 273 Unionists were returned to the Commons, but this was 2 short of the Liberal total. With the support of the Irish Nationalists and the Labour party, Asquith still had a secure majority with the result, however, that the issue of Irish Home Rule was once again forced into the forefront of British politics.

Opposition to the budget having been safely dissipated, Asquith turned to the constitutional issue. In April 1910, he introduced into the Commons the Parliament Bill, which proposed to remove the power of the House of Lords to interfere with money Bills and to limit their Lordships' powers to block legislation for more than three sessions of Parliament. Should the Lords reject the Parliament Bill, Asquith held out the threat of a mass creation of peers to overturn the in-built Conservative majority. The Bill safely passed the Commons and was sent up to the Lords, where opinion was bitterly divided. Lord Halsbury led a recalcitrant group prepared 'to die in the ditch' ('Ditchers'), Lord Landsdowne a group prepared to compromise ('Hedgers'). Predictably, Austen followed Joe in his support of the 'Ditchers', prepared to reject the Bill and to damn the consequences.

The issue was complicated by the death of Edward VII, who had been reluctant to sanction the mass creation of peers, on 6 May 1910. In deference to the new monarch George V, the party leaders agreed to a Constitutional Conference to seek a solution. Balfour led the four-man Unionist delegation which included Austen. Between June and November, the Conference met on no less than twenty-two occasions before breaking up without agreement on 10 November. Lloyd George emerged as the most flexible and constructive of the eight delegates. Advocating the formation of a Coalition Government, he surprised the Unionist quartet by expressing willingness to contemplate imperial preference, a scheme of compulsory military service and a federal solution of the Irish problem. In the course of the conference, in a speech to the Liberal Christian League, he praised Joe Chamberlain for his contribution to the welfare of the masses by his support for state action. He even went so far as to draw up a proposed list of Cabinet offices, with Austen Chamberlain pencilled in as First Lord of the Admiralty. Although Austen retained his basic distrust of Lloyd George, he could not help but be impressed, reporting to his father that Lloyd George had acted 'with great force and sincerity'. Lloyd George was less impressed with Austen's contribution to the discussions: 'such a slow and commonplace mind that he didn't count', he commented.[21] The conference broke down mainly on the question of Ireland. Lloyd George proposed something close to the Chamberlainite model of the 1880s, 'Home Rule All Round', but Balfour feared further splits and upheaval in his party. Asquith reported the failure to come to an agreement to the King and at the same time asked for a dissolution.

The December 1910 election was a desultory affair, with public involvement at a low ebb. In an attempt to improve his party's standing, Balfour made a speech in the Albert Hall pledging to hold a referendum on food taxes should the Unionists form a government. The Chamberlains were predictably angry. Austen confided to Landsdowne that Balfour's declaration was 'a great blow to me—the worst disappointment that I have suffered for a long time in politics'. But Balfour's pledge, evidence of the deep divisions in his party, had little effect on the result and there was only a tiny shift in the relative strength of the parties, the Unionists gaining a mere two seats.

Asquith reintroduced the Parliament Bill in the House of Commons in February. It was passed in May and sent up to the House of Lords. On 25 July 1911, the Ditchers staged a dinner at the Hotel Cecil in honour of Lord Halsbury. Joe sent a telegram urging 'No surrender' while Austen made a speech in which he spoke of 'this revolution, nurtured in lies, promoted by fraud and only to be achieved by violence'. Asquith, he argued, had 'tricked the Opposition, entrapped the Crown and deceived the people'. He had thus played the part his father had decreed for him, but one suspects that in his head he would have preferred to be in the camp of the compromisers led by Balfour and Landsdowne. In the course of the debate in the Lords on 10 August, Morley revealed that Asquith had secured the King's agreement to the creation of peers should the bill be rejected. In the division, 13 bishops and 37 Unionist peers voted with the Government, while Landsdowne and others abstained. The Bill was passed by 17 votes.

A defining moment

Upheaval in the Unionist Party was by no means at an end. What was perceived as failure in Balfour's leadership incited a demand, led by Leo Maxse, owner and editor of the *National Review*, for his replacement. Although Austen had identified himself completely with the Ditchers, he refused to join the attack on Balfour, admitting to F. E. Smith, 'I am too much attached to him ever to join any combination against him or his leadership'. But, weary of perpetual strife, Balfour resigned on 7 November 1911. Rather than perceiving an opportunity, Austen expressed his dismay to Mary:

> The blow has fallen and I am sick as a man can be.... I love the man, and though as you know he has once or twice nearly broken my heart politically, I now can think of nothing but the pleasure of intimate association with him, the constant personal kindness he has shown to me and the great qualities of mind and character he has brought to the discharge of the tremendous duties of his post.

Austen was, as David Dutton wrote, 'the obvious choice' of successor. He had the support of Balfour himself, of the Chief Whip Balcarres, other party managers and of a majority of the Shadow Cabinet. It soon became apparent, however, that there were elements in the party who were critical of his 'diehard' stance over the Parliament Act and his membership of the Halsbury Club, which had mobilised opposition to Balfour. Ironically, they accused Austen of disloyalty to a man he revered and had not wanted displaced. Although the Liberal Unionists were by now well integrated into the party, some still saw his Liberal Unionism and Unitarian background as a disqualification. But the largest body of opposition came from those heartily sick of dictation from 'the crippled giant of Highbury' and of the havoc that tariff reform had spawned in the party.

These strands of opposition were mobilised by Walter Long, who disliked Austen and was jealous of his influence in the party. His parliamentary record pre-dated Chamberlain's and he also enjoyed front-bench status. Nobody in the party leadership believed him more suitable than Austen, but his landownership and hunting-and-fishing lifestyle united the squirearchy behind him. Garvin, editor of *The Observer*, noted 'a curious lot of old Tory and Anglican feeling against Birmingham and Unitarianism coming out'. But there was a final factor that defeated Austen—his diffidence and his self-doubt made him his own worst enemy. Though confident of his ability to lead the party, he wanted the leadership simply handed to him and was not prepared to fight for it. It was this lack of verve which made even the tariff reformers lukewarm about his qualities: Austen was their leader, but not the one they wanted. Explaining himself to Joe and Mary, he wrote, 'I was appalled by the difficulties of the position and well aware how many of the necessary qualities I lacked'.[22]

In the circumstances, with Austen and Long neck and neck, it was perhaps inevitable that a third party should snatch the prize. Andrew Bonar Law, a Scottish-Canadian former ironmaster, urged on by Max Aitken (later Lord Beaverbrook), threw his hat in the ring and although junior to both Long and Chamberlain and with no ministerial experience, he refused to withdraw. He had recently joined the Shadow Cabinet, was a strong tariff reformer and had already earned respect as an able debater with a phenomenal memory. It was most unlikely that he expected to win against Austen, but rather was putting down a marker for the future. It was Austen himself who opened the door. Though he later calculated that he would have won a ballot, Austen was unwilling to divide the party and he therefore proposed to Long that they should both withdraw in favour of Bonar Law. Long, whose main object was to stop Austen, agreed. Bonar Law, proposed by Long and seconded by Austen, was elected leader without opposition at a party meeting in the Carlton Club on 13 November 1911.

Although there were those who were impressed by Austen's self-sacrifice and meticulous sense of honour and who respected him for the way he had behaved, the hard men in the party had their doubts about his character confirmed. Among his sternest critics was Leo Amery, elected MP for Birmingham at a by-election that year and a fanatical disciple of Joe Chamberlain. In his autobiography, *My Political Life*, he wrote:

> The trouble with Austen was not undue humility or diffidence. He had quite a good opinion of himself. But he had an exaggerated fear of being regarded as pushful ... or other than scrupulously correct and loyal in all his personal dealings; a weakness that was to stand in his way on more than one occasion.[23]

Did this stem from a consciousness that his father, 'Pushful Joe', had acquired a very different reputation? More plausibly, these objections had genuinely to do with his nature. Such a conscientious character put him at a disadvantage when contrasted with men of more robust ambitions. News of Austen's self-denial was badly received at Highbury. Although Joe professed to endorse his actions, he had begun to perceive that it was Neville, rather than Austen, who was made of sterner mettle. Perhaps, from Austen's personal point of view, it was all for the best. From 1912 to 1914, the country experienced a period of acute turbulence: industrial unrest, Suffragette militancy and division over Ireland. Given Austen's poor health and lack of stamina, it may have been more than he could have handled, even as leader of the Opposition as opposed to the Government. But he would soon have good reason to regret the decision he had made in 1911.

Bonar Law was a confirmed tariff reformer and he withdrew Balfour's Albert Hall pledge to hold a referendum on food taxes. But he found himself under strong pressure from disillusioned Tories, who had become convinced that the party could never win an election while advocating taxes on food. The pressure came especially from Lancashire where Lord Derby, aided by the Cecils, orchestrated contention. Austen attempted to keep Bonar Law up to the mark, but the pressure became too intense and he offered to resign. A memorial to him was organised and signed by the great majority of Unionist MPs urging him to stay. In January 1913, he and Lord Lansdowne, party leader in the Lords, announced that food taxes would be dropped from the Unionist agenda. Austen was devastated and wrote forlornly to Highbury:

> I have done my best but the game is up. We are beaten and the cause for which Father gave more than life itself is abandoned.[24]

Nearly blind and deeply depressed, Joe Chamberlain made the decision that he would not again contest West Birmingham and demanded that Austen be his successor. Somewhat reluctantly, Austen agreed to abandon the leafy lanes of Worcestershire for the smoke-filled alleys of industrial Birmingham.

The disposal of the food tax issue enabled a united party to turn its attention to Ireland. On 11 April 1912, Asquith had introduced the third Home Rule Bill into the Commons and barring unforeseen circumstances, under the Parliament Act, Irish Home Rule would become a reality in 1914. Bonar Law took a rigid and unyielding line in support of Sir Edward Carson, who was organising resistance in Ulster. The signing of the Covenant and the formation of the Ulster Volunteer Force made civil war a real possibility and the so-called Curragh Mutiny—with officers in the Irish garrison opting to resign if called upon to deal with the Ulstermen— underlined the danger. When Carson had paid a visit to Highbury, Joe Chamberlain had signified his support for the policy of 'No Surrender'. Austen, however, was more equivocal and searched for constitutional solutions. But his efforts to revive Joe's federal formula of the 1880s found little echo in the Unionist Party, in which Bonar Law, Carson, and F. E. Smith made all the running. Recognising Austen's instinct for conciliation, Asquith, with whom Austen enjoyed cordial relations, twice offered him the Chairmanship of Royal Commissions. The first, on the Civil Service, Austen refused but the second, on Indian Finance and Currency, he accepted. Although Austen's status in his own party had slipped following his failure to seize the leadership and his clear differences with Bonar Law, whom he was coming to despise as 'an amateur', Asquith's offers were a confirmation of Austen's reputation as a competent administrator. As with Asquith, he continued to enjoy good personal relations with Joe's old friend and then rival, Lord Morley, and also Winston Churchill. For the time being, however, he drew the line at Lloyd George. Once when invited to dinner by Churchill, he replied,

> [...] though always delighted to see you and Morley on any pretext I should prefer not to be asked to meet Lloyd George—at present.[25]

Despite his reservations, one detects in this reply all the symptoms of a potential Coalitionist who would one day even reverse his opinion of the family's principal *bête noire*.

The death of Joe Chamberlain on 2 July 1914 was for Austen both a sorrow and a liberation. He would henceforth be his own man. It also led to a severing of the family's connection with Birmingham, only Neville remaining resident in the city. Joe left £125,000 in his will, the bulk of the money going to Mary and his surviving daughters. A mere £12,000 remained for his sons, of which three quarters went to Austen. He and Mary agreed that Highbury could no longer be maintained and by the autumn Mary had disposed of the estate and the contents of the house, herself taking up residence in Prince's Gardens. Beatrice bought a house close to Austen's in Egerton Place and Hilda and Ida a substantial house in Odiham in Hampshire. In August Austen transferred constituencies and was returned unopposed at a by-election in West Birmingham. Although Joe's intention was to ensure Austen's leadership of the Birmingham caucus, his status became largely nominal and it was Neville, the man on the spot, who was increasingly perceived as the heir to Joe's position.

War and return to government

When war broke out between Germany and France on 2 August 1914, Austen was in the forefront of those Unionists demanding an immediate declaration in support of France. He urged party leaders to put pressure on Asquith, who was contending with divisions in his Cabinet. The invasion of Belgium, however, resolved the issue and a British declaration of war on Germany followed on 4 August. The Chancellor, Lloyd George, invited the two surviving former Unionist Chancellors, Lord St Aldwyn and Austen, to act as Treasury advisers. Austen responded with some enthusiasm and found himself impressed with Lloyd George's acumen and energy. These, comments Peter Dutton, were 'the first tentative steps in Chamberlain's association with Lloyd George'.[26] Austen did not yet perceive him as a replacement for Asquith, but responding to military setbacks, he, in conjunction with Curzon and Lord Robert Cecil, was among those pressing the Prime Minister to form a coalition and establish a small War Cabinet to facilitate a more efficient management of the war.

In May 1915, Asquith bowed to pressure and formed the first coalition, though the disposition of offices made it clear that he had no intention of relinquishing control. Bonar Law was, somewhat contemptuously, appointed Secretary of State for the Colonies, Balfour First Lord of the Admiralty, and Austen Secretary of State for India. Although peripheral to the main issues of the conflict in Europe, Austen was at least back in Cabinet after a decade in the wilderness and thankful to receive a ministerial salary. He did not, it seems, inspire his Liberal colleagues, Lord Runciman describing his contributions to Cabinet debate as insignificant and unsuggestive. But the key appointment was that of Lloyd George, who courageously abandoned the Exchequer for the new post of Minister of Munitions and soon began transforming the British war effort on the supply side.

The office of Secretary of State for India was a high-status, yet curiously hybrid role. Real decision-making was done on the spot in India, where the Viceroy at this time was Lord Hardinge. The Indian Army was similarly beyond the reach of the War Office in London. When Britain declared war on Turkey in November 1914, an operation was begun in Mesopotamia to secure the oilfields at the head of the Persian Gulf. The initial success of the expedition encouraged the Cabinet to stiffen this largely Indian force with a British division and to authorise a push on Baghdad. This proved to be a step too far. Gen. Townsend's force was defeated by the Turks and retreated to Kut, where, on 16 April 1916, it was forced to surrender and 6,000 Indian troops and 3,000 British were taken prisoner. The furore resulting from this fiasco was compounded by rumours of inadequate medical services and the suffering of sick and wounded troops. The Mesopotamian campaign inevitably reflected on the Secretary of State. Nobody considered Chamberlain responsible for the military disaster, but provisioning and medical services were considered to be the responsibility of the India Office. Austen had received reports of their inadequacy and had repeatedly taxed Lord Hardinge with the complaints which had reached him, only to be reassured that these were baseless rumours and these assurances he had passed on to the Commons. Austen was as shocked as anyone by the extent of the revelations that followed, regarding it as 'an absolute scandal'. Heads would have to roll.

The Asquith Government set up a commission to investigate the issues under Lord George Hamilton, a former Secretary of State for India. The Commission's report, published in June 1917, contained only minor criticisms of the Secretary of State whom, it was felt, should have made his concerns about the state of affairs in Mesopotamia more public. His fault lay in trusting the men on the spot. Austen made an effective defence of his role in the House of Commons, but nevertheless insisted on resigning on 12 July 1917. His resignation was widely regarded, especially in political circles, as a further indication of Austen's naïve over-sensitivity to his 'honour'. It may also have been motivated in part by his feeling of utter exhaustion and the threat of breakdown in his health. He looked forward to a period of recuperation in the Sussex countryside, but even there, issues of state pursued him. He refused his successor's request to visit India, but he did accept membership of two parliamentary committees. His return to office was regarded as only a matter of time.

He had been appointed to the India Office by Asquith. His resignation, however, was presented to a different leader—none other than David Lloyd George, who had replaced Asquith upon his own resignation in December 1916. Austen had taken little part in the internal conflicts and intrigues leading to the fall of Asquith and, though he shared many of the criticisms made of the Prime Minister, he regretted it on personal grounds. To his sister Hilda on 14 December, he confessed:

> I take no pleasure in a change which gives me a chief I profoundly distrust—no doubt a man of great energy but quite untrustworthy, who doesn't run crooked because he wants to but because he doesn't know how to run straight.[27]

Although Lloyd George tried to dissuade Austen from leaving his post and even offered him the Paris Embassy, which he declined, it would be a while before Austen called time on the family feud and began to succumb to the Welshman's notorious charm. Tolerable relations were nevertheless established and by March 1917, Austen was reporting to his sister Hilda,

'Lloyd George dined in my house last night! Such are Time's strange reverses'.

To many in the political establishment, a Coalition Government without Austen seemed unthinkable and his name was connected with every vacancy that occurred. Though enjoying greater leisure, as always the pull of office was strong and he remained confident that he had a contribution to make, especially in keeping Lloyd George on the straight and narrow. Shortly before re-joining the Government, he reflected on the character of the man he had come to regard as indispensable, though flawed.

> With all his faults he has certain qualities especially valuable at this time and I want not to destroy him but to save him from his own folly and crookedness.[28]

In April 1918 the inevitable invitation came and Austen was invited to join the War Cabinet of six as a minister without portfolio. His return to government was generally welcomed, apart from vitriolic attacks in the *Daily Mail* in retaliation for the trenchant criticisms he had recently made of the pretensions of the press barons in the House of Commons. The paper lampooned Austen as 'an ineffective mediocrity' and his career one of 'amiable insignificance'.[29]

From the very beginning, Austen's chief preoccupation as a Cabinet member was with the developing crisis in Ireland and the search for a solution. As a member of the Home Rule Committee set up to draft legislation, he reverted to his father's ideas of the 1880s 'to federalise the whole UK'. Unfortunately, he met with intransigence both from Unionists and Irish Nationalists, lamenting that 'Ireland is full of unreason'. His continued advocacy of a federal solution found scant support. His administrative skills were nevertheless in demand in a range of committees and he assured his sisters that he was making a difference. In June he expressed pessimism about the chances of an end to the war. 'The end', he told his sisters, 'is far off I fear'. However, Austen's mood changed following the British victory at the Battle of Amiens in August, followed by a string of victories on other fronts, which he described to them as 'prodijeous' [sic]. He began to contemplate the shape of a peace settlement, which he feared would be complicated by President Wilson's naivety. He let rip his contempt for Germany in a letter to Hilda:

> Truculent in success, overbearing and brutal in victory, when they find the game is up they collapse morally as a people....

When contemplating the future shape of British politics, Austen was firmly convinced that the continuance of the Coalition under Lloyd George's leadership was essential. He feared for a future which seemed full of dangers—'strikes, discontent and much revolutionary feeling'. Socialism, which he associated with the Labour Party and the trade union movement, had to be kept at bay and out of power.

The return to peace and the Coalition Government

As the general election of December 1918 loomed following the Armistice of the previous month, Austen grew alarmed by the state of the once formidable Unionist organisation in Birmingham, which had largely disintegrated in the course of the war. He need not have worried. Lloyd George basked in popular approval as 'the little man who had won the war', while the Unionist Party was boosted by the division of the Liberals between the 'Coalies' and 'Squiffites'. The main challenge, therefore, came from Labour, which had itself so recently been split by the issues of the war. Birmingham stood out once again as a Unionist stronghold. The Representation of the People's Act of 1918 had considerably increased the electorate, enfranchising women of 30 and over. It had also increased Birmingham's divisions from seven to twelve, all of which were won by Coalition supporters, their majorities ranging from 4,000 in Yardley to over 12,000 in Moseley. Once again, Austen enjoyed the luxury of an unopposed return, his Labour opponent having failed to get his deposit in on time. For the Chamberlain family this was a time of sadness, Austen's sister Beatrice having succumbed to Spanish flu in the previous month. Though there was some consolation in Neville's successful return to Parliament, for the very first time, as MP for Ladywood.

The Coalition leaders had every reason to be pleased with the result of the 'Coupon Election'. 338 Conservatives and 136 Coalition Liberals were returned, to be confronted by 59 Labour representatives and a paltry 26 Squiffites, not including their leader. Austen regretted Asquith's defeat and perceived peril in the magnitude of the Coalition majority. In the re-shuffle that followed and against the instincts of the PM, Bonar Law pressed for Austen to replace him at the Exchequer. It was not merely Lloyd George, however, who raised objections, but Austen himself, for this office was offered without a place in Cabinet and without tenure of 11 Downing Street, which Bonar Law intended to continue occupying. The intention seemed to be that Lloyd George and Bonar Law would run the Government as a duumvirate, the former dealing with the many international issues thrown up by the war and the latter with domestic policy. Not only was Austen's *amour propre* offended, but his sense of constitutional propriety. He complained that he had been offered the post like a dog might be thrown a bone, to which Lloyd George riposted that there was quite a lot of meat on the bone in question![30] Austen conceded No. 11 to Bonar Law, but insisted on the restoration of normal Cabinet arrangements. A compromise was reached. For the time being, the War Cabinet of which Austen was a member would continue. In October 1919, the old Cabinet arrangements were restored, with Austen and Lord Curzon the dominant members in the frequent absence of Lloyd George and Bonar Law.

It was little wonder that Austen approached his new role with reluctance. He knew from his earlier experience how heavy was the burden carried by the Chancellor and the problems faced in the wake of this, the 'Great War' were many times worse. The national debt was ten times higher than it had been in 1903 and servicing it swallowed 52 per cent of Government revenue in his first budget. Heavy external debt, mostly to the US, had also been incurred. The pensions of some 2 million men wounded in the war were an unavoidable cost, while Lloyd George, with his promises of 'homes fit for heroes', had committed the Government to welfare reforms. On the other hand, entrepreneurs were pressing for reductions in tax, especially Excess Profits Duty, which had reached 80 per cent. Orthodox financial policy dictated balanced budgets, debt reduction and eventually a return to the gold standard. How was Austen to square these circles? It was small wonder that as early as April 1918 he was writing despairingly to Ida, 'I wish I could chuck the whole business', and the family was once again worried about the state of his health. Twice Lloyd George offered him relief from his burdens: in July 1919 he was offered the Washington Embassy, and in October 1920 the Viceroyalty of India. Both were exceedingly prestigious posts, yet Austen declined. His morale was undoubtedly improved by his purchase of Twitt's Gyll, a small estate in Sussex, to which he could escape with his wife and children.

Sharp fluctuations in the state of the economy, a period of buoyant activity followed by a sharp decline accompanied by rising unemployment, complicated Austen's task. In his first budget he was obliged to raise the level of taxation though halving Excess Profits Duty. He took great satisfaction from a modest measure of imperial preference, making tea and other products imported from around the Empire cheaper. This measure, of course, was accompanied by the obligatory genuflection to his father. In his second he was able to make a modest start on debt reduction and had the satisfaction of abolishing the famous land taxes which had caused such a furore in the People's Budget of 1909. By that time Austen was beginning to feel equal to his unenviable task. 'Give me three more years and short of unforeseen catastrophe in Europe or Asia we will have our finances in a thoroughly sound position,' he boasted to his sisters. He described his second budget as 'my triumph' and congratulated himself on his growing ascendancy in the Commons: 'I have a position quite of my own and the pleasant feeling that men of all parties like and respect me'.

In Austen's third year as Chancellor, he faced a number of pressures. Churchill was demanding funds to aid the White Russian armies, Addison was intent on implementing what turned out to be a very expensive housing programme and while parts of the press were demanding reductions in Government expenditure, Lord Rothermere was going to such extremes as to sponsor Anti-Waste candidates in by-elections. Austen found support from an unlikely quarter. 'Curiously enough', he told sister Ida, 'my only ally is the Prime Minister'. Remaining doubts about the PM were further dispelled when, in February 1921, Lloyd George was made a Freeman of the City of Birmingham and delivered a very flattering speech about the contribution made by the city to the war effort. That evening Austen joined Lloyd George at a dinner given by the Jewellers Association, subsequently reporting to his sisters:

> Whatever his past and present faults, I do not regret it and I would not have absented myself if I could, for he has great qualities and has rendered great services. No living Englishman can compare with him and when the history of these times comes to be written can you doubt that he will stand out like the Younger Pitt if not with the effulgence of Chatham.

Soon after the Birmingham visit, Austen's wearisome burden of the Exchequer was lifted from his shoulders. In March Bonar Law was obliged by illness to resign his offices of Lord Privy Seal and Leader of the Unionist Party in the House of Commons. Though other names were canvassed, there was no concerted opposition to Austen and he was elected leader by acclaim at the Carlton Club. True to form, instead of seeing this role as a glorious opportunity, Austen responded gloomily to his elevation. It was, he told his sisters 'an obvious duty but without any pleasure or any great expectations except trouble and hard duty'. Within days, however, he was becoming almost jaunty, confessing to Ida, 'I am beginning to like it, and I hope you will consider that a healthy sign'. Perhaps to his surprise, his promotion to leader brought congratulations from all sides and met with general approval in the press. At the outset Lloyd George was equally apprehensive. He had enjoyed excellent relations with Bonar Law in and out of Parliament and regretted his absence. His mistress Frances Stevenson's diary recorded the PM's view of Austen as prickly, pompous and wooden. Yet he soon warmed to Austen, describing him to Bonar Law as 'loyal, straight and sensible', while Frances confided in her diary:

[Lloyd George] certainly gets on better with him than he expected to. Austen plays the game and he sees that he can trust the PM who conceals nothing from him.[31]

And yet, Austen's leadership of the Unionist Party was destined to be the shortest on record. His failure to convert it into the Premiership would once again confront his family with grave disappointment.

The lost opportunity

Although regretting the loss of Bonar Law, the transition to Austen at least made it easier to achieve a negotiated settlement of the Irish question, which had reached an acute phase. The Government's tactic of meeting terror with terror was causing widespread revulsion and damaging Britain's reputation both at home and abroad. In his study of the Coalition, Lord Morgan summarises its attitude thus:

Ireland was the blackest chapter of the government's policy in any theatre, a monument to ignorance, racial and religious prejudice, and ineptitude.[32]

Bonar Law was identified with the diehard position on Ireland, but from the time he had re-entered the Coalition, Austen had insisted on a search for a political solution through his resurrection of his father's old proposal of devolution. 'Home Rule All Round' found little support from colleagues and did him harm in some quarters of the party. However, it prompted Lloyd George into a more pragmatic stance and a mixture of cajolery and threats brought Sinn Fein to the table. In December 1921, a treaty was signed recognising the independence of the twenty-six counties of Southern Ireland, the six counties comprising Ulster remaining part of the United Kingdom, with its own Parliament in Belfast. Many Irish Nationalists refused to accept the treaty both in part and its entirety and a bloody civil war ensued. The Anglo-Irish Treaty was far from a final settlement of the Irish question, but at least—from the British Government's point of view—it had been removed from the top of the political agenda.

There was little else of which the Coalition could boast. At home the state of the economy remained bleak and the 'Geddes Axe' destroyed hopes of social reform, while abroad Lloyd George's attempts at finding solutions to problems attached to the Treaty of Versailles came to naught at the Genoa Conference. Lloyd George's talisman status was fading fast. Rank-and-file Unionists were beginning to ask what the Coalition was for and why the party, with overwhelming ascendancy in Parliament, should not have one of its own in No. 10 Downing Street. The party managers reported a strong grass-roots reaction to rumours that the Government intended to go to the country once more on a Coalition ticket and revulsion at any suggestion of 'fusion' between Unionist and Coalition Liberals. In an ironic twist of fate, it was the latter group which, reluctant to close the door on future re-union with the Squiffites, snuffed out this possibility. A gap was steadily opening up between the 'Cabs' and the mass membership of the Unionist Party: coalitions did indeed coalesce at the top. Austen had little to offer the party beyond his anti-socialism and fear of a Labour Government. He was dedicated to the continuance of the Coalition and to the leadership of Lloyd George and in this he did have the support of the senior Unionists in the Cabinet—Balfour, Churchill, Sir Robert Horne and Birkenhead (the Lord Chancellor). Failing to put a credible case to party members, he depended heavily on his authority as leader. Birkenhead caused particular offence by his strident and offensive attacks on doubters who happened to include a number of junior ministers. Chamberlain's intimacy with Birkenhead did him no small harm both in the final stages of the Coalition and later. David Dutton's analysis of Austen's failure to manage the party is a devastating catalogue of insensitive errors, lending confirmation to the view that Austen was never cut out for leadership. Though few outside the magic circle at Westminster would have known of Lloyd George's adulterous relationship with Frances Stevenson, among them were members of 'the Respectable Tendency', of which Stanley Baldwin was an outstanding representative. Birkenhead's dissolute private life was also the subject of disgrace. More widely known, however, was Lloyd George's practice of selling honours to fill his own and the party's coffers, with the Unionists taking their cut, leading to a series of grants to dubious recipients. What finally destroyed Unionist support for him, however, was his determination to back the Greeks in their war against Turkey. When Mustapha Kemal Atatürk expelled the Greeks from Asia Minor in September 1922, his forces came face to face with a small British garrison at Chanak in the approaches to Constantinople. France and Italy refused their support, as did Dominion governments, with the exception of New Zealand and Newfoundland. Only the coolness of Gen. Harrington, in command at Chanak, saved this encounter from outright conflict and the diplomats were left to resolve the issue at the Lausanne Conference. For many Unionists, Chanak was the final straw and the return to politics of Bonar Law gave them a leader to rally around. In a letter to *The Times* on 6 October, Law argued that Britain was in no position to act alone as the world's policeman.

Strong hints that the Government intended to hold an election in advance of the annual National Union meeting in November led to an explosion of angry protests. Austen agreed to hold a meeting of Unionist MPs in the

Carlton Club on 19 October 1922. He put the case for coalition in a speech which he described as 'firm but conciliatory', but which has in fact been judged by his biographers to have been intransigent and insensitive. His tone offended even those who were supportive of his leadership and hoped to hear a reasoned explanation of his policy. A key speech was made by Stanley Baldwin, who famously described Lloyd George as 'a dynamic force … a terrible thing'. He made it clear that he would resign from Government should the decision go in favour of continuing the Coalition under the Welshman. The presence of Bonar Law was decisive, taken as evidence of his willingness to resume the leadership. On a motion proposed by Ernest Pretyman to go to the country as an independent party, the MPs present voted 187 to 87 in favour. A humiliated Austen resigned the leadership and when the news reached Lloyd George, he promptly went to the Palace to resign as PM. The King sent for Bonar Law, who undertook to form a government. This he managed to do with difficulty. All the 'Great Ones' stood out with the exception of Lord Curzon, the Foreign Secretary, who had had his differences with Lloyd George but had previously signalled his solidarity with Austen and Co. Contemptuously dismissed by Birkenhead as 'a government of the second eleven', it consisted largely of former under-Secretaries. Baldwin, who had served under Austen as long ago as 1903, became Chancellor of the Exchequer. Austen was upset by Neville's decision to accept the post of Postmaster General, but reluctantly agreed that if Neville did not accept office at the age of fifty-three, he had no future in politics. Bonar Law was as conscious as anyone of the weakness of his Cabinet and hoped to bring back Austen as soon as possible. But Austen felt embittered and humiliated. In his letters to his sisters, he vacillated between a total refusal to serve under Bonar Law and willingness to return to government on condition that the ex-Cabs came in with him: 'I won't go back without my friends,' he told Ida, and boasted that 'If Neville had not joined the Government, I'd have them out in six months.' Seeing little future for himself in politics, Austen briefly contemplated retirement, but that mood soon passed. He remained an unrepentant Coalitionist: 'I shall try to keep the way open for a new coalition,' he told Ida. Its intended leader was of course Lloyd George, whose magic never faded for Austen. Little did either man realise that Lloyd George, the most charismatic politician of his generation and one of Britain's greatest Prime Ministers, would never again hold office. For the remainder of the inter-war years, Britain would be ruled by the Respectable Tendency, who would ensure Lloyd George's confinement to the back-benches. It seemed more than likely that Austen would suffer the same fate. He had twice been thwarted by Bonar Law and, looking back, he regretted the decision he had made in 1911, finding it hard to suppress his acrimony:

He is a weak man and I thought him strong. He has little experience, but I thought he would learn. He does not learn and he will remain an amateur to the end of his days.[33]

Gardening Leave

To describe Bonar Law as an 'amateur' was a serious underestimation. Here was a politician who had timed his coup impeccably. In the general election which he called immediately—under the slogan 'Tranquillity'— it was apparent that the electorate shared the Conservative Party's disillusionment with the Coalition. Law's Conservatives, with 345 seats, secured a comfortable majority over Labour (142 seats) with the Liberals attempting unconvincingly to present a united front under the label 'National Liberal Party', the main losers with 116 seats. Disagreements at the summit of the party, with Neville Chamberlain, Leo Amery and Arthur Steel-Maitland all supporting Bonar Law's Government in spite of Austen, seemed to have little impact on the results in Birmingham. Austen defeated Frank Smith, a Labour veteran with a long string of electoral defeats behind him, by 5,806 votes. His own election at least gave Austen pleasure. It was 'a real triumph and largely, very largely a personal one for Ivy and me ...' he boasted to his sisters, 'I am a biggish man when I get to work'. Austen was relieved to find that the Chamberlain tradition was still alive and kicking in Birmingham, though he was shocked by the social conditions prevailing in his inner-city constituency: 'why anyone who lives in such slums should not be a Socialist, a Communist or a Red Revolutionary I am at a loss to say'. It was the comment of an outsider, criticised by his brother for his infrequent visits to and neglect of his constituency. However, it was Neville's shrinking majority in Ladywood rather than Austen's in West Birmingham which gave cause for concern and would continue to do so. The events of 1922 had driven a wedge between the two brothers: Bonar Law had carefully cultivated Neville, who had accepted the post of Post-Master General in his Government. Yet in fairness, once he had become a fixture in Bonar Law's and then Baldwin's Cabinets, Neville did do his best to pave the way for Austen's return.

Bonar Law was no more impressed by the calibre of his Cabinet than Austen was, even going as far as to criticise his Chancellor of the Exchequer, Stanley Baldwin, in an anonymous letter to *The Times* for the unsatisfactory nature of the debt settlement the latter had negotiated in Washington. The Conservative motto, 'when in doubt send for Austen', operated yet again. In the spring of 1923, Bonar Law approached Austen through his friend Lord Beaverbrook with a tempting offer which once again held out the promise of a possible reversion to the Premiership. If Austen would return to the Cabinet as Lord Privy Seal, Law would promise to resign in his favour in the autumn. Austen, still harbouring deep resentment, made it clear that he would not return without his friends. While many in the party and in government would have welcomed him back, Birkenhead, whose corrosive tongue and dissolute lifestyle had alienated many, was altogether a different case. So Austen remained content to observe events from the sidelines, enjoy his alpine garden at Twitt's Gyll and make the most of this accidental opportunity for frequent holidays. In May 1923, events took a dramatic turn when Bonar Law, diagnosed with cancer of the throat, was forced to retire. He died in October, having been Prime Minister for a mere 209 days. Austen acted as one of the pall-bearers at his funeral in Westminster Abbey. With Austen and his friends still on the outside, the choice of Bonar Law's successor was between Baldwin and the Foreign Secretary, Lord Curzon, who in the view of the exiled ex-Cabs had 'ratted' in joining Bonar Law's Cabinet the previous year. They now had the satisfaction of seeing a mortified George Curzon passed over for the less distinguished Stanley Baldwin whom, in his chagrin, Curzon described as 'a person of the utmost insignificance'. Swallowing his pride, Curzon agreed to stay on as Foreign Secretary and even to propose Baldwin's election as leader at the ensuing party meeting.

At the time of Law's resignation, Austen was holidaying in the Pyrenees and characteristically refrained from rushing home lest he be perceived as seeking office, or even the Premiership. Baldwin's instinct was to re-unite the party, but he encountered strong opposition from existing Cabinet members, more so to Birkenhead than Austen. He did, however, offer Austen the Washington Embassy, an offer which was angrily rejected. Austen turned to Neville to pour out his feelings of injustice and wounded pride, coupled with criticisms of Baldwin's shortcomings.

Bonar Law had bequeathed to Baldwin a secure parliamentary majority and an assured tenure of some four years. In a rare burst of initiative, however, which took the political world by storm, Baldwin declared in a speech at Plymouth on 25 October that he needed weapons to fight unemployment and would therefore seek an electoral mandate for the introduction of a programme of tariff reform. Austen was critical of Baldwin's lack of preparation and of the limitations of his proposed tariffs, which excluded staple foodstuffs. But, as his father's son, he was bound to give his support. His doubts proved to be justified. In the general election of December 1923, the Conservatives lost their overall majority, their 258 MPs outnumbered by a combination of the free trade parties, 191 Labour and 158 Liberals. In Birmingham the Unionists once again held all twelve seats, though with reduced majorities, Austen polling 2,000 fewer votes than in the previous year.

For the last time, Asquith had a vital role to play. Although pressed by Austen and others to support an alliance with the Conservatives, he decided to allow the installation of a Labour Government under Ramsay MacDonald, an outcome that Austen had long feared. He mounted a furious and effective attack on Asquith in the House of Commons, correctly prophesying the eclipse of the Liberal Party:

> He has taken his choice and he has by that choice constituted his own immortality. He will go down in history as the last Prime Minister of a Liberal Administration. He has sung the swan song of the Liberal Party.[34]

This speech confirmed Austen's effectiveness as a parliamentary performer and the way was clear for him to return to the Tory front bench—but he made it clear that he would not return without his friends. After a difficult series of exchanges, Neville arranged a dinner at his house on 5 February 1924 at which a reconciliation took place, Baldwin agreeing to Austen's terms. No sooner was he back in the Shadow Cabinet than he began to dominate discussions, Lord Derby commenting that had an outsider entered the room, he would have thought that Chamberlain, not Baldwin, was party leader. This was a tense time for Baldwin, who functioned more effectively in office than in opposition. Many in the party were embittered by the manner of their recent defeat and would gladly have seen the back of Stanley. A significant number would have preferred Austen, but he refused to campaign against a man he had—reluctantly—accepted as leader.

The performance in office of the Labour Government made a nonsense of Austen's virulent fear of socialism, though it was true that radical measures were not possible while Asquith was in a position to pull the plug at any time, which he did in October 1924, precipitating the third general election in little more than two years. As Austen had predicted, the Liberal Party was squeezed between the Conservatives and Labour, returning only 40 MPs. Labour increased its vote by a million but lost forty seats and the Conservatives increased theirs by over 2 million, returning 419 MPs. Baldwin again became PM with a secure majority and every prospect of serving a full term. In Birmingham, the Unionist vote increased healthily— Austen's by over 3,000—but Labour at last made a dent, taking the King's Norton division from an unpopular and inactive Tory, Herbert Austin.

Austen was offered and accepted the post of Foreign Secretary, which he had for so long coveted and Baldwin also gratified him by naming him Deputy Leader of the House of Commons. Number Two once more. With Neville becoming Minister of Health, there were two Chamberlains in the Cabinet once again. With Leo Amery and Arthur Steel-Maitland also in the Cabinet, Birmingham was well represented, though neither of the

Chamberlain brothers were very enthusiastic about these appointments (especially that of Steel-Maitland as Minister of Labour). The surprise appointment, not least to himself, was that of Churchill as Chancellor of the Exchequer. Although he had at last attained the office which fitted him best, Austen approached his duty as Foreign Secretary with his usual apprehension. 'I feel no elation,' he lamented to Hilda, 'but only a sobering sense of great difficulties in my path.' His comments to his sisters on the subject of Baldwin were often corrosive, reflecting his impression that he had been usurped by a man of inferior ability and less distinguished service than himself. 'I do not think him competent for his position', 'a conceited ass' and 'stupid and uncommunicative' were among his derogatory remarks. Once in office, however, and finding that Baldwin was only too willing to give him a free hand, he tempered his criticisms and began to appreciate Baldwin's emollient handling of domestic issues and in particular the General Strike of 1926. As he had so often done in his career, he ultimately warmed to his task and the tone of his letters to his sisters changed. He was finding the work of the Foreign Office 'congenial', 'profoundly interesting', even 'terrific'. The aura of respect and dignity which enveloped a British Foreign Secretary at this time in history exactly suited his proud and prickly temperament, though he was often troubled by the accompanying costs which left him feeling impoverished at the end of his tenure.

A Round Peg in a Round Hole

Austen's appointment was welcomed by the permanent staff at the Foreign Office, still smarting from the vagaries of the previous Conservative Foreign Secretary, Lord Curzon. An initial problem was the pretensions of Lord Robert Cecil, Chancellor of the Duchy of Lancaster, appointed to deal with League of Nations affairs. Cecil represented the idealism of the League of Nations lobby and Austen, whose attitude to the League was more pragmatic, had to make it clear that there would be no dualism in the operation of British foreign policy.

For all Britain's world-wide interests, it was European affairs which absorbed the greater part of the Foreign Minister's attention. Austen was a traditionalist whose role-model was Castlereagh, who had battled to maintain the balance of power in Europe more than a century earlier. He aspired to do likewise, which meant primarily acting as an 'honest broker' between France and Germany. Austen's whole instinct was to sympathise with France and to regard Germany as a continuing threat to the peace of Europe. His preferred line of action was to renew the Entente and to offer France the security pact which the US and Britain had withheld following the Treaty of Versailles, in the belief that this would persuade the French Government to pursue a more emollient policy towards Germany. Cabinet colleagues and elements of the press, however, did not share Austen's perception. Relations between Britain and France had turned sour in the wake of the war, as a result of rivalries in the Middle East and France's desertion of Britain during the Chanak Crisis. The previous Conservative Foreign Minister, Curzon, had warned the Cabinet that 'the great power from whom we have most to fear in future is France'. The League of Nations lobby blamed the French for foot-dragging over the issue of disarmament and the Franco-Belgian occupation of the Ruhr in 1923 (as a response to the German default of reparations) was widely condemned in Britain. For all these reasons, Austen's hopes of a new Franco-British Entente were a non-starter, encountering strong opposition in Cabinet. Another route had to be found and the prospects were not altogether bleak.

In France, Poincaré's Cabinet broke up in 1924 and the far less intransigent Aristide Briand replaced him as the dominant figure in French foreign policy. Austen and Briand became firm friends and in his memoirs Austen speaks of Briand with great affection. Importantly, the German Government was also reviewing its foreign policy and Gustav Stresemann emerged as the main advocate of a policy of 'fulfilment' rather than confrontation as a means of obtaining a revision of the more hated features of the Treaty of Versailles. Austen never entirely trusted Stresemann, whom he recognised as both a revisionist and a nationalist. At times he became very critical of the German Foreign Minister, denouncing him as 'niggling, provocative, crooked'. But he worked patiently to win his confidence and to hold a fair balance between Germany and France. In this he succeeded. Stresemann found him 'straight' and trustworthy and became convinced of his goodwill towards Germany. Austen was the catalyst that made the Locarno Treaties possible. The authoritative diplomatic historian Zara Steiner takes a more favourable view of both Austen and the Locarno achievement than others have done:

> The somewhat cold and reserved British foreign secretary, unfairly judged a political washout, helped to create the conditions for what was seen as a new chapter in European diplomacy.[35]

Austen was the key member in the trio who were to dominate the European stage in the latter half of the 1920s, a time when British prestige was high in Europe and in the world.

The conference convened in the congenial surroundings of the small Swiss lakeside town of Locarno from 5 to 16 October 1925. It resulted in a series of agreements which were initialled in the town's *Palais de*

Justice on 16 October, Austen's sixty-second birthday, and finally signed in London on 1 December. The most important of the treaties was the one guaranteeing the frontiers of Germany, France and Belgium, with Britain and Italy acting as guarantors. Locarno was the first occasion at which Austen met the Italian dictator, Benito Mussolini and the pair struck up an unlikely friendship. Austen eventually made five visits to Rome—four in two years—and his approval of Mussolini may have materially helped the latter consolidate his regime as well as advance his status in European affairs. Ivy Chamberlain notoriously became a fan and 'prominently displayed the gift of a fascist pin'—a friendship which looked innocent at the time, but would assume more sinister connotations a decade or so later. Stresemann irritated Chamberlain by trying to extract more concessions at the last moment, including the cancellation of article 231 of the Versailles Treaty, the infamous 'War Guilt' clause. But he had made substantial gains, including an agreement to bring forward the evacuation of the forces occupying the Rhineland and a relaxation of the reparations burden. Germany's economic position was also eased by the Dawes Plan, the work of the Chicago banker Charles Dawes, which opened the way for substantial American loans. In return for these concessions, Germany agreed to enter the League of Nations and to take its place on the Security Council, a decision which was enthusiastically applauded by the many supporters of the League, particularly numerous in Britain. What seemed so significant was that, unlike the *Diktat* of Versailles, the German Government had voluntarily agreed, even initiated, a settlement which held out the promise of a peaceful Europe. It seemed like the end of the dismal chapter which had begun in August 1914 and the dawn of a more optimistic era. *The Times* caught the mood, proclaiming 'Peace at Last', and popular approval manifested itself in the plethora of cinemas and dance-halls named or renamed 'Locarno'.[36]

Locarno, of course, was not without its critics. Austen himself feared that public hopes were set too high. 'There is bound before long to be a reaction from the present exaggerated expectations,' he wrote to Ida. He was, if somewhat overly sombre, essentially correct. The pundits were quick to point out that Locarno had dealt only with Europe's western frontiers and ignored the eastern, where there were still many causes for friction between Germany and the successor states. Indeed, it was argued that Locarno could be interpreted as a sign that Britain was abandoning any commitment in the region, a sense reinforced by Austen's declaration that the Polish Corridor was a cause 'for which no British Government ever will or ever can risk the bones of a British grenadier'—a prophecy which spectacularly unravelled a decade or so later and at the instigation of his own brother. It was also pointed out, then and since, that the

1. The Chamberlain family: Neville, Austen, Joseph, Beatrice and Mary *c.* 1900.

2. A picture of elegance. Joe as
a successful young entrepreneur.

THE MODERN SAMSON.
(WHAT HE HAS DONE)

3. Joe the iconoclast tearing down the pillars of society.

4. Joe in 1888.

5. Joe and Mary, a couple of swells.

6. Joe at the despatch box, by 'Spy' (Sir Leslie Ward).

7. Joe as first Chancellor of Birmingham University, 1900.

8. Joe, accompanied by Mary, courageously visited South Africa in the immediate aftermath of the Boer War.

9. Joe changes the political agenda, 1903.

10. Controversy over food taxes, 'the big and little loaf'.

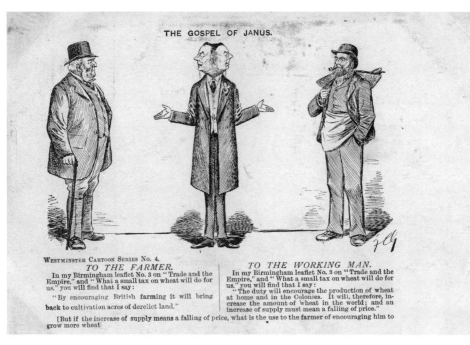

11. Joe spins it both ways.

12. In goal for England.

13. Joe, Austen and Joe's grandson, little Joe, born in 1907.

"TO LIVE IS CHRIST, AND TO DIE IS GAIN."
IN
MEMORY OF
HARRIET,
WIFE OF JOSEPH CHAMBERLAIN,
AND
DAUGHTER OF ARCHIBALD KENRICK,
DIED OCTOBER 22ND 1863, AGED 27 YEARS.

"THERE IS NO DEATH! WHAT SEEMS SO IS TRANSITION;
THIS LIFE OF MORTAL BREATH
IS BUT A SUBURB OF THE LIFE ELYSIAN,
WHOSE PORTAL WE CALL DEATH."

ALSO OF FLORENCE, DAUGHTER OF
TIMOTHY KENRICK,
AND SECOND WIFE OF THE ABOVE
JOSEPH CHAMBERLAIN,
AND THEIR INFANT SON,
WHO DIED FEBRUARY 14TH 1875.

ALSO OF
JOSEPH CHAMBERLAIN
BORN JULY 8TH 1836,
DIED JULY 2ND 1914.

14. The Chamberlain gravestone in Key Hill Cemetery, Ladywood.

15. Austen, a chip off the old block.

MR. & MRS. AUSTEN CHAMBERLAIN.
BY SPECIAL PERMISSION

16. Austen and Ivy, married in 1906.

'FOLLOWING IN FATHER'S FOOTSTEPS'

Scott Russell & Co Bham No 927

AUSTEN CHAMBERLAIN ESQ. elected
M.P for E. Worcestershire Jan.22. 1906.
Majority- 4366.

17. Sustaining the Chamberlain image.

18. Austen with Andrew Bonar Law, who supplanted him as leader of the Unionist Party in 1922.

19. Foreign Secretary 1924–1929.

An unconventional pose of Austen Chamberlain, British Foreign Secretary, at his country home, "Twitts Chyll," Five Ashes, Sussex. 1925 International.

20. Austen at his fireside at Twitt's Gyll, his unfortunately named country house in Sussex.

21. Austen electioneering in Birmingham.

22. The monocle washerman canvassing for votes, 1931.

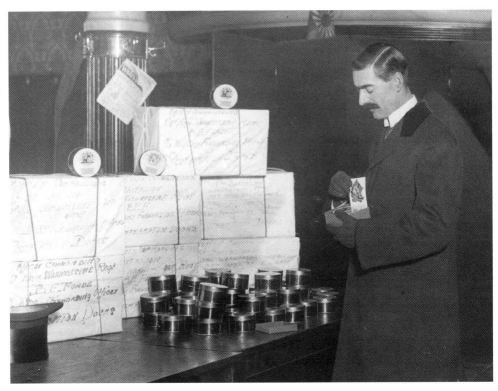

23. Neville, Lord Mayor of Birmingham, helping to despatch 'goodies' to the Royal Warwicks.

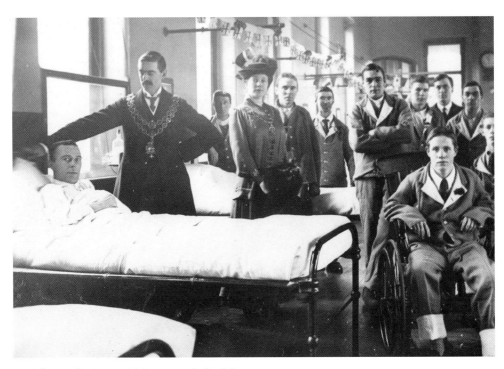

24. The Lord Mayor visiting wounded soldiers.

25. Neville electioneering in Edgbaston with Annie.

26. Neville at work.

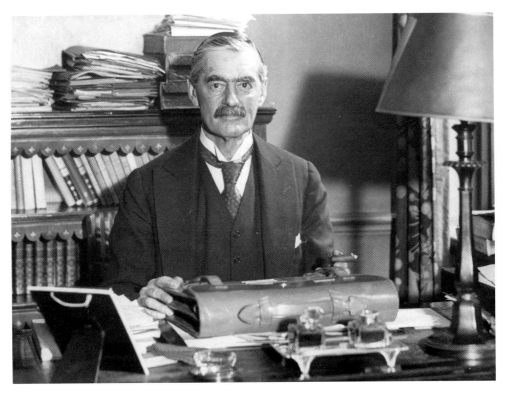

27. Neville, Chancellor of the Exchequer.

28. Neville with Ramsay MacDonald.

29. Neville, Prime Minister 1937.

30. Neville with Adolf Hitler.

31. Neville sharing a pleasantry with Benito Mussolini.

32. Blue plaque on Edgbaston High School, Westbourne Road, the site of Neville's Birmingham House.

British guarantee of Europe's Western frontiers was more symbolic than real. There were no military preparations, no staff talks, nor anything suggesting that Britain could or would intervene in the event of aggression. With hindsight it was easy for historians to dismiss Locarno as relatively insignificant, a mere episode in the European thirty years' war. This is to read history backwards and in disregard of how so many people felt at the time. In fact, 'This was not a time of illusions; it was a time of hope'—hope that was brutally shattered beginning in 1929, that *annus terribilis*, a year which also marked the eclipse of the three statesmen of Locarno.

Back in England, Austen was showered with congratulations. The King pressed him to take an honour and he agreed to become a Knight of the Garter. Recognising this as a violation of the family tradition, he justified himself by arguing that a title would make him more effective in his role as Foreign Secretary. Perhaps this was the moment that he finally emerged from his father's shadow. Other honours followed: Birmingham gave him the Freedom of the City, as did the City of London. The French Government offered him the Grand Cross of the Legion of Honour, an award he coveted but felt obliged to refuse. Most prestigious of all was the Nobel Peace Prize, jointly awarded to Austen and the Chicago banker Charles Dawes. In the following year, the prize went jointly to Briand and Stresemann. 'It rains gold boxes!' Austen exulted to Mary.

Locarno had enhanced Britain's prestige in Europe as well as that of its Foreign Secretary.

> Chamberlain went on to create a unique place for himself at Geneva and, in contrast to Lloyd George after the peace conference, enhanced his reputation by careful statesmanship and an attention to detail that won trust and professional acclaim.

But even at Geneva problems arose, such as the bitter disputes over membership of the Security Council. Austen valued the League and did his best to make it viable, but at heart he was a traditionalist who thought primarily in terms of relations between powers. This put him at odds with Robert Cecil, who resigned in 1927. Yet the League was the least of his troubles. Both Egypt and China were trouble spots which posed acute dilemmas, as did the perennial problem of relations with Russia. There was also friction with the US which, in David Dutton's opinion, sent Anglo–US relations plummeting to a new low. As the rising spirit of nationalism made Egypt increasingly challenging to govern, Austen's response was to concede as much independence as possible without compromising Britain's control of the Suez Canal. The High Commissioner, Lord Lloyd, pressed for sterner measures and found support from Churchill, Amery, Birkenhead and others. Austen had grown used to Amery's pinpricks but found Birkenhead's criticism especially hurtful, bearing in mind the political sacrifices he had made to save the Lord Chancellor's career and to bring him back into power. The rise of national resentment against foreigners, especially the British, was also causing grief in China and here Austen supported a firmer line. Violent attacks forced the abandonment of a British concession at Hankow, but a force of 20,000 men, tanks and aircraft were despatched to defend the far more valuable concession at Shanghai.

Austen became increasingly frustrated by the attitude of the US Government to whom he looked for support and co-operation. Britain had ended its treaty relations with Japan at America's behest, but found little response to requests for joint action. He came to the conclusion that American policy was basically anti-British and vented his frustration and contempt in his correspondence for 'the smug, self-interested isolationism of US policy'. He reserved his most censorious remarks for Frank Kellogg, Secretary of State for Foreign Affairs and joint author with Briand of the vacuous Kellogg Peace Pact, for which he received the Nobel Peace Prize. 'Kellogg', he complained to Ida, 'is an old woman without a policy and trembling at every breeze that blows from the Senate.' He felt obliged to sign the Peace Pact on behalf of Britain in 1928 but regarded it as an irrelevant and unwanted interference from a rich and powerful, yet unreliable state. Mussolini, on the other hand, he was finding 'most cordial personally', telling his sisters of 'our pleasant personal relations'.

In May 1927, Britain broke off diplomatic relations with Russia against Austen's advice. His view, that it would make it more difficult to deal with the complex problems of Eastern Europe, was rejected in Cabinet. This was evidence of the decline of Austen's influence. His firmest support, somewhat to his surprise, came from Baldwin, who had little interest in foreign affairs and trusted Austen's judgement. For much of his time as Foreign Secretary, Austen felt energised and sent surprisingly positive reports of his state of health to his sisters. However, in July 1928 he succumbed to pneumonia and it was not until November that he was fully back in harness, his recuperation including a three-week convalescence in California. Baldwin resisted siren voices suggesting that Austen be replaced, maintaining that he was irreplaceable. Austen's earlier misgivings about the expenses inseparable from the office of Foreign Secretary proved all too justified and it was with deep regret that he was obliged to sell Twitt's Gyll in 1929. Henceforth, he would be confined to London hotels and apartments and a small house with garden at Rutland Gate. It came as something of a relief to Austen when Baldwin's term of office came to an end in May 1929 and a general election ensued.

A second round in opposition

The Chamberlain brothers could face the election with justified confidence. In so far as the Baldwin Government could claim success, this was largely due to their efforts. But Austen soon found out how little issues of foreign policy counted in the backstreets of West Birmingham. He came within a whisker of losing his seat for the first and only time in his career, credited with a majority over his Labour opponent of a mere 43 votes. 'The old people still supported us,' he informed his sisters, 'but the young were sullen and voted socialist almost solidly.' His neglect of his constituency, its dismal housing conditions and rising unemployment all contributed to this poor result. It was not only Austen who suffered. Sir Oswald Mosley had organised and energised the Birmingham Labour Party (BLP) and had Neville not switched from Ladywood to Edgbaston, he would surely have been unseated. As it was, Labour made its long-awaited breakthrough, winning six of Birmingham's twelve seats. Among the fallen was Sir Arthur Steel-Maitland, though he was soon re-elected at a by-election in Tamworth. There seemed to be every justification for Mosley's boast that 'the Chamberlain tradition' had lost its potency.

The Conservative vote had held up reasonably well, but its total of 260 MPs was eclipsed by Labour's 288. The Liberals, who by general consent had produced the most exciting manifesto—the work of Lloyd George and Keynes—increased their representation from 40 to 59 and once more held the balance of power. Ramsay MacDonald returned to Downing Street for the second time, while Arthur Henderson stepped into Austen's shoes at the Foreign Office.

Austen's narrow squeak in Birmingham and his expectation that this time Labour could expect a long-ish term in office forced him to think hard about his future. His letters to his sisters reveal that he did not again expect to hold office and was even contemplating a life outside politics: 'the temptation to chuck in my hand is very great'. His presentiment that his career as a front-bench politician was over was deepened by the deaths of the men with whom he had gone into the wilderness in 1922 — Balfour and Birkenhead in 1930 and Worthington-Evans ('Worthy') in 1931. His laments at their passing reveal the essential sweetness of Austen's nature, old rivalries forgotten. Balfour was 'the last man to whom I looked up in the political world' and Birkenhead 'impossible not to like and even love'. I shall 'never find a truer or more affectionate friend,' a judgement which would not have been widely replicated in Conservative ranks. Austen's affection for and loyalty to the louche Birkenhead has often been puzzled over, as have his friendships with men of as suspect a reputation as Warden Chilcott, so dissimilar in personality from Chamberlain.

It is hard to take too seriously Austen's musings about exiting politics, for he was soon heavily engaged in the internecine strife which afflicted the Conservative Party in opposition. He did not give active support to the campaign of the press lords, Rothermere and Beaverbrook, neither for imperial free trade nor for their strident challenge to Baldwin's leadership—though he shared their sense that Baldwin was an incompetent leader. Correspondence with his sisters echoed with all his old contempt for Baldwin, guilty of 'dull egoism and vanity' and 'blind complacency'. Baldwin, bemoaned Austen, 'was not a leader and nothing will make him one.' With his own ambition waning, Austen worked hard to promote Neville's chances of succession and this became the major concern of these years: 'Neville has got to do the job,' he told Ida. Baldwin, however, fought back against his critics, eloquently denouncing the press lords; and when in March 1931 Duff Cooper defeated an anti-Baldwin candidate in a by-election, Baldwin's tenure of the leadership was made secure. Neville would be obliged to wait and meanwhile the two half-brothers pooled their strength to draw up an 'unauthorised programme' for their party. 'Neville does the heavy work and I do the trimmings,' Austen told Ivy. Austen also took a prominent part in the debate over the future of India. His criticisms of the Viceroy, later Lord Halifax, provoked the latter into comparing Austen to 'a log of wood'.

By the summer of 1931, the Labour Government was entering a critical juncture, with unemployment hovering around 2½ million and with the May committee demanding substantial budget cuts. Yet Austen played no part in the events that followed. When the Cabinet failed to agree, Ramsay MacDonald went to the Palace to offer the resignation of his Government. However, he was persuaded on a temporary basis to form a coalition in order to present a united front in the crisis. The new Cabinet consisted of ten members, four each from the Labour and Conservative parties and two Liberals. Austen harboured little hope of returning to the Foreign Office but was incensed when the appointment went to the Marquess of Reading, the Liberal leader in the Lords, a man with no experience of foreign affairs who last served in government as Attorney General in 1913. To add insult to injury, following Baldwin's hint that Austen was now too old to fill a major Cabinet post, Reading was, at seventy-one, three years his senior. Austen was incensed and stricken with emotion at this news and had to be calmed down by Mary and Neville. His brother also persuaded him to accept the consolation post that Baldwin held out, First Lord of the Admiralty, outside the Cabinet. The wheel had come full circle: Austen's ministerial career had begun at the Admiralty in 1895 and would end there. He found the Admiralty very congenial, but was soon complaining to his sisters that he did not have enough work to occupy him, his administrative appetite apparently undimmed.

Austen's tenure lasted for only ten weeks and ended on a sour note. The National Government implemented a series of budget cuts which included reductions in public sector salaries. The sailors reacted angrily to the manner in which the cuts were applied and on 17 September sailors of the Atlantic fleet refused duties, returning to work only once the cuts were adjusted in a way that seemed fairer. The so-called 'Invergordon Mutiny' was a relatively trivial and short-lived demonstration and had little political significance: 'the general spirit was not revolutionary or Bolshevist,' Austen reported to Hilda. Nevertheless, the news of discontent in the world's greatest navy reverberated overseas and possibly had an adverse effect on the exchange value of the pound. Although Austen had not been involved in the apportionment of the cuts, he could fairly be accused of taking his eye off the ball and the incident cast a shadow over his last ministerial role.

The Invergordon Mutiny was but a minor incident within a broader crisis. The Government failed in its attempt to defend the pound and was forced to abandon the gold standard and to devalue. The Cabinet became bitterly divided over the issue of whether finally to abandon free trade and to extend Protectionist measures. In October 1931, MacDonald and Baldwin agreed to go the country as a National Government, appealing to the electorate for a 'doctor's mandate'. The event left the Labour Party demoralised. In essence, the election was an invitation for the electorate to deliver a verdict on the Labour Government and this turned out to be a severe one. Only 52 Labour MPs survived and MacDonald's National Labour supporters numbered a mere 13. The Liberals, meanwhile, had fragmented into three factions—National Liberal (35), Liberal (33) and Independent Liberal (4). The Conservatives returned a massive 473 MPs, but until 1935 had to suffer the anomaly of serving under a Labour Prime Minister, although real power lay in the hands of Baldwin, Lord President of the Council and Neville Chamberlain, Chancellor of the Exchequer.

In Birmingham, the Conservatives registered a victory of overwhelming proportions over a Labour Party deflated by the desertion of Oswald Mosley and his acolytes. All six seats lost in 1929 were regained. Austen, opposed by the candidate, O. G. Willey, who had pressed him so close in 1929, this time recorded a majority of over 11,000. 'The size of my majority eclipsed all my expectations...' he exulted to his sisters. 'We are twelve. I had not hoped to see that again.'

For some time following the general election, Austen's morale was nevertheless at rock bottom. Much as he loved Parliament and its arcane procedures, he felt under-employed and complained to his sisters that he was 'bored stiff'. He informed Baldwin that he would not again be a candidate for office and his sisters that he would not again stand for West

Birmingham. The National Government depressed him and his comments on it were almost entirely negative. MacDonald he characterised as woolly, devoid of ideas and 'physically worn out'. Almost inconceivably, he found MacDonald even worse than Baldwin, but he reserved his most severe strictures for the Liberal leader, Herbert Samuel, whom he judged 'a dirty dog' with 'the most dishonest mind of any politician with whom I am acquainted'. He was singularly unimpressed by Sir John Simon at the Foreign Office, whom he described sadly as 'very bad'. In March 1932 he crossed the Channel to attend the funeral of his favourite Frenchman, Aristide Briand and grieved at the loss of 'a very true and real friendship'. The other member of the trio which had dominated European diplomacy post-Locarno, Gustav Stresemann, had preceded Briand to the grave in 1929. Austen's black mood became increasingly impenetrable. 'I eat my heart out in idleness and uselessness and see my work undone and feel myself unwanted and unregretted,' was his *cri de coeur* to his sisters. The one bright spot was Neville's growing authority as Chancellor. The introduction of the Import Duties Bill in February 1932 and the negotiation of imperial preference at the Ottawa Conference was seen by the Chamberlain brothers and family members as the belated realisation of Joe's dream.

It seemed unlikely that a man of Austen's pedigree would be left in idleness for long and soon various offers came his way, lifting his spirits. In October 1933, Ramsay MacDonald offered him the Wardenship of the Cinque Ports, a sinecure which carried with it residence at Dover Castle. Austen was tempted, especially by the extensive gardens, but calculated sadly that the £1,500 to £2,000 a year which it would cost to maintain was beyond his means. He was predictably in demand for various committees, the most satisfactory of which was one which played an active role in the preparation of the India Act of 1935. The least pleasing was his experiences on the executive committee of the League of Nations Union, 'a collection of cranks and ill-mannered and churlish cranks at that'. He found its members unrealistic and out of touch with the real world outside Geneva. 'Oh! these peace lovers. They are far worse than the men of war', he grumbled.

It was the men of war who fully re-ignited his interest in politics. Following the advent to power of Adolf Hitler in January 1933, Austen began to warn of the renewed danger of German aggression. In this he was in advance of Winston Churchill, who enjoyed considerably less credibility in the party than Austen and was widely regarded as the maverick who had twice 'ratted'. To Hilda, Austen expressed his disgust with the brutality of the Nazi regime and of the folly of allowing Germany to re-arm while the League was still pressing others to disarm: 'there should be no running after Germany and no payment of blackmail this time'. Austen saw that 'the possibility of war was nearer than at any time since 1914' and called for accelerated rearmament. In March 1935, in a debate on the Government's White Paper on Defence, he made a devastating attack on Attlee, then Labour deputy leader, for his party's continued resistance to rearmament.

The man whom many in the party had come to regard as a charming anachronism, with his old-fashioned dress and his old world courtesy, began once again to command attention. Robert Self argues that Austen was never more influential than in his final years in the Commons, the growth of his stature 'truly remarkable'.[37] Yet a party led by Stanley Baldwin, who replaced MacDonald as PM in 1935 and with Simon at the Foreign Office, was unlikely to generate the response to the German threat that Austen now advocated and his influence tended to be confined largely to the younger cohort of Tory MPs—men such as Eden and Macmillan.

In October 1935, hoping to take advantage of the improved economic situation, Baldwin dissolved Parliament. In the general election Labour recovered to a certain extent, mainly at the expense of the fragmented Liberals, returning 154 MPs. But the result left the Conservatives with a commanding majority. Few could have predicted that this would be the last general election for ten years. Reversing his earlier intention, Austen stood again and faced the same opponent as in 1931. His majority was reduced but was still in excess of 7,000. He sensed that things were looking up in the constituency. Housing, in which he had taken a belated interest, was improving, though unemployment less so. He also sensed that the old Chamberlain loyalty was still alive in Birmingham, which again returned twelve Conservatives. 'Bravo, Birmingham,' Austen exulted. 'There's not another city like it.'

In the post-election Cabinet reshuffle, Austen welcomed the replacement of Simon at the FO by Sir Samuel Hoare. But Hoare soon became embroiled in the crisis precipitated by Mussolini's brutal invasion of Abyssinia. Supporters of the League called for sanctions against Italy, but the governments of both Britain and France were wary of driving Mussolini into Hitler's arms. The British Government was also reluctant to assume what would have been the major role in enforcing sanctions. Hoare and the French Foreign Minister, Pierre Laval, cobbled together an agreement which would have left Mussolini with the greater part of his ill-gotten gains. When a French newspaper leaked the terms of the agreement, there was an outcry in Britain which shook the Government. Faced with this dilemma, the Cabinet decided that Hoare must fall on his sword. In this crisis Baldwin recognised that Austen's views would carry great weight in the Commons and slyly hinted that Austen would be a candidate to replace Hoare. Austen had no doubt that Hoare had been betrayed:

'Laval has behaved treacherously,' he told his sisters, 'but I fear that Sam Hoare blundered badly.' In the ensuing debate in the Commons, he pulled his punches. He condemned the Hoare-Laval Pact as 'a betrayal of the League', but switched his attack to the Labour opposition and assisted the Government to emerge unscathed.

Fully expecting to return to government, the old war-horse was interviewed by Baldwin on 20 December, only to be told that the PM considered him too old to carry the heavy responsibility of the FO. To soften the blow, Baldwin offered him a post as Minister of State outside the Cabinet with a salary of £3,000, which he subsequently raised to £5,000. This offer must have been a sore temptation. Austen was in dire financial straits, having moved out of Rutland Gate into the Goring Hotel pending a further move to a smaller house in Egerton Terrace. Recognising it for what is was, a bribe to keep him onside and having consulted Ivy, Austen sent a dignified rejection. Smarting from this episode, Austen's contempt for Baldwin plumbed new depths. 'He told me I was ga-ga,' he complained to his sisters. Baldwin was 'self-centred, selfish and idle,' he fulminated, 'yet one of the shrewdest not to say the slyest of politicians but without a constructive idea in his head.'

Freed of his illusions about returning to office, Austen became more outspoken and in February 1936 astonished the House of Commons by an uninhibited attack on Baldwin for his Government's lack of policies. His anxiety about developments in Germany and the state of British re-armament brought him closer to Churchill. Tory dissidents called for the creation of a Minister of Defence and in Austen's opinion there was only one possible candidate for the job—Churchill. His continuing admiration for Lloyd George also surfaced and he called for a post to be found for him. This caused something of a rift between Austen and Neville, who, like Baldwin, would never countenance the return to Government of Lloyd George.

In March 1936, Hitler sent his troops into the Rhineland in defiance of both the Versailles and Locarno treaties. Austen immediately perceived the gravity of the situation and called for a response. Hitler, he believed, had acted against the advice of at least some of his generals and, if he was not opposed, his prestige would soar and encourage him to pursue further adventures. Britain's reputation would inevitably suffer:

> [...] every country in Europe will feel that England is a broken reed and the end can only be the complete triumph of Germany and I fear our own ultimate ruin.[38]

Austen saw this move as part of a planned pattern for the achievement of a greater German Reich, the next likely target being Austria. 'The independence of Austria,' he stressed, 'is the key position.' 'If Austria perishes,' he told the Commons on 1 April 1936, 'Czechoslovakia becomes indefensible.' His attitude was summed up in the mantra, 'To a peaceful Germany much, to this Germany nothing'.

His response to German aggression was to advocate old-fashioned collective security, a position decried by the League of Nations and the pacifist lobbies. The key to the defence of Austria was, in Austen's view, the re-creation of the Stresa Front with Italy and to this end he called for the abandonment of the sanctions which were driving Mussolini into the arms of Hitler. Although he was in this period inclined to pull his punches so as not to damage Neville's prospects, he became increasingly critical of Baldwin's Government and moved closer to the Churchill group. Churchill, of course, was unpopular with the bulk of the Conservative Party, which retained what to Austen was an inexplicable loyalty to Baldwin. The PM's devotees denounced 'the Anti-Baldwin Shadow Cabinet' and Sir Henry 'Chips' Channon spoke for this group in denouncing Austen as 'ossified, tedious and hopelessly out of date'.[39] They would have good reason to change their minds.

In his final months, Austen renewed his contacts with leading French politicians. In November 1936 he received an honorary degree at the University of Lyons and in January 1937 he visited Paris for the last time. In March Austen suffered a minor heart attack and on the 16th he died in the bathroom of his new home in Egerton Terrace. Tributes were duly paid to him at a memorial service at Westminster. Lloyd George spoke of his loyalty and integrity, describing him as 'a man who strained the point of honour always against himself'. But it was Baldwin who paid the most eloquent tribute, describing Austen as 'a great Parliamentarian who excelled in loyalty and integrity'. In a letter to Ivy, Winston Churchill declared that Austen's 'life added lustre to the famous name he bore'.[40]

In death, Austen's separation from his father became absolute. He was buried not in Birmingham among his close relatives but in St Marylebone cemetery in London. Ten weeks later his half-brother became Prime Minister, attaining a position which could, for better or worse, so easily have been Austen's 'who always played the game and always lost'.

Arthur Neville Chamberlain

Introduction

Neville Chamberlain was, by dint of offices held, the most eminent of the Chamberlains, surpassing both his father and half-brother. Coming late to national politics, he rose rapidly in the Conservative hierarchy. Appointed Post-Master General by Bonar Law in 1922, he was successively Minister of Health, twice Chancellor of the Exchequer and finally, after years of waiting in the wings, successor to Stanley Baldwin as Prime Minister. His appetite for power was at least equal to that of his father and infinitely stronger than his half-brother's. His legislative achievements also far outweighed those of Joe Chamberlain, making him the most outstanding social reformer of the inter-war years, bridging the gap in this regard between Lloyd George before the First World War and Clement Attlee in the wake of the second.

Many of these achievements, however, have been overshadowed by his record as the exponent of British foreign policy during his period as Prime Minister between 1937 and 1940. The events of that time have made Neville by far the most controversial of the Chamberlains. The immense popularity he had gained as the champion of peace in Europe in 1938 was followed, as in a Greek tragedy, by ignominy two years later, when his world fell apart. However unfair the portrait of Neville in the work of 'Cato', *Guilty Men* (1940), it proved a highly influential tract and was followed by a torrent of condemnation by historians, diarists and articles in the press. A later phase of revisionism was followed by post-revisionism, but little it seems could alter Chamberlain's image, summed up by the American historian Larry Fuchser as that of 'a pathetic old man, one of the great losers of history'.[1] Chamberlain's great failure, the attempt to appease Hitler and Mussolini, has greatly influenced post-war foreign policy as a paradigm of how *not* to do it. In public opinion polls Neville has been bracketed with Lord North, who blundered into war with the American colonies in the eighteenth century, as Britain's worst ever Prime Minister. Even in Birmingham, the city of his birth on which he lavished so much effort and attention, a veil has been drawn over Neville. It is his father who is honoured and commemorated. No fountains or squares are dedicated to Neville, nothing beyond a blue plaque on his former home in Edgbaston and the odd foundation stone. Sir David Cannadine, distinguished Birmingham-born historian, offers no defence. By 1929, he wrote, Neville was already

> [...] in a rut of self-righteous narrow-mindedness which hardly equipped him to cope at ever higher level with the tumultuous decade that was to come. As a person and a politician, he was just like his umbrella, stiff and rolled up tight.[2]

Detractors, such as Lloyd George, delighted in depicting him as a narrow provincial, viewing the world through the wrong end of a municipal drainpipe. This was far from the truth. Neville was a cultivated and well-travelled man with a passable facility in both French and German, in contrast to Lloyd George himself.

Neville's lack of personal charisma, however, contributed to the ignominy which was to be his lot. Lacking the easy charm of Baldwin, his gloomy aloofness and smug self-confidence alienated many, though close colleagues were drawn to him by the certainty and rationality which he radiated. But Neville's was never a personality to inspire sympathy. Winston Churchill, who had often spoken in his defence during his lifetime, commented slyly after his death in 1940, 'Poor Neville, he will come badly out of history. I know for I shall write the history'. Neville has indeed come badly out of history which has rarely given him his due. As one historian has pointed out, Neville, like Pontius Pilate, is known for one big thing. The strenuous efforts of a lifetime have tended to fade into the shadows, his role that of scapegoat for disasters in 1940.

Early life and career

Arthur Neville Chamberlain was born on 18 March 1869, the eldest of four children sired by Joe Chamberlain following his second marriage in 1868 to Florence Kenrick, the cousin of his first wife Harriet Kenrick. Neville's birth was followed closely by that of three daughters, Ida, Hilda and Ethel. Never robust and perhaps worn down by childbirth, Florence died in February 1875 giving birth to a fifth. Joe Chamberlain, left with six children from his two marriages, turned to his sisters Caroline and Clara for their care and upbringing. Joe senior had moved his family from London to Birmingham in 1863, Joe's brothers—Richard, Arthur, Walter and Herbert—all becoming immersed in local business enterprises. Arthur especially, but Walter also enjoying conspicuous success. Richard and Arthur followed Joe into local politics, becoming town councillors. Richard succeeded Joe in the office of Mayor from 1878 to 1880, his mayoralty being generally considered a distinguished one. The Chamberlain brothers married and produced families of their own, Arthur, who married Louisa Kenrick, twin of Joe's second wife, proving especially fecund. With their extensive family connections forming what they called the 'click', the Chamberlain children grew up surrounded by uncles, aunts and a numerous cousinhood, this network representing the aristocracy of Birmingham. Their material surroundings could reasonably be described by provincial standards as opulent.

Neville was brought up first at Southbourne in Augustus Road, Edgbaston, one of a group of large houses with ample gardens in the heart of the Calthorpe estate and from 1880 at Highbury, Joe's brother Walter taking over the tenancy of Southbourne. Living on an estate initially of 18 acres and thereafter expanded, Neville and his siblings had ample space in which to develop their hobbies and interests. In Neville's case this meant 'bug-hunting' accompanied by his adoring sister, Ida. From an early age he developed an interest in natural history which never left him. He saw little of his father, who was immersed in his political concerns and spending the bulk of his time in London, where he acquired a property at Prince's Gate in Kensington and close to Hyde Park. The main point of contact between Joe and Neville, when Joe was resident at Highbury, was in the orchid houses which they inspected together, a mutual love of flowers being one of the few things the two appeared to have in common. Joe did not share Neville's love of natural history, nor his developing interest in Darwinian theory. Whereas Neville cultivated a deep love of music and especially Beethoven, Joe was tone deaf. It would be true to say that Neville took after the Kenrick side of the family and was well-liked by his Kenrick uncles and especially his bachelor uncle George, who inducted him in shooting and fishing and left him a substantial legacy when he died. Unlike Austen, Neville was not drawn to politics, not least because his elder brother so obviously filled the slot as his father's apprentice. Not merely indifferent, he expressed an aversion to politics, complaining to a school friend that the whole atmosphere of the house became arctic when his father was preparing for a big speech. 'Wretched man, he never knows what he is going to say,' sniffed Neville dismissively—words that could never have been uttered by Austen.

In his brilliant biography of Joe Chamberlain, Peter Marsh emphasises the lack of empathy between Joe and Neville and suggests that he was 'emotionally scorched by his father'.[3] Others have drawn similar conclusions about their relationship in order to explain some of Neville's later characteristics—his self-sufficiency and his limited capacity to make friends, the rather grim and saturnine appearance that earned him the sobriquet 'the Coroner'. But Neville's introversion stemmed more from his nature than his nurture. Keith Feiling, his first official biographer, rejected a common view of a troubled childhood, writing that Neville's childhood 'was neither spoilt nor moody ... he was a happy and normal creature'.[4] Neville was well loved in his family circle, especially by his sisters, but found it difficult to socialise outside the family, attributing this to 'accursed shyness'. In spite of the obvious advantages, it can never have been easy to be the son of Joseph Chamberlain and Neville would have been less than human if he had not experienced jealousy at the close relationship between his father and 'the special one', Austen. His relationship with his father improved with the years, however, and towards the end of his life Joe came to perceive the streak of toughness and determination in Neville and to expect more of him than of Austen.

It is true that Joe felt disappointment in his younger son's childhood and adolescent development. After a short spell at a school in Southport, Neville was sent to a preparatory school before following Austen to Rugby, where the two briefly overlapped. It cannot have been easy to be the younger brother of one as grand and as senior as Austen and it seems that Neville was bullied by an older boy who bore a grudge against his brother. Having no enthusiasm for sports, preferring bird-watching and bug-hunting, Neville never became part of the mainstream and made few friends. Nor did he distinguish himself academically. As Joe contemplated the limited progress made by Neville he decided to remove him from classical studies and transfer him into the recently formed 'modern' stream, as a preparation for business rather than for political or public service. Given the prominence of the classics in the education of gilded youth in Victorian Britain, this was a distinct demotion and was compounded for Neville by the fact that most of his fellow 'modernists' were younger than himself. Joe removed Neville from Rugby at the end of the autumn term of 1886, when Neville was seventeen. He left without regret and without a backward glance. Unlike Austen, who loved his old school and later became chairman of the governors, Neville never again visited the place. Sending his sons to Rugby may have been the appropriate choice for the conservative and Establishment-minded Austen, but in the case of Neville, Joe had made a distinct error.

To facilitate a career in business Joe now despatched Neville to Mason's College in Edmund Street, Birmingham, there to study metallurgy and engineering. The magnificently appointed college, founded by the wealthy and philanthropic pen manufacturer Sir Josiah Mason, offered a rigorous education in the subjects essential to the continued vibrancy of Birmingham industry and among its teachers were Nobel prize winners. For a time Neville overlapped with Stanley Baldwin who, after Cambridge, was sent there by his father Alfred, an ironmaster and MP for Kidderminster in Worcestershire, to prepare him for a career in the family firm situated not far away at Wilden near Stourport. It is surely a tribute to Mason's College that two future Prime Ministers should have studied there in the 1880s, though there is no evidence that they were aware of one another. Neville was able to live at Highbury, often in a solitary state since the family lived in London during parliamentary sessions and Joe enjoyed spending vacations in the south of France during the long periods of recess. Again, biographers have emphasised the lonesomeness of his existence, though tempered by the close proximity of abundant relatives.

Neville attended Mason's College for two years, from 1887 to 1889, studying maths, metallurgy and engineering design, none of which fully engaged his interest. Again, he seems to have made few friends, a teacher describing him as 'modest almost to shyness'. Like his father before him he taught Sunday school at the Unitarian church in Broad Street but, also like his father, he lacked deep religious belief. His step-mother's sociability drew him more into the family circle, though he and Mary never developed the deep mutual friendship which characterised her relations with Austen. Travelling overseas in a family group, Neville began to enlarge his horizons but still did not share his father's political obsessiveness. While at a dinner in Cairo he sat next to Gen. Kitchener and discussed—flowers.

Leaving Mason's College, Neville was apprenticed to a firm of accountants, Howard Smiths. He found the work not uncongenial and enjoyed visiting parts of the Midlands for auditing purposes. After only one year he was offered a junior partnership but, as it transpired, his career as an accountant was about to come to an abrupt end. After a family trip to France and Egypt, Joe and Mary went to the US to visit the Endicotts. Their itinerary took them into Canada, where they encountered Sir Ambrose Shea, Governor of the Bahamas, who was staying in the same hotel. Sir Ambrose painted a glowing picture of the development prospects of the islands and specifically of their suitability for growing sisal, the raw material for the manufacture of rope. Joe summoned Neville to join them in New York and sent both his sons on a voyage of investigation to the Bahamas, travelling on the weekly mail boat to Nassau, the capital. Austen furnished Joe with a glowing account of the prospects and Joe, against the advice of shrewd brother Arthur, decided to plunge in. With Austen about to embark on a parliamentary career, it fell to Neville to carry through the scheme. In April 1891, the twenty-two year old Neville arrived back in the Bahamas with instructions to find suitable land and to purchase an initial 10,000 acres.

Sisal

The Andros Fibre Company was an astonishing piece of speculation which sheds interesting light on Joe Chamberlain's character. It was a gambler's throw, intended to repair the family fortunes which were causing him sleepless nights. Neither he nor Austen were at this time in receipt of ministerial salaries and the cost of politics was not inconsiderable. Besides, the outgoings of two well-staffed homes were high. Both Mary and Austen had expensive tastes, while the upkeep of four daughters imposed a considerable drain on his resources. To cap it all, his investments, especially in South America, were performing badly. This formed the backdrop to his quixotic decision to pursue Shea's dream of mouth-watering profits to be made by growing sisal in the British Bahamas. Neither he nor his two sons had any experience of managing tropical plantations, for which tending the gardens of Highbury was no sort of preparation. Yet it was Austen and Neville who were sent to explore the scene without expert help apart from what Shea could offer on the spot. Austen, who took the lead in reporting enthusiastically to his father, had no relevant knowledge, while Neville had at least the experience of studying engineering at Mason's College and nearly two years of practical experience as an accountant. 'The cultivation of the hemp plant appears extremely simple,' reported Austen naively.[5] Joe accordingly took the plunge.

In April 1891, Neville packed his bags, bade farewell to his adoring sisters and set off *en route* for Nassau via New York. The site chosen for the plantation was on Andros, the largest of the islands and about 20 miles by sea from Nassau. An initial purchase of 10,000 acres was arranged through the district surveyor, the site adjacent to a harbour at Mastic Point. 'I am confident', wrote Neville to Joe, 'that I have secured the best site available in the Bahamas.'[6] As soon as he had acclimatised himself, Neville began to assemble a team of local labourers to clear the land and prepare for eventual planting, his labour force at its maximum numbering some 800 men. He himself laboured alongside his 'darkies', gratified to find that he possessed the necessary physical stamina to withstand the inevitable hardships. At first Neville's living-quarters were no better than a hut and remained so until he could get a house built and employ a housekeeper and house-boy. Loneliness was a major problem. There were no white neighbours within miles. Because of the swarms of mosquitoes, it was impossible to work outside much after 4 p.m. and Neville spent the long evenings indoors, reading and writing voluminous letters to his family and reports to his father. Life brightened a little when his manager Michael Knowles brought his wife and children to the plantation. Neville formed an affection for Mrs Knowles and was upset when she died suddenly in childbirth. Her death had a devastating effect on Knowles, who took to the bottle, suffered from acute sleeplessness and eventually had to be sent away to Nassau for treatment.

At first the tone of Neville's reports was optimistic in spite of the many hardships and inconveniences he was obliged to endure. Joe's hope was that, once the plantation was firmly established, local management could be employed, leaving Neville free to return home for lengthy periods. As it was, Neville's visits home were limited to the summer months when the temperatures on Andros reached unendurable levels. After a two-month break in the summer of 1892, Austen, a newly-minted MP, returned with him and stayed until Christmas. In the following year Joe himself travelled out but was afflicted by headaches and toothache and did little serious exploring. In October he sailed for New York, but was sufficiently satisfied with progress to invest a further £20,000 in the enterprise by way of issuing debentures.

Neville pressed on. He now had a comfortable house with servants, a store, and a boat called 'Beatrice' in which he was learning to sail. The extra capital was employed in constructing a light railway, improving roads and on the purchase of bailing machinery. From that point on, however, Neville's confidence began to fade. The plants were not growing as well as expected and a would-be American purchaser rejected samples as being too stiff and of poor quality. To cap it all the price of sisal in the market began to fall dramatically. Neville's despair for the future of the enterprise was complete when the bailing shed and its contents were destroyed by fire. In a letter to his father in February 1896, Neville sounded a note of despair and personal reproach:

> [...] the plants don't grow ... all the order and discipline that I have worked up will be lost ... this is my failure, I can't bear to think of it.[7]

In his reply Joe pointed out that he had invested £50,000 into the project: 'this would indeed be a catastrophe', one he would have to bear if Neville's forebodings proved correct.[8]

By April 1896 Neville believed that the end-game had indeed been reached and he reconciled himself to the abandonment of the scheme to which he had devoted five years of his life.

> I no longer see any chance of making the investment pay ... I cannot blame myself too much for my want of judgement.[9]

He returned to Highbury in the summer of 1896, when the final decision to abandon was made. He then returned to Andros in the autumn to tie up loose ends and conduct a fire sale of assets, which fetched less than £1,000. There were no buyers for the land itself. Neville had gallantly taken upon himself the responsibility and though he had undoubtedly made mistakes and misjudgements, he knew in his heart that he had been saddled with an impossible task. This disaster did not prove as fatal to the Chamberlain finances as Joe had feared. From 1895 Joe and Austen were both in receipt of ministerial salaries and the family's investments were looking up. The Chamberlains continued to indulge their affluent lifestyles. As his sense that he had let his family down began to fade, so Neville reflected on the experience, telling a friend

> [...] in spite of all the disappointments, it was a great experience, and I know I am much the better and stronger for it.[10]

The mature Neville of 1896 was a character far removed from the diffident youth of twenty-one who had been launched on mission impossible by his impetuous father. While the experience deepened his reserve and introversion, it also hardened him and endowed him with a strong sense of his own capabilities and will to survive. Years later, when Neville and Winston Churchill served in the same Cabinet, the former recounted tales of his colonial adventure to an astonished Churchill, who reflected that few people knew that this Englishman, so often depicted as a 'governessy' provincial by his critics, had once been a hard-bitten colonial pioneer. It was a formative experience which left its mark for better or for worse.

The Birmingham businessman

Neville never visited Andros again, turning his back on that 'accursed island' as he had on Rugby school. He returned to his father's house at Highbury without professional qualifications and with little money of his own, having been paid the princely sum of £200 a year to manage the Andros Fibre Co. For the next decade he lived at Highbury and for lengthy periods was the only member of the family in residence. Joe's and Austen's political involvement kept them in London, which Mary much preferred to Birmingham, and in the winter his father and step-mother headed for the Riviera. Neville, cared for by the housekeeper Kate Bird, lived among the dust-sheets in the huge and under-populated house, though, given his nature, he was not greatly troubled by loneliness. At 28 he had to make a fresh start and where else to turn but to his uncles, especially Arthur, who lived close by at Moor Green Hall.

Arthur Chamberlain was one of the most successful professional managers of his era in Birmingham. The most important of his entrepreneurial concerns was Kynochs at Witton, makers of cordite and ammunition, which he rescued from bankruptcy. Arthur was willing to find a place for Neville, but Joe thought it politically inexpedient to link Neville too closely to a firm contracting with the Government. Instead, Arthur used his influence to obtain a slot for his nephew at Elliott's, a metal-processing firm large in terms of the Birmingham economy at that time, employing a workforce of between 800 and 1,000. Neville joined the board as a director, a post which occupied him for no more than one day a week. Elliott's was conveniently placed at Selly Oak, within an easy bike ride of Highbury. Characteristically, Neville took his role seriously, poking into every nook and cranny and filling notebooks with his comments. Once again, Uncle Arthur came up with a proposal for his under-employed nephew. He knew of a small company in Bordesley, also within easy bicycling distance of Highbury, which employed between 100 and 200 people in the manufacture of ships berths. The firm was Hoskins and Son: the son had died and his father had become anxious to sell. The company had been well managed, held contracts with shipping companies and the Admiralty and was making steady profits. This plan was accepted and the purchase price raised by a combination of family money and a bank loan. While Neville was left free to manage, he remained under the scrutiny of his father, who held the purse-strings and determined Neville's salary and bonuses: an initial £500 per annum raised to £600 in 1900, with £250 bonuses from time to time. By the time Neville was in full control a decade later, Hoskins was providing him with something closer to £5,000.

As anyone who knew Neville would have expected, he paid meticulous attention to business. A paternalist employer in the strong tradition of Birmingham family firms, he paid careful attention to the needs and welfare of his workers, paying them above the going rate and introducing bonuses. Like Uncle Arthur at the Witton works, he was averse to the development of the trade unions and hoped to avert the growth of trade unionism in his firm through the good terms of employment offered. His biographer, David Dilks, wrote that he managed Hoskins with 'a mixture of discipline and informality', and that by the standards of the time, he was 'an exceptionally good employer'.[11] Early on in his management Hoskins was affected by a Birmingham engineering strike, but it was never again affected by strike action while Neville was in charge. Although Hoskins was not a large firm, even by Birmingham standards, Neville's budding reputation as a manager and his extensive and influential family connections, ensured his rise in the entrepreneurial hierarchy. Other opportunities inevitably came his way, notably the chairmanship of Elliott's and a directorship of Birmingham

Small Arms (BSA). He also became an influential member of the Council of the Birmingham Chamber of Commerce. Like his father before him, he rubbed shoulders with other rising entrepreneurs and professionals in the Birmingham and Edgbaston Debating Society.

The success of Hoskins was balm to Neville's soul, his sense of failure put behind him. He found it particularly gratifying that it enabled him to play a full part in repairing the family finances. With Joe's resignation in 1903 and Austen's loss of office from December 1905, profits made at Hoskins made a vital contribution—the more so following Joe's stroke, with its concomitant medical and nursing expenses and the lengthy sojourns in Cannes. Taking charge of the family's disordered assets, Neville dared to complain to Hilda of Mary's extravagance.

While the family spent much of the year in London and on the Riviera, Neville became more immersed in business and the affairs of Birmingham. Neville kept up the Chamberlain habit of exchanging letters with family members, the main recipient of his doings and his innermost thoughts being his sister Hilda. His rather chilly, reserved and fastidious character proved an obstacle to the married life he craved. In 1903, he fell deeply in love with a friend of Hilda's, the singer Rosalind Craig Sellar, who performed at the Birmingham Triennial Festival in 1900 and 1903. When she rejected him, he consoled himself by taking a lengthy trip to India accompanied by his cousin Byng Kenrick. On the outward journey, he found himself sleeping in one of his own ships berths.

In the course of this trip, news reached him of the death from TB in Switzerland of his youngest sister Ethel, who was married to Lionel Richards, a barrister and close friend of the family. They had presented Joe with his first grandchild, Hilda Mary. In 1906, Neville acted as best man for Austen on the occasion of his marriage to Ivy Dundas. At last Neville found the partner for whom he longed in Anne De Vere Cole, niece of his Aunt Lilian, the widow of Herbert Chamberlain who had married again into the Cole family and acted as matchmaker. They were married in London in January 1911. Although Annie and Neville were of contrasting temperaments—she was brittle and of nervous disposition—it was a lifelong partnership which brought Neville great happiness and two children.

His letters to his sisters were full of praise for the contribution Annie made to his career. Unlike him, she was sociable and outgoing and so proved effective at electioneering and rallying women to the Unionist cause. Marriage entailed leaving Highbury at last. They moved to a house in Westbourne Road, Edgbaston, in the heart of the Calthorpe Estate and adjacent to Birmingham's Botanical Gardens. This was to be their main home for the next quarter century.

Community and politics

Becoming involved in the management of the Botanical Gardens in Edgbaston was a labour of love and the least onerous of Neville's contributions to the community. As a Chamberlain and in the tradition of Birmingham's wealthy Nonconformist families, he was in great demand for all manner of social and philanthropic activities. Not only did he respond positively, giving much of his spare time to various causes, but by his very nature he found it difficult not to take the leading role. Somewhat surprisingly he took an interest in the Territorial Army, becoming chairman of the board which managed the City's units. Although 'a reverent agnostic' like his father, he taught Sunday school at the Unitarian Church of the Messiah in Broad Street as his father had before him and he also inherited Joe's commitment to Birmingham University, joining the Board of Governors, sitting on the Buildings Committee and taking a particular interest in the establishment of a Department of Mining. But his greatest concern was with hospitals and medical services. He became an official visitor to the General Hospital and chairman of its committee in 1908. In typical style, he overhauled its organisation, in particular urging improvements in its outpatients department. His sister Ida shared his commitment and was especially keen on the appointment of almoners. Neville advocated extending the charity-funded provident dispensaries, of which there were three in the city. He became President and by the end of his tenure the service covered the whole city. Working people were able to consult competent doctors who accepted reduced fees for their work. Such experience was later to serve Neville well as Minister of Health.

Given Neville's commitment to welfare and education, it is hardly surprising that his name became linked with every political vacancy. But his reluctance to take an active part in politics persisted, partly because he felt that two high-profile politicians in the family was enough and partly because of his own diffidence. Dilks commented that Neville 'loathed making speeches and facing audiences', an aversion he never entirely conquered.[12] Playing a modest part in the general election campaign of 1900, he was like the rest of the family, incensed by Lloyd George's insinuations on the issue of Government contracts. He and Uncle Arthur successfully sued the Liberal newspaper *The Star*, receiving modest damages. His attitude became more positive in the wake of Joe's launch of the tariff reform campaign in 1903. Like many Birmingham businessmen involved in the metal trades, Neville had long been a convert. An important moment arrived in 1904 with the death of Joseph Powell Williams, a key aide in the management of the Liberal Unionist Party. Joe now demanded that Neville play a more active role, especially in managing and promoting the tariff reform cause in the area. In January 1906, Neville took a more prominent part than hitherto in the general election campaign and the incapacity of Joe from July 1906 onwards drew him further into commitment. He had effectively become the manager of the Liberal Unionist Association in Birmingham. In April 1911 the parliamentary seat of South Birmingham fell vacant. As usual, Neville's name was mooted and Annie was keen for him to put his name forward, but he rejected the opportunity and instead gave his backing to Leo Amery, a tireless journalist and propagandist who came to see himself as the true heir of Joseph Chamberlain. Amery was duly elected and remained MP for Birmingham until 1945, his lively career often criss-crossing with the Chamberlain brothers'. Neville would on occasion have cause to regret his patronage of Amery, of whom it was said that, had he been six inches taller and his speeches thirty minutes shorter, he might have been Prime Minister.

Rejecting openings to Parliament, Neville did decide at last to stand for the City Council and in November 1911 was duly returned for All Saints' ward, part of his father's constituency of West Birmingham. His decision had a lot to do with his ambition for his native city, which was experiencing a spectacular expansion and the management of which he wished to be involved in.

For years Birmingham had been bursting at the seams, surrounded by a collar of independent authorities in districts which were economically and socially integrated with Birmingham. In the 1890s the city had begun to reel them in. By the turn of the century, the Garden Suburb movement was fashionable and Birmingham produced two notable examples of enlightened town planning in George Cadbury's Bournville Village Trust and J. S. Nettlefold's Harborne Tenants Ltd., responsible for the model development of the Moorpool Estate. A little later the Ideal Benefit Society produced a plan for a 'workmen's garden colony' at Bordesley Green. The town planning movement was motivated not only by economic and aesthetic considerations, but also by the perceived connection between housing and health. Though health statistics had been improving decade upon decade, there was a stubborn core of infant mortality and premature death in the crowded inner city. Neville Chamberlain espoused both sides of the argument. Intimately involved in schemes to improve the city's health, as a member of the Council of the Chamber of Commerce he gave evidence to the parliamentary enquiry into Birmingham's plans for expansion. In May 1911 the Greater Birmingham Act, a truly radical measure, completed its passage through Parliament. The city was nearly tripled in size, giving it control of an area three times the size of Glasgow and twice the size of Manchester or Liverpool. Its population increased accordingly to 840,000. Joe Chamberlain's boast that Birmingham was 'the second city of the Empire' had become reality.

The man most responsible for this transformation was John Sutton Nettlefold, councillor for Edgbaston and Harborne ward, chairman of Birmingham's first Housing Committee from 1901 and author of *Practical Housing* (1908). Nettlefold had put Birmingham in the forefront of the town planning movement which induced Parliament to pass the Housing and Town Planning Act in 1909, giving Birmingham the green light for expansion. Ironically, in the municipal elections of 1911 which increased the size of the council to 120 members, Nettlefold lost his seat and was driven to the political margins. It had nothing to do with his pioneering efforts for town planning, but everything to do with Unionist politics. For Nettlefold had crossed his wicked uncle Joe. Nettlefold was married to Arthur Chamberlain's daughter, Margaret, and had followed his father-in-law's course in opposing tariff reform. His belief in free trade led Arthur to re-join the Liberal party and to become President of the Birmingham Liberal Association. Nettlefold confined himself to organising a Unionist Free Trade Association in his ward but, as treasurer of the Birmingham LUA, he had refused to sign cheques which he deemed were being misdirected for the purposes of tariff reform propaganda. He had first been removed from the treasurership and then, in 1911, removed from the council. His cousin, Edward Nettlefold, took over his role as treasurer while cousin Neville took his place as chairman of the Housing and Town Planning Committee. The family feud was never healed. Joe and Arthur had for many years been close but now bickered like schoolboys, Neville reporting that their Sunday dinners *en famille* had become a scene of conflict and ill-feeling.[13]

Neville had found himself a new plantation—Greater Birmingham. He now had ample scope for his rationalistic and systematic turn of mind. A series of plans were produced for the city's future development based on the concept of 'zoning', dividing it into areas of industry, business and residence, with the aims of producing a more efficient and cleaner environment and of 'decanting' population from the inner city into more spacious zones where provision could be made for gardens, allotments and parks. Appropriately, Neville combined his chairmanship of the Housing and Town Planning Committee with that of Health. In 1913, he chaired a special committee formed to investigate the city's housing conditions. The report furnished a comprehensive picture of Birmingham's 43,000 back-to-backs and has been much used by social historians. His rising status in the City Council was marked in 1914 by his appointment as an alderman, which saved him from seeking re-election that year and in 1915 he was chosen to be Lord Mayor, following in the footsteps not only of his father, but of ten other relatives who had served in that office.

The office of Lord Mayor of Birmingham was by no means a merely ceremonial one. The great cities of Britain at that time exercised very considerable powers and Birmingham could reasonably be described as a city-state, exercising control over its own utilities, local transport and education and welfare systems. Beyond its boundaries, it owned farms in Wales and sanatoria in the Cotswolds. The bulk of the finance to support these activities was raised from its own resources. Accordingly, a Birmingham Lord Mayor was potentially a powerful and influential figure should he have the will and the ability to carry the council with him. Neville, like his father, had both in abundance.

On 2 July 1914 Joe Chamberlain died and a few days later his body was driven through the packed and silent streets to be buried among his former wives and relatives in Key Hill cemetery in Icknield Street, Ladywood. A month later, Britain declared war on Germany, marking the beginning of years of social and economic strain and upheaval. Birmingham, at the heart of Britain's industrial economy, boomed and all the businesses with which the Chamberlains were connected expanded their profits. It was against this background that Neville became Lord Mayor in November 1915. He found ample scope for his energies and his inventive and active mind. 'Perhaps these were the most contented years of Chamberlain's life,' speculated biographer David Dilks.[14] What was notable was that, at this stage in his life, he was not the divisive figure that he was so frequently accused of being in later years. Dilks claims that he 'had pleasant relations with his Labour colleagues and found some of them helpful later'.[15] In September 1916 the TUC held its annual meeting in Birmingham, which was welcomed with a speech in which the Lord Mayor pleaded for co-operation between capital and labour and laid before the delegates the prospect of far-reaching societal changes in the future. It was the speech of a thoughtful social reformer and not a dyed-in-the-wool Tory, which Neville Chamberlain never was.

The wartime mayoralty

Birmingham was as well governed as was possible in the chaotic conditions of war. The City Council was anxious to keep the city as productive and as stable as possible. A Citizens' Society was formed with the task of bringing relief to distressed families, while a Civic Recreation League did its best to keep up the morale of the people. Neville took a particular interest in the latter, rising in full regalia in the interval of a concert given by the Hallé Orchestra to advocate the establishment of a permanent city orchestra. His aspiration would become reality in 1919 with the founding of the City of Birmingham Symphony Orchestra (CBSO) with the aid of a council subsidy. This was to be Neville's permanent memorial, but at the time there were more immediate and serious matters to deal with. Shortages of milk and coal were answered with a system of rationing to become more familiar in the Second World War, the council using its purchasing power to buy in supplies and to sell them at cost. In January 1916, Birmingham experienced its first air-raid and Neville turned his mind to organising a system of defence which he pressed on the Home Office. Highbury, deserted by the family and unsaleable, was turned into a convalescent hospital for wounded soldiers and Neville persuaded the university to do likewise with its Great Hall. Considerable effort was also made to provide relief for Belgian refugees. But apart from the CBSO, the most enduring of Chamberlain's efforts was the establishment of a unique institution, the Birmingham Municipal Bank.

One of the main ways in which the Government financed the war was through the sale of war bonds, a form of saving which left untouched the wages of working people, many of whom were enjoying inflated wage packets. Anxious to tap this resource and to encourage thrift among the workers, Neville suggested a savings scheme which would collect small sums at source. His draft bill immediately ran into a barrage of objections—from the Friendly Societies, the banks and not least from the Treasury—and by May 1916 he was ready to admit defeat. 'I am beat,' he reported to Hilda, 'and the Savings bank is dead.'[16] His scheme was saved through the support of a number of Labour leaders and especially of Eldred Hallas, leader of the Municipal Workers' Union, who made numerous speeches in its favour in the factories of Birmingham. Initially suspicious of any proposition which involved employers interfering with their wage packets, attitudes changed when Hallas suggested that they might buy stamps or coupons. Opposition crumbled, a Bill came before Parliament in July 1916 and received the royal assent a month later. Hallas, a patriotic Labour leader who was battling with pacifists in the Birmingham Trades Council, would receive a political reward in 1918.[17] The first premises of the bank were established in the basement of the Corporation Water Department. Interest on deposits was paid at 3½ per cent guaranteed by the corporation and within two years it had attracted 30,000 depositors. After the war ended, the bank became permanent under the terms of the Birmingham Corporation Act of July 1919. Smart headquarters were opened in Broad Street and branches established across the city. Asa Briggs, official Birmingham historian, credits the scheme with great success, as do most of Neville Chamberlain's biographers, with the exception of Nick Smart, who asks sceptically why the Birmingham Municipal Bank remained unique and was not copied by other municipalities.[18]

Neville revelled in the office of Lord Mayor and in the scope which it gave him for initiative. He felt compensated for the perceived misfires of his early manhood. On the occasion of his forty-seventh birthday he replied smugly to a letter of congratulation from Mary: 'if the good things came to me rather later in life than they do to some I am making up now for lost time'. His career, however, was about to take a dramatic and life-changing turn, which would shatter his cocoon of self-satisfaction.

In and out of Cabinet

On 19 December 1916, Neville Chamberlain went to London for consultations with the Local Government Board. Boarding the train at Paddington for his return to Snow Hill he was intercepted by a messenger sent by Austen and asked to go immediately to the India Office. Central Government was in turmoil as the new Prime Minister, David Lloyd George, was shaking things up and bringing down the curtain on the somnolent Asquith regime. Among his new appointments he was seeking a man of 'Push and Go' to head the Department of National Service. Edwin Montagu had turned the job down and Austen had suggested to the War Committee that Neville would be a suitable alternative. Both Lord Milner and Sir Edward Carson supported the idea and Austen passed the suggestion on to Lloyd George. After a ten minute interview at the Prime Minister's office in the House of Commons, Neville was offered and accepted the post of Director General of National Service. Lloyd George, a believer in phrenology, later claimed that he was immediately put off by the shape of Neville's head, but this claim was made years after the event in his *War Memoirs* (1934) and was just one of the many insults traded between the pair over the years.

Within hours Lloyd George had announced the appointment to the House of Commons. Neville was left in a state of mental turmoil. He was extremely reluctant to resign the role of Lord Mayor of Birmingham, to which he had just been elected for a second term and was unclear about many details of the new appointment, including the salary attached. Crucially, he would be dealing directly with the Cabinet but, not being an MP, he would not be able to defend his proposals on the floor of the House, which he came to recognise as a fatal flaw in his position. A second drawback was that he was required to put together his department from scratch, the St Ermin's Hotel being earmarked for the purpose. Unused to the devious ways of Whitehall, Neville desperately needed an experienced chief of staff, yet he preferred to call on men he trusted and had worked with in the administration of his home city, in particular Ernest Hiley, former town clerk. His sisters, seasoned in the way of politics, were uneasy about the nature and the manner of the appointment, Hilda commenting, 'your title, magnificent and comprehensive as it sounds, is yet a trifle vague'.[19] This turned out to be an understatement.

With the Army demanding half a million new recruits to be trained in time for the next 'big push', Neville was under pressure to produce quick results. His instinct was to bring to an end the system of exemptions, but here he met obstruction from a number of other ministries, including the Ministry of Munitions, the Ministry of Agriculture and the new Ministry of Labour, which all had their own agendas. The introduction of conscription was still strongly resisted by many Liberals and by a substantial section of the Labour movement. Caught up in the complexity of the issues and ministerial rivalries, Neville struggled manfully to find a practical solution, but soon found that he could not rely on the support or the sympathy of the Prime Minister. Discouraged, he very soon began to contemplate resignation, Lord Milner's friendly advice to 'get out of it' chiming with his own bruised feelings. Under fire from the press and in face of the indifference or worse from the Prime Minister, Neville resigned on 8 August 1917. It was galling to see his successor, Aukland Geddes, being given many of the powers of which he had been denied.

Neville returned to Birmingham chastened and depressed. Although he knew he had not been given the powers needed to succeed in the allotted task, he was left with an exaggerated sense of personal failure. His smouldering feelings of hostility to Lloyd George, 'that mean little skunk', were shared by his sisters.[20] Neither could he avoid resentment of his 'damned well meaning brother' who had bounced him into the role. Only the team of civil servants he had assembled at St Ermin's hotel in Victoria Street showed any appreciation for his efforts. He was offered but rejected a knighthood. To Neville, this was Andros all over again. He returned to Westbourne to resume his life and to contemplate the future. With the encouragement of Annie he determined to seek a parliamentary seat, although he realised that, with the age of 50 fast approaching, his political prospects were dwindling.

His mood that year was made all the bleaker by news of the death in action in December 1917 of his cousin Norman, son of Herbert Chamberlain and the second of Neville's cousins to die, Arthur Chamberlain's son John having been killed in the previous May. It was the loss of Norman that affected Neville the most deeply. After attending Eton and Oxford, Norman had been set on a political career and suffered honourable defeat in the strong Liberal seat of Camborne in Cornwall in 1910. In 1909 he was elected to the Birmingham City Council two years ahead of Neville. The two cousins became very close, Neville describing him as 'the most intimate friend I had'.[21] Norman served as chairman of the Parks Committee and dedicated his life to the service of youth. In his will he left money for the provision of playing fields and this legacy came to fruition on an estate in Shard End. A number of historians and notably

Iain Macleod have considered that Norman's death had a profound effect on Neville, for whom it encapsulated the waste and futility of war and therefore had an important bearing on future policy. Neville's profound love of peace and hatred of war were personified in Norman, the subject of the only book he ever wrote. Closer to home, the influenza pandemic which swept Europe at the very end of the war claimed the life of Beatrice, Neville's half-sister and the eldest of Joe Chamberlain's six children.

Neville's first task on his return was to regain his position of leadership in Birmingham's municipal politics. For the duration of the war there had been a moratorium on elections, the eight vacancies which occurred on the City Council being filled by co-option. No parliamentary vacancies had cropped up during that time. As an elected alderman, Neville was entitled to resume his place on the City Council. He re-joined the Town Planning Committee, became chairman of the Citizens' Committee and in November 1917 became deputy Lord Mayor. In June 1918 he was offered, but declined, the opportunity to become Lord Mayor again in the following year. The reason for his refusal was his wish to keep his options open. He had already signalled to Charles Vince, chief agent of the Birmingham Liberal Unionist Association (BLUA), that he wanted a parliamentary seat, but neither the 74-year-old Sir Ebenezer Parkes nor the 86-year-old Jesse Collings were willing to make way for him. He had no choice but to be patient. Meanwhile there was much work to do, not only in the municipal context but also in preparation for the return of normal party politics.

The Unionist party machine had virtually disintegrated in the course of war. Negotiations over the fusion of the Conservatives (BCA) and the Liberal Unionists (BLUA) had stalled in 1914. These were resumed in the summer of 1918 with Neville in the chair. He had to repel a challenge for the leadership from Sir Arthur Steel-Maitland, currently an undersecretary at the Board of Trade and formerly a Conservative party chairman, together with some back-biting from Sir Frank Lowe, veteran leader of the BCA. However, he successfully upheld the Chamberlain birthright. A joint management committee was set up under Neville as chairman. Exuding self-satisfaction and with a sly sense of humour, he reported to Hilda,

> [...] this decision practically places the direction of Unionist politics in my hands. I am not sure whether all those present perceived this, I didn't mention it.[22]

Neville was determined to centralise the Unionist party, overcoming resistance from ward associations in Aston and Erdington. A new central office was established in Edmund Street and there followed a steady appointment of professional agents. A Women's Association and a Junior Unionist Association were also established. The Unionist party and Neville personally could rely on the steady support of the *BDP* and *The Birmingham Mail* (*BM*) whose editor, A. H. Hubbard, had been installed at Joe Chamberlain's instigation during the tariff reform controversy earlier in the century. Whatever the shortcomings of the Unionist machine, they paled into insignificance compared to the weakness of the BLP, which was riven with ideological conflict and whose only full-time secretary was shared with the Trades Council. The Unionist Association under Neville, who in this respect as in others was following closely in father's footsteps, never lost its grip on Birmingham politics in the years between the wars and was recognised as probably the most powerful in the country. Even in his busiest Westminster days, Neville never relaxed his control of the Birmingham party or of the Midland Union.

It was high time for the political machine to be renovated and reactivated. Not only had wartime emergencies changed the social and economic face of Britain, but the political system had been substantially recast by the Representation of the People Act of 1918. The Birmingham electorate, a mere 95,000 in 1914, had expanded to 427,000 by 1918, of which 165,000 were women over 30. When conceded the vote on the same terms as men in 1929 women would come to constitute more than half of Birmingham's electorate of 660,000. Conscious of this electoral shift, Neville pressed for the foundation of a Women's Association and looked to Annie to play a leading role, which she did resolutely and with charm. In 1922, a full-time female organiser was appointed at a salary of £250 per annum. Birmingham's seven pre-war divisions were increased to twelve, in proportion to the increase in its population. Neville stood for the Ladywood constituency, a stone's throw from his home in Edgbaston. He would have much preferred the Edgbaston constituency, but this remained firmly in the hands of Sir Frank Lowe, much to the irritation of the Chamberlain family. Ladywood was a challenging constituency. It contained pockets of slum housing and poverty and an overwhelmingly working-class electorate. He and Annie were obliged to spend much time and energy in what he described as 'slumming'. Neville took no pleasure in electioneering, which he tended to regard as an unfortunate necessity imposed by the parliamentary system and he viewed with a jaundiced eye the way of life and the habits of many of his constituents—even their food he found distasteful. It would have been surprising if some of his constituents had not sensed this patrician, or rather bourgeois, disdain. Lack of rapport with ordinary people was a flaw in his political make-up. Austen reported to his sisters on one occasion that 'Neville's manner freezes people'.[23] His diffidence, his reserve and his disdain for small talk meant that, however much respect he garnered, whether in the Birmingham Council House or at Westminster, he would never inspire the affection of which Stanley Baldwin and even Austen proved capable.

In the aftermath of the greatest war in history and on an untried register, it is hardly surprising that the general election of December 1918 was the most confused of the century. It went down in history as the 'Coupon Election', the 'coupon' being the contemptuous label given by Asquith to the letter of endorsement signed by Lloyd George and Bonar Law to supporters of the Coalition. Neville received the 'coupon' but claimed he never used it. Of more utility was a letter from W. J. Davis ('Brassy', as he was known in the Chamberlain family), which praised Neville and damned pacifist Labour men of which Neville's opponent was one. Davis was the founder and leader of the Brassworkers' Society, an ex-chairman of the TUC and the most prominent labour leader in Birmingham. Neville had Davis' letter printed and distributed in the constituency.

Neville was opposed in Ladywood by an Asquithian Liberal from Sussex, Mrs Margaret Corbett Ashby and by a city councillor, John Kneeshaw, calling himself 'the people's dreadnought'—an ironic title for an active member of the Union of Democratic Control and conscientious objector during the war. Campaigning on a programme of nationalisation and a capital levy, Kneeshaw was just the sort of Socialist the Chamberlain brothers, and especially Austen, feared in the tempestuous aftermath of the war. Neville responded with a radical programme of his own. Not opposed in principle to nationalisation, as in the case of canals, he advocated a minimum wage, reductions in working hours and state intervention in the housing market. His election was made all the more secure by the continued recrimination in the ranks of Labour between pacifists and 'patriots'. Neville's majority on a low turn-out (barely reaching 50 per cent) was a little under 6,000. All twelve candidates endorsed by the Unionists were elected. Two of these were Labour leaders, Arthur Jephcott in Yardley and Eldred Hallas in Duddeston. Jephcott was a long-time Liberal Unionist but Hallas, a leader of the Municipal Workers' Union, was a member of the British Workers' League (BWL), which had supported the war and battled those elements in the Labour movement which opposed it. The BWL had influential patrons headed by Lord Milner, a member of Lloyd George's War Cabinet. Its leading members, standing as the National Democratic Labour Party (NDLP), received their reward with a handful of parliamentary seats in 1918. Neville had received valuable support from Eldred Hallas in his campaign to establish the Birmingham Municipal Bank and he managed to persuade the Duddeston constituency to adopt Hallas as their candidate—although by the time of the general election he was beginning to have second thoughts, concerned by the stridency of the latter's tone, which Neville feared would drive moderate workers into the arms of the Labour party. The NDLP, however, proved ephemeral. Within a year Hallas had 'ratted', crossing the floor of the House of Commons and taking the Labour Whip. It was agreed that he should remain MP for Duddeston until the next election, when he would stand down. In these peculiar post-war circumstances, Hallas could fairly claim to be Birmingham's first Labour MP, even if he had been elected predominantly by Unionist votes. The election of prominent Labour leaders such as Jephcott and Hallas was a signal that Birmingham Unionism, a label preferred to Conservatism, was socially progressive. Neville himself admitted loathing the label 'Conservative', much preferring 'Unionist' in his father's image.

The Coupon Election spawned an unbalanced Parliament. 338 Conservatives and 136 Coalition Liberals were opposed by a mere 59 Labour MPs and 26 Asquithian Liberals, Asquith himself having been beaten at East Fife. On the overcrowded government benches there seemed to be only one clear objective—to keep Lloyd George in power. Many Unionists had no great love for the Welshman, only a grudging respect for his achievements, while their leaders, Bonar Law emphatically supported by Austen Chamberlain, regarded him as indispensable. His admirers contemplated either the creation of a new centre party or the ultimate fusion of the two wings of the Coalition Government, Unionists and Lloyd George Liberals. Oddly, it was the rank-and-file Coalies who proved the most resistant to this course of action and thus doomed their own political futures. Such an unstable situation could not last. By 1921 Lloyd George had ceased to pull rabbits out of the hat in ether foreign or domestic affairs and it was only the support of leading Unionists which stemmed the tide of Unionist revolt.

Neville of course was no admirer of the Prime Minister. At moments he expressed respect for his skills but he harboured an intense dislike of the 'dirty little Welsh attorney'. Among the latter's admirers, of course, was his brother Austen, whom Neville was anxious not to embarrass by out-and-out criticism of the Government. He recognised that there was no room for both brothers in the administration, and in any case he had no intention of once again serving under Lloyd George. Curiously, Bonar Law, who developed a high opinion of Neville's manifest talents, sounded him out in March 1920 as to his willingness to serve in a junior office, perhaps at the Ministry of Health. He hinted that, at his age, he might never get another chance. Neville refused the offer and rehearsed all his well-known grievances against Lloyd George, but he did so politely out of respect for the Unionist leader. These were, however, very frustrating years for Neville, his career apparently going nowhere. The two brothers seemed increasingly to inhabit different political universes. Not only did they differ radically in their perception of the Prime Minister, but their approach to policy differed markedly. Austen took no interest in Neville's schemes for larger state investment in housing and other socially progressive policies, while Neville increasingly came to regard his brother as unconstructive and even reactionary. As he complained to his sisters, 'he thinks me wild and I think him unprogressive.'[24] Intensely irritated by Austen's air of negative condescension, on one occasion Neville gave vent to his feelings to Hilda: 'I have made a firm resolution never to be so foolish as to ask him to do anything for me or for Birmingham again'.

In the circumstances Neville found it expedient to cultivate his Birmingham businesses, maintain involvement in Birmingham's civic affairs and to continue to improve the finances and organisation of Birmingham and Midland Unionism. Westbourne rather than Egerton Terrace, his London address, remained the focus of his activities and his family life. In February 1921, much to Neville's frustration, the Birmingham City Council made Lloyd George a Freeman of the City. Accompanied by Austen, Lloyd George made a highly complimentary speech at a dinner in his honour arranged by the Jewellers' Association. Neville slunk away to Sidmouth, writing sarcastically to Ida, 'to think that at this moment our pure souled Prime Minister is receiving the freedom of Birmingham. I can scarce restrain a tear.'[25] It would be five years before Austen was similarly honoured and eleven years before Neville joined his father and brother on the City's Roll of Honour.

Neville had entered Parliament in a somewhat negative frame of mind, fearing that at fifty years of age he was too late to achieve much. Once installed, however, he began to enjoy the experience, reporting to Ida, 'I begin to feel the fascination of the House of Commons'. Not being a confident speaker himself, he admired the oratory and debating skills of Churchill, Austen and others, including his *bête noire* Lloyd George. But, if he did not shine in debate on the floor of the House, he more than made up for it in his assiduity in committees. The demand for his services mounted steadily, biographer David Dilks commenting

> [...] the subjects ranged from the development of waterways to the condition of life in canal boats, from Ministers' salaries to electricity supply, housing and town planning.[26]

It was housing above all that preoccupied him and he became chairman of the Unhealthy Areas Committee which reported in 1921. Neville was in favour of the nationalisation of land but advocated local authority control of housing development. A distinctly personal initiative was his effort to improve the legal status of illegitimate children, dealt with in what became known as the 'Bastardy Bill'.

Neville built for himself a solid reputation as a reliable and constructive committee man, always on top of the issues and always ready to take a lead in formulating solutions. For him administration was the essence of politics. At this stage of his career, his 'accursed shyness' and reluctance to socialise with fellow MPs was less evident than it later became and he reported to his sisters that he lunched and dined regularly in the House, making friends and acquaintances. His progressive ideas carried him well to the left of the party, though his rejection of 'fusion' and dislike of Lloyd George and the Coalition aligned him with Robert Cecil's die-hards on the right of the party. He did not, however, see eye to eye with them in their opposition to the Irish settlement of 1921 and for Austen's sake kept a discreet distance.

Neville and Annie were on a six-week tour of Canada when the Coalition collapsed on 19 October 1922 as a result of the revolt against Austen at the Carlton Club meeting. For obvious reasons he had stood clear of the turmoil in the party and played no part in the Government's downfall. The fall of Lloyd George's Ministry was a key event in British political history between the wars. For the Conservative Party, too, this was a crucial event, 'a slice off the top'. Into the wilderness with Lloyd George went Austen, Balfour, Churchill and other Ministers who had hitherto dominated British politics—only Lord Curzon held out in the hope of the succession to the premiership. Bonar Law became Prime Minister and, apprehensively, he was obliged to fill these posts with lesser men, forming what Lord Birkenhead called 'the second XI'. These lesser figures subsequently proved immovable, the futures of the ex-Cabs now in the hands of Bonar Law and his successor Stanley Baldwin, a relatively junior figure who had gone to the Carlton Club meeting set on going out of politics if Lloyd George, whom he derided as a danger to the Conservative Party and the country, survived. Neville, though sympathising with the obvious setback to Austen, was delighted with the fall of Lloyd George. Writing to Hilda he recorded 'his profound thanks to Providence for delivering us from the goat'.[27]

Upwardly mobile

Although it was not obvious at the time, Neville was also to be a major beneficiary of the change of regime. Promotion would soon be his and the two men, Baldwin and Chamberlain, would establish a firm grip on British politics in the ensuing decades. Neville's and Austen's status in the party was soon reversed and while Austen retained his position as a

Conservative 'Grandee', when he and other ex-Cabs returned to office it was on Baldwin's terms. Relations between the two half-brothers, however much they assured each other of their mutual affection, would never be without tension.

Within days of becoming Prime Minister, Bonar Law approached Neville via Leo Amery with an offer of the office of Postmaster-General, to be held outside the Cabinet. The offer presented Neville with a dilemma, since he knew well how much it would upset his brother but, in truth he barely hesitated. In the face of Austen's angry protests he threatened to leave politics altogether if required to refuse office. On the plus side he argued that he might act as a bridge between Bonar Law and Austen, enhancing the prospect of party re-union. For the subsequent six months Neville, with his usual assiduity, immersed himself in postal charges, the parcel post, telephone provision and the mysteries of wireless telegraphy. Law showed an increasing respect for his judgement, consulting him on foreign as well as domestic issues, while Neville found Law's gloomy and pessimistic outlook not uncongenial. Law soon added to Neville's portfolio the role of Paymaster General, which increased his salary and provided him with an office commanding a magnificent view over Whitehall.

Ironically, since the revolt against Lloyd George had partly stemmed from Conservative rank-and-file opposition to an early general election, Law decided to dissolve Parliament and seek a popular mandate. The general election of November 1922 was the first of a sequence of three general elections in three years. The electorate obliged by returning 347 Unionists, giving Law a secure majority. In Birmingham, all twelve seats were comfortably held by Unionists. Four were returned unopposed and in the remaining seats majorities ranged from Herbert Austin's 1,853 in King's Norton to Oliver Locker-Lampson's 6,069 in Handsworth. Sir Ernest Hiley, former town clerk and Neville's Chief of Staff in his brief tenure as Director of National Service, took Hallas' place in Duddeston. Neville could take satisfaction from the smooth functioning of the Unionist machine, but was disappointed with his own result in Ladywood, his majority of 2,443 being more than 3,000 less than Austen's in neighbouring West Birmingham. This was in spite of his and Annie's intense efforts in the constituency, the Chief Agent commenting that 'there wasn't a dog hanging that they didn't attend'.[28] Clearly, Austen's fall from party grace had not affected his popularity in Birmingham, something of both a puzzle and an irritant to Neville.

In March 1923, Law promoted Neville to the Cabinet post which he admitted should have been his in the first place, though first refusal had gone to former Chancellor of the Exchequer, Sir Robert Horne. There was no post which Neville would find more congenial than Minister of Health, covering a range of domestic issues with which he had long been engaged and especially housing. Neville revelled in his new-found status, reporting smugly to his sisters:

> [...] it seems my fate is to be given the most dangerous and responsible position in the front line and probably the fate of the Government will now depend on poor me.[29]

Immediately he applied himself to the problems of housing supply and the issue of rent restriction, a wartime measure about which many landlords were complaining and which was widely considered to contribute to the on-going housing shortage. The policies of a former Minister of Health, Dr Christopher Addison, had failed to produce the quantity of houses needed to accommodate a growing population and to make possible measures of slum clearance, Addison houses being among the most expensive built between the wars. Neville's Housing Act sought both to accelerate supply and to reduce costs, which were in any case falling. It offered a subsidy of £6 for each house built to specified dimensions for a period of twenty years and was open to both private builders and local authorities, the offer to be time-limited to two years. It was private builders who responded most positively. Of the 438,000 houses built under the act, 362,700 were by private builders. This accorded well with Neville's general philosophy. Wherever possible, he favoured house ownership by those workers who could afford it, both as fostering a 'property-owning democracy' and as the most expedient means of decanting population from run-down city centres. The thrust of the post war policy of Neville's creation, the Birmingham Municipal Bank, was to provide mortgages for relatively affluent workers. At the same time he was never an opponent of state interference, though preferred its source to be local authorities rather than central government. His Housing Act had critics, mainly on the Left, from which quarter he was attacked for fostering the construction of reduced-sized, non-parlour houses. Neville's Labour successor, the formidable John Wheatley, would increase subsidy, extend time limits and shift the emphasis from private to council house construction, but Neville's Act was generally well received. His thorough grasp of the issues impressed even his critics and enhanced his reputation as a capable administrator. On the issue of rent restriction it was necessary to proceed cautiously. Neville would have preferred to have abolished controls but accepted the need 'to protect the tenant from the extortionate landlord when control goes'.[30] His Rent Restriction Continuation Act relaxed but did not rescind controls.

In May 1923 Bonar Law's ill health—followed swiftly by his death from throat cancer—forced his retirement. The rival candidates for the succession were Foreign Secretary Lord Curzon and Chancellor of the Exchequer Stanley Baldwin. Somewhat surprisingly, Neville confided to his sisters, 'I had rather hoped that Curzon would have been Prime Minister but I had not realised the extent of his unpopularity in the country'.[31] In spite of the similarity in their backgrounds, Neville did not hold Baldwin in high esteem and was always ready to itemise his shortcomings: their outlook on politics was very different. Where Neville was a carnivore, keen to forge a 'New Conservatism', Baldwin was a herbivore, emollient and anxious to calm the climate of class conflict. A Baldwin premiership offered the possibility of healing the rift in the party, but when Baldwin belatedly consulted Austen, the leader of the ex-Cabs, he mishandled that prickly man, who became infuriated by the suggestion that he might like to become His Majesty's next Ambassador in Washington. The reality Baldwin faced was that many of his Cabinet colleagues were not yet ready to welcome Austen back and were even more hostile to Birkenhead, a loose liver whose caustic tongue had given offence. Neville did his best to mollify his brother, who was threatening to leave Parliament altogether at the time of the next dissolution. Meanwhile, an unwelcome offer came Neville's way. On 16 August, while fishing in Scotland, he received a letter from the Prime Minister's office offering him the post of Chancellor of the Exchequer, which had been offered to but turned down by Sir Robert Horne. Neville was enjoying his job at the Ministry of Health and, together with his civil servants, had prepared detailed legislative plans for the next two years. Accordingly he declined the promotion and somewhat bizarrely for a man who had studied accountancy and was the director of a number of Birmingham firms, protested that he had no gift for finance, 'which I have never been able to understand'. Annie, while keen for Neville's advancement, was also reluctant to move from their newly acquired house in Eaton Square, Belgravia, to number 11 Downing Street. Baldwin, however, brooked no refusal and with genuine reluctance Neville gave way. He need not have worried. He was one of the few Chancellors in history who was never called upon to present a budget in this his first spell as Chancellor.

The Labour experiment

For the one and only time in his life Stanley Baldwin shocked the political world by taking a bold initiative. In a speech to NUCCA at Plymouth on 25 October, he declared that the Government was powerless to tackle the crisis of unemployment without tariffs. Since Law had pledged that a Conservative Government would not introduce further measures of protection without an electoral mandate, an early dissolution of Parliament was required. Both Chamberlain brothers were delighted by this turn of events and it is possible that one at least of Baldwin's motives was to bring about re-union in the party. His decision also caused a degree of turmoil in the party. Whereas Austen and his followers were at first enthusiastic, their eagerness faded somewhat as it became clear that Baldwin's proposal would not include the food taxes necessary to act as a platform for imperial preference. At the same time there were many in the party, especially in Lancashire, who retained a stubborn belief in free trade and, indeed, a majority of the Cabinet probably shared this view. It was also clear that Baldwin had made little preparation for the campaign, Austen and Co. scathingly contrasting his efforts with Joe Chamberlain's two decades earlier. A further negative factor was that both the Labour and Liberal parties immediately affirmed their allegiance to free trade. For the Liberals in particular, Baldwin seemed to have thrown them a lifeline as Joe had done in 1903. In these circumstances it was not surprising that the Conservatives lost 80 seats, mostly in Lancashire, in the general election of December 1923. They remained the largest party in the Commons with 258 seats, but the two free trade parties together, Labour with 191 seats and the Liberals with 158, outnumbered them. Heated negotiations ruled out a new Conservative-Liberal Coalition and Baldwin resigned on behalf of his Government. The King sent for James Ramsay MacDonald to form the landmark first Labour administration. For Conservatives there could hardly have been a better time to try the experiment of a Labour Government. Should it attempt to introduce the radical policies demanded by the Labour Left, the onus would fall on Asquith, who held the balance of power, either to acquiesce or to pull the plug. As Austen and others clearly perceived, this would be the swansong of the Liberal Party and would mark a further trend towards a dominant, two-party system.

Relegation to the Opposition at least raised the prospect of the re-union of the Conservative Party. Although Baldwin's programme had fallen short of the hopes of the tariff reformers such as Austen and Amery, they unhesitatingly supported the campaign. General sentiment in the party favoured the return of Austen and Horne, but strong objections to Birkenhead persisted. Yet Austen stubbornly refused to return to the Shadow Cabinet without Birkenhead. Neville made it his business to smooth the way and he brought Baldwin and his brother together at a dinner party in his house at Eaton Square in February 1924. What started as a frigid affair began to thaw and Neville reported to his sisters that, by the end of the evening, it was 'My dear Stanley and My dear Austen as if they had never been parted'.[32] At midnight the two left Eaton Square together, if not arm-in-arm at least reconciled. Baldwin agreed to take Birkenhead back and, on this assurance, Austen attended the Shadow Cabinet the next day, was named deputy leader and took the lead in discussion. So, reported Neville, 're-union has come at last, thanks, I think I may say, to me'. This proved to be a shrewd move by Baldwin. With both Chamberlain brothers in his camp he was better able to resist pressures, especially from the press barons Beaverbrook and Rothermere, to resign. He was far less confident in opposition than in government and there were those in the party who would have preferred Austen Chamberlain as leader, but such a transition was now made unlikely by Austen's acceptance of Baldwin's leadership.

In October 1924, Asquith pulled the plug on Ramsay MacDonald's Government, precipitating the third general election in three years. Although enjoying only a brief spell in office, Labour had gained from the experience and had dissipated fears of a 'red tide'. Nevertheless, though the Labour party had generally strengthened its position in the country, it was the Conservatives who were returned to office with a comfortable majority—415 MPs against 152 Labour MPs and a mere 42 Liberals. In Birmingham the Unionists, as they still preferred to call themselves, had faced an unexpectedly tough challenge. Neville was uneasy about his position in Ladywood and looked enviously at the neighbouring constituency of Edgbaston where his cousin Byng Kenrick was chairman. Sir Francis Lowe signalled his willingness to retire but too late to make the necessary arrangements. However, Neville felt confident of victory in Ladywood: 'I feel more confident this time than I did last about my own seat and Birmingham generally,' he told Hilda, 'I shall be disappointed if I don't increase my majority'.[33] He acknowledged that 'Labour is making a tremendous effort here', but underestimated the Mosley effect. Oswald Mosley, formerly a Conservative and then an independent MP before hitching his star to the Labour Party, had chosen to contest Ladywood as the quickest and most spectacular route to political stardom, much as Lord Randolph Churchill had done by standing against Bright in Central Birmingham in the 1880s. Mosley was only adopted as a candidate in July but made an instant impact. He brought with him to the city two expert organisers, John Strachey and Allan Young. Strachey was at this time a Marxist and later a Minister in Attlee's post-war Government. He was adopted for Aston while Allan Young became a full-time organiser for the BLP. Mosley dispensed ample funds to oil the wheels of the impoverished BLP. The Labour newspaper, *The Town Crier*, was soon full of his doings and singing his praises. He was without doubt one of the most charismatic orators of his time, beside whom Neville looked somewhat drab and unexciting. 'In Birmingham,' wrote Mosley's biographer Robert Skidelsky, 'it was Mosley, not MacDonald who ruled'.[34]

The count was perhaps the most dramatic in Birmingham's political history. Several recounts were called for and the result was not declared until 4.30 a.m. At one point Mosley left the Town Hall to announce to the waiting crowd that he had won, but Neville was finally declared to be the winner by 77 votes. For years afterwards rumours circulated that a vital bundle of votes had been flushed down the toilet. Neville was in by the skin of his teeth but Herbert Austin was out, Labour winning its first Birmingham seat. Even Neville admitted that Austin well deserved his fate. He was 'the worst representative I have ever come across,' he told Hilda, 'never attending the House or doing anything in his constituency'.[35] Labour had closed the gap on the Unionists in all the inner-city constituencies except in West Birmingham, where Austen increased his majority by some 2,000—a result which must have been galling for Neville who, in contrast to his largely absentee brother, had gone to great lengths to cultivate his constituents. With Mosley rampant and the morale of the BLP's supporters sky-high, it was evident that it was time for Neville to beat a retreat to Edgbaston. His discomfort, however, was not mirrored in the party generally, the Conservatives returning to Westminster with a large majority.

The brothers together in Cabinet

When putting together his new Cabinet, Baldwin first offered Neville the chance to return to the Exchequer. Neville demurred, 'I ought to be a great Minister of Health but I am not likely to be more than a second-rate Chancellor,' he told his sisters.[36] Baldwin did not insist on this occasion and agreed to Neville's request. To his own surprise as well as that of the political community and the fury of many Tories, who regarded him as a dangerous renegade, Baldwin appointed Churchill to be his next Chancellor. His motives were obscure, but he probably intended it as another step in the restoration of party unity and an indication to the electorate that he accepted the rejection of tariff reform, since Winston remained a firm free trader. The appointment also brought about an accession of strength to the Conservative front bench in the Commons. Neville, in contrast to Austen, was disapproving, doubting whether he and Churchill could work amicably together. Winston 'lacked judgement,' he complained to Hilda, 'he is a very dangerous man to have in the government'.[37] Amid the inevitable tussles between these two strong characters there were from time to time expressions of admiration for Churchill's energy, flashes of genius and his power of debate, but his judgement of Churchill never substantially changed. In the new Government Birmingham had never been better represented. Alongside the Chamberlain brothers were Leo Amery, Colonial Secretary and Arthur Steel-Maitland, Minister of Labour, although relations between the quartet were never entirely amicable.

Neville set about his new job with a zeal amounting almost to fanaticism. He presented his staff with a four-year programme covering the whole field of the ministry's wide responsibilities: housing, rating and valuation, the Poor Law, medical services, pensions and health insurance. He envisaged a programme of no less than twenty-five Bills to bring about the changes he had in mind. In November he secured the Cabinet's acquiescence. 'My staff are quite convinced that no Minister is so hard working as theirs,' he told Hilda, 'and I believe they aren't far wrong'. In the next four years he would enact legislation in twenty-one of those twenty-five areas.

It is hard to think of a parallel to such legislative fecundity, a physical as well as intellectual feat. Neville worshipped hard work and application. David Dilks described his physical energy as 'perhaps equal to Churchill's, superior to Baldwin's and by any standard exceptional'. He impressed by his mastery and by his clear exposition of what he intended to achieve. He dealt summarily with anything slipshod or superficial and this often led him into bitter exchanges with his political opponents. He received an oft-quoted reprimand from Baldwin, which he reported to Ida and left him unrepentant.

> I always gave him the impression when I spoke to him in the H. of C. that I looked on the Labour Party as dirt. The fact is that intellectually, with a few exceptions, they are dirt.[38]

As minister in charge of a spending department in a government which felt obliged to make cuts in public expenditure, clashes with Labour were inevitable. He had a long-running dispute with the Poor Law Guardians of West Ham and other authorities, described as 'Bolshie Paradises', which were resisting the standardisation of welfare payments and in Neville's view, overpaying at the expense of the ratepayers. In housing policy, while doing his utmost to increase production, he was also intent on reducing the level of subsidy. A consistent theme in his letters to his sisters was contempt for his critics on the Labour benches:

> You have no idea how difficult this [sic] Labour men are to deal with. They will never give you a straight answer to a straight question. They always reply at interminable length in sentences which have no grammatical ending and leave me in a hopeless fog.[39]

On another occasion, at a time when a section of the Opposition had taken to hissing him, he expressed his 'utter contempt for their lamentable stupidity' as well as for their 'pothouse manners'. He was particularly incensed when the sensitive issue of Government contracting was raised, particularly galling since Hoskins lost £8,000 that year. It was not only Neville's sarcastic manner that Labour resented, but their sense that he was the epitome of a capitalist employer who, in spite of his apparent paternalism, had no real feeling for the lives of the poor and down-trodden, except as objects of his legislative experiments. Had they been able to read his correspondence with his sisters, their prejudices would have been confirmed. As the time of the miners' strike, which persisted for months after the collapse of the General Strike of May 1926, he wrote to Ida complaining that the miners 'are not living too uncomfortably at the expense of the ratepayer while the nation is gradually overcome by creeping paralysis'.[40]

The culmination of Neville's work as Minister of Health came towards the end of the Baldwin administration in the form of the Local Government Act. An immensely complicated piece of legislation, it contained 115 clauses and 12 schedules, the general thrust of which was to increase the powers and responsibilities of local authorities and to standardise and rationalise the rating system. Perhaps the most eye-catching reform was the abolition of the Poor Law Guardians, who had presided over the distribution of relief to the poor since 1834 and were widely detested by the working classes. *The Times* described the Act as 'one of the most outstanding legislative achievements of the twentieth century', a verdict endorsed by some of Neville's principal biographers. In 1944, Keith Feiling described it as 'massive and unquestioned, the chapter of his public life least contraverted'. In 1961, Iain Macleod defined it as 'one of the most far reaching complicated programmes of legislation any Minister had attempted before or since' and characterised Neville as the link between the pre-1914 Liberal social reforms and the establishment of the Welfare State by Attlee's Government from 1945. With his own background of Ministerial experience, MacLeod recognised 'the hideous strain' such a complex piece of legislation must have imposed on its author. David Dilks (1984), while emphasising that the act was a work of consolidation rather than innovation, was equally impressed by Neville's achievement.

> By universal consent, Chamberlain's speech of two and a half hours on
> 26 November 1928 provided one of the most memorable parliamentary
> occasions of that session and perhaps of the whole inter-war period.

Robert Self (2002) takes a more nuanced view. While acknowledging that the Act of 1929 'represented a fitting culmination of Neville Chamberlain's reforming record,' he doubts whether the act wrought the changes on the ground to the extent Neville intended.

> [...] the extremely hierarchical administrative structures and
> authoritarian attitudes acquired in Poor Law years too often persisted
> into the newly-created PACs and NHS.

Nevertheless, it can be said that the act of 1929 was Neville's *magnum opus*—his finest hour as a social reformer.[41]

The end of Baldwin's second Government—a fortunate defeat

Baldwin dissolved Parliament in May 1929 and his party prepared for a general election. The Tories held high hopes of victory, feeling that they had a good story to tell. Spending on welfare, on pensions and on education had all risen, Churchill's latest budget had included modest reductions in taxation, while Austen Chamberlain's achievements in foreign policy had earned popular acclaim. Baldwin's cautious slogan of 'Safety First' seemed not inappropriate, though it contrasted markedly with the adventurous proposals concocted by Lloyd George and Maynard Keynes in 'We Can Conquer Unemployment'. And it was unemployment that proved to be the Government's Achilles heel. Returning to the gold standard in 1925 at an overvalued rate, Churchill's decision as Chancellor—but a consensual one—had handicapped British industry and contributed to a steady decline in exports, with malign consequences for the labour market and wage levels. The electorate turned again to Labour and returned 287 Labour MPs to the Conservatives' 261. Once again the Liberals, with 59 MPs, held the balance of power. On 5 June 1929, Ramsay MacDonald formed his second administration. The victory was to prove a poisoned chalice as the world economy began plunging into the downward spiral known as the Great Depression.

The shock was greater in Birmingham than anywhere else in the country. The achievements of the Chamberlain brothers were perhaps too abstract for an electorate that Neville described as 'a large mass of uneducated and credulous people'. Although Mosley had won a by-election at Smethwick in 1926, he had not abandoned his assaults on the Chamberlain citadel in Birmingham. The combination of Mosley's oratory, his money and the organisational skills of his team did much to eliminate the inferiority complex from which the BLP suffered. On 31 May 1929, *The Town Crier* proclaimed 'Labour's Smashing Victory' in Birmingham. Although King's Norton reverted to the Conservatives, no less than six seats fell to Labour. The most spectacular result was the defeat of Sir Arthur Steel-Maitland in Erdington by Jim Simmons, the one-legged military veteran. More humiliating was the near-defeat of Austen in West Birmingham, in by a mere 43 votes. Neville could watch proceedings with dismay but in personal comfort, having transferred to leafy Edgbaston, Birmingham's Belgravia. Mosley, 'that viper', could plausibly boast that Birmingham's days as a Unionist stronghold were over:

[...] the father's fortress has been seized from the nerveless grasp of
the sons. Birmingham once followed a man and has now dismissed his
plaster effigies.[42]

The shock of defeat spread despondency through the ranks of the
Conservative Party. As usual, discontent focussed on the defeated leader
for what was seen as Baldwin's inertia and lack of constructive ideas. The
old slogan of 1911, *BMG* ('Balfour Must Go') seemed equally appropriate
to Baldwin in 1929. The anti-Baldwin feelings were fanned by the press
lords Beaverbrook and Rothermere. Once again Beaverbrook set out to
convert the country to tariff reform, launching the Empire Free Trade
Movement and following it up with the formation of the United Empire
Party, making for some interesting by-elections. Both Chamberlain
brothers, of course, favoured tariff reform but Neville's efforts to form a
concordat with the Beaver proved fruitless. Should the attempt to remove
Baldwin succeed, the two most likely candidates for the leadership were
Winston Churchill and Neville Chamberlain. Perhaps for the first time
Neville saw himself as a potential Prime Minister. Of the two, Churchill
was the more charismatic and the better parliamentary performer, but
his history of switching parties had not been forgiven by many Tories
and he clung to free trade at a time when party sentiment was moving
against it. He subsequently weakened his case by identifying with Tory
diehards in opposition to political plans for devolution in India. Neville at
this stage believed that his best tactic was to uphold Baldwin against his
critics, calculating that being a loyalist offered the best hope of stepping
into the leader's shoes when his seemingly inevitable retirement occurred.
In December 1929, he and his family embarked on a three-month trip
to East Africa. When he returned in March 1930, Neville became Party
Chairman and assumed control of the Conservative Research Department,
work he found congenial though it was against the advice of Austen,
who was openly calling for his brother's succession and regarded these
offices as diversionary. Baldwin came very close to retirement at this
point. Neville in his letter to Hilda on 1 March 1931 wrote: 'Very Secret.
S. B. has decided to go at once'. But next morning, he had changed his
mind and somehow found the energy to fight back against his critics,
famously denouncing the press lords and comparing them to harlots
who throughout the ages had exercised power without responsibility. In
crucial by-elections, Baldwin loyalists rebuffed Beaverbrook's candidates,
making his leadership secure. For a time relations between Baldwin and
Neville were bad. The former suspected him of being among the plotters.[43]
To his sisters, Neville expressed 'resentment and indignation'. But soon
it was Ramsay MacDonald's position that began to look insecure as the

country moved inexorably into industrial depression and financial crisis. A world crisis, not of the Labour Party's making, MacDonald and his Government were nevertheless blamed for a bankruptcy of ideas. Not the least of their critics was Sir Oswald Mosley, who resigned from his Cabinet post to form the New Party in 1931, advocating a pot-pourri of policies derived from Joe Chamberlain and John Maynard Keynes. On the road to fascism, he launched the British Union of Fascists (BUF) in 1932. Mosley was a minor symptom of what was happening across the globe. Opinion was polarising away from traditional Conservative, Liberal and moderate Socialist parties and towards the extremes of fascism and communism. The devil's decade was underway. What preserved the British system more or less intact was not only a political culture steeped in the parliamentary tradition and the rule of common law, but also a relatively benign experience of depression—far less severe than it was to prove, for instance, in Germany and the US, where unemployment reached 6 million and 15 million respectively, compared to a peak of 2.3 million in Britain. Nevertheless, a fall of nearly 6 per cent in GDP and 11 per cent in wage levels between 1929 and 1932 and a sharp reduction in gold reserves was sufficiently serious to cause a political crisis, which led to the exclusion of the Labour Party from power for a decade and to the hegemony of the Conservative Party, lightly disguised as a National Government.

The formation of the National Government

August 1931 was the storm centre of a political crisis that transformed the shape of inter-war politics. The banking crisis afflicting Europe and the US had reached Britain's shores. The deficit soared, international credit was exhausted, sterling in deep difficulty and gold reserves leaching away. Faced with demands for deep cuts in public expenditure, the Labour Cabinet split, several of its members refusing to countenance the level of cuts demanded by the Conservatives. With Baldwin enjoying one of his perennial sojourns in Aix-les-Bains, Churchill sunning himself in Biarritz and Lloyd George recuperating from a prostate operation, Neville Chamberlain, firmly ensconced in the Conservative Central Office, was in strategic command of Opposition policy. No friend of coalitions, he did not at first welcome the idea of a National Government. 'I hate the idea and hope it won't come to pass,' he told his sisters, preferring to put pressure on the Labour Government to make necessary cuts and relishing the thought of a split in Labour ranks.[44] However, as the crisis developed he came round to an acceptance of the idea of an all-party coalition as the most reassuring way of tackling the crisis, at least in the short term. On 23 August, a weary Ramsay MacDonald announced his intention to resign on behalf of his Government, but was persuaded by the King to remain in office and to form a National Government, which he managed to do. The new Cabinet of ten members consisted of four Labour representatives, four Conservatives and two Liberals. Baldwin, who had expected to succeed MacDonald as PM was an obvious loser, together with those Conservatives who had an expectation of office, but most accepted the logic of forming a coalition to meet with the emergency.

MacDonald called for a 'Doctor's Mandate' for his Government, in which Neville went back to his old job at the Ministry of Health. Cuts in public expenditure, which provoked a degree of unrest and notably the Invergordon Mutiny, enabled Philip Snowden, the Chancellor to balance the budget. But the run on the pound was not stemmed and on 21 September Britain abandoned the gold standard. The National Government had failed to save the pound but, to the general surprise, no dire consequences followed. The main adjustment, a fall in the rate against the dollar, was overdue and offered British exporters a greater chance of recovery from the slump. Logically, the Coalition should have ended at this point, especially as there were sharp divisions in the Cabinet over whether to continue with free trade or to adopt a policy of protective tariffs.

However, the decision was made that the National Government should remain in being and should submit itself to a general election. The election, held in October 1931, was in essence a punitive exercise aimed at the Labour Party from which MacDonald, Snowden and their handful of followers had been expelled. It resulted in a massive landslide: 558 Government supporters were returned to Westminster, all of them Conservatives, except for 35 Simonite Liberals and 33 Samuelite Liberals. The Opposition consisted of a mere 52 Labour MPs and Lloyd George's family group of four. The result was a severely unbalanced Parliament.

In Birmingham the Conservatives reversed all the losses of 1929 and the Chamberlain brothers were once again able to boast, 'We are twelve'. The Labour vote fell by nearly 70,000 and its share of the poll fell from 40 to 26 per cent. Massive majorities for the Conservative candidates included Austen's 10,000 in West Birmingham. Labour's disarray was caused not only by the defection of MacDonald but by that of Mosley, who was given a violent reception when he held a rally in the Rag Market on 18 October. His two New Party candidates fared abysmally, polling less than 1,000 votes between them. Neville, secure in Edgbaston, could afford to observe matters in comfort, although his majority of 28,000 was eclipsed by Patrick Hannon's 39,000 in Moseley. For the remainder of the decade, the BLP was unable to mount more than a feeble challenge to the BCA, although it deserved much credit for its repudiation of Mosley and subsequently having no truck with either his New Party or with the British Union of Fascists.

Chancellor of the Exchequer

The new Cabinet was confronted with internal division over trade policy, with Snowden and Samuel holding out against the adoption of protection. However, the appointment of Neville Chamberlain as Chancellor on 5 November 1931 clarified what direction policy would move in. The first step was the introduction of a temporary measure, the Abnormal Importations Act, aimed at stopping the inflow of 'dumped' goods by subjecting them to a tariff of up to 100 per cent. Neville then chaired a Cabinet Committee, which prepared a more permanent response to the crisis in the balance of trade. 4 February 1932 was Neville's date with destiny, 'the great day of my life'.[45] Using the battered box his father had used for his last performance in the Commons, he removed his notes and unveiled his Import Duties Bill to the House, with Mary and Hilda listening intently in the Gallery. It was a key moment in British economic history, the point at which Britain abandoned free trade after a century of firm commitment marked by the repulse of every assault mounted by its critics, the most serious of which had been Joe Chamberlain's TRL. Neville struggled to control his emotions as he genuflected to his father's memory, presenting the Bill as the culmination of the cause for which Joe had given his life. As his speech came to an end, Austen came forward to shake his hand. The BDP reported,

> [...] there was an extraordinary demonstration of enthusiasm by members who rose in their places, waved order papers, and cheered and cheered again. Labour members alone remained seated.[46]

The Bill, passed by a massive majority of 454 to 78, proposed a basic, 10-per-cent tariff on most imports, subject to preference for Dominion and colonial products but with the Board of Trade empowered to raise that level as and when it seemed necessary. The future of the British economy would rest primarily on the home market and, it was hoped, the expansion of trade with the Empire.

Negotiation of imperial preference was the next stage of Neville's strategy and to that end a conference was convened to meet in Ottawa on 20 July. But before that conference met Neville had two immediate hurdles to overcome. The first was to formulate and pass his first budget in April 1932. Neville's objective was to balance the budget and to bear down on the imbalance in Britain's trade. This allowed neither for tax cuts nor for the restoration of the level of public sector salaries, cut by his predecessor Snowden in 1931. Roy Jenkins described it as a 'hair-shirt budget', while *The Times* remarked on Chamberlain's 'puritanical severity'.[47] Shortly afterwards, however, he carried through a strategy which became central to economic recovery. The interest rate on the War Loan was reduced from 5 to 3½ per cent, a conversion which saved the Treasury some 30 million a year. Coupled with a reduction in bank rate from 6 to 4 per cent, this inaugurated a period of cheap money, which stimulated investment and in particular triggered a boom in house-building. Neville also sought solutions to the international debt problem which was repressing trade. At a conference in Lausanne, he proposed the mutual cancellation of war debt and declared himself willing to forego the considerable sums owed to Britain if the US was prepared to do the same. The French Government reluctantly agreed to accept a final payment of 3 million gold marks in reparations from Germany, but the deal collapsed in the face of American intransigence, both on the part of the Hoover administration and that of his successor, Roosevelt. By this time the overworked Neville was suffering from one of his periodic attacks of gout, so severe that he had to resort to a bath chair. This attitude of the Americans hardly improved his health or his temper. They were 'a nation of cads', and members of Congress 'pig-headed and righteous nobodies'.[48] The retreat of the US into isolationism and economic nationalism also ruled out co-operation with the British in any attempt to curb Japanese aggression in the Pacific, which began in Northern China but rapidly spread south, threatening British interests and those of other countries including the US. The Cabinet contemplated defaulting on the British debt to the US, a measure which Neville regarded as well justified, but to act unilaterally offended his sense of financial probity. Full payment was made in gold in December 1932 and a payment in silver equal to about half of what was due in 1933, after which Neville suspended further payment. A hostile Congress passed the Johnson Act in 1934, which prohibited future loans to states which had not paid in full. The refusal of Roosevelt's administration to play a full and active part in international diplomacy was obviously a key factor in shaping the course of events and a source of encouragement to those powers challenging the status quo.

The Imperial Economic Conference opened in Ottawa on 20 July 1932 and lasted for a full month. The British sent a large delegation which included Baldwin as well as Chamberlain, still oppressed by the gout induced by overwork. Between the opening of the conference and its closure on 20 August, the British delegation attended no less than one hundred and twelve meetings. The lack of consensus and the visible absence of the imperial spirit which Joe Chamberlain had worked hard to inculcate dismayed the British negotiators. The conference was marked by huckstering, with each Dominion seeking to protect its own interests and reluctant to concede anything substantial to British manufactured exports. Bennett, the Prime Minister of Canada, became a particular thorn in Neville's flesh. He possessed, Neville told Hilda, 'the manners of a Chicago policeman and the temperament of a Hollywood film actor'.[49] In his diary he described Bennett in even more severe terms, as 'a sharper and a crook'. The conference ended with a series of bilateral agreements falling well short of the imperial *Zollverein* of Chamberlainite dreams. The visit to Canada was the last time that Neville set foot in any of the Dominions. Among the severest of Neville's critics was fellow Birmingham MP Leo Amery.

It was all a great disappointment, but in the atmosphere of fear and *sauve qui peut* which prevailed at the time, it is hard to see what more the British delegation could have achieved. Trade patterns in the following years showed a small increase in British exports to the Dominions, but the main beneficiaries were dominion primary producers, who enjoyed preferential access to the British market. If Ottawa showed how fragile imperial sentiment had become, the system of agreements put in place did at least ensure that the Dominions pegged their exchange rates to the pound and kept their considerable sterling balances in London. Ottawa made it clear to Chamberlain that it was primarily to the recovery of the home market that Britain must look and here he would enjoy greater success.

The proceedings at Ottawa had the advantage from Neville's point of view of ridding the Cabinet of the remaining free traders, principally Snowden and Samuel, which strengthened his grip on policy. His first two budgets established him as a rigidly orthodox Chancellor firmly supported by his officials at the Treasury. His determination to balance the budget and to make room for a measure of debt reduction left no room for tax cuts or increases in public expenditure. The austerity of his message, together with his somewhat gloomy appearance and Victorian style of dress, would earn him sobriquets such as 'the coroner' and even 'the undertaker' from Birmingham. His 'hair-shirt' management of the economy naturally attracted criticism, though conspicuously not from the City. The most vociferous of his critics included his old enemy, Lloyd George and a leading economist, J. M. Keynes, who was given strong support in the columns of *The Times*. Basically what his opponents advocated was deficit financing to alleviate chronic unemployment in the depressed heavy industry regions of the north. The critics called in aid Roosevelt's New Deal, launched with such razzmatazz in the US. Chamberlain remained unimpressed. Believing that Roosevelt was more of a showman than an economist, he dismissed the New Deal as the 'poorest stuff imaginable, vague, rhetorical and containing not a single new idea'.[50] Those 'idiotic Yankees,' he told Hilda, 'simply infuriate me'. Nor was he much enthused by Maynard Keynes.

After a face-to-face discussion with him in March 1933, he told his sister 'his ideas were worse than I had supposed'. Spending money on doubtful schemes simply to create employment he believed to be futile: 'the policy of public works is always disappointing,' he told the Commons. He resented the criticisms that his policies were purely negative and unimaginative. Although the 'Special Areas' policy he introduced for four areas of heavy unemployment was underfunded, there were a number of positive initiatives to which he could point in answer to his critics. Among them were funding to improve the telephone system, a £4½-million subsidy to complete the *Queen Mary* and to promote the merger of the Cunard and White Star Lines and the £35 million invested in London Transport, which helped to establish arguably the best underground system in the world. Industrial recovery was principally the task of industrialists and to this end he encouraged producer groups to modernise and to cartelize their industries, with some success as in the case of the iron and steel industry. Economic historians, especially when writing at times when Keynesianism was fashionable, have been critical of Neville's Chancellorship, but it seems not unreasonable to conclude that there was no credible alternative to what one historian has described as his 'non-Keynesianism managed economy'. There was at the time no coherent Keynesian model and Keynes himself was notorious for changes of mind, for instance veering away from his free trade advocacy to a reluctant endorsement of protectionism as the Great Depression struck. Not until 1937 had he formulated his much-vaunted General Theory.

By 1934 the climate of opinion was changing and the economy recovering. Introducing his 1934 budget in the Commons, Neville announced it as 'the end of Bleak House and the beginning of Great Expectations'.[51] He was able to remit the extra 6d off income tax imposed in 1931, restore the cuts in unemployment benefit and halve the reduction in public sector salaries made by Snowden in 1931 and to record a £31-million surplus. In his budget in the following year Neville was able to restore the other half of the cuts, increase tax allowances and put aside an additional £23 million for public spending and still managed to squeeze out a surplus. Unemployment, which had reached nearly three million in 1932, was falling steadily to under two million and the low cost of borrowing money and reductions in the price of food and commodities gave people in work a sense that the Depression was behind them. The Special Areas remained a black spot, their sad condition so often taken to characterise the 1930s.

There was another factor that cast a shadow. In 1932 spending on armaments had reached its lowest level between the wars, a fraction of what it had been in 1918. In that year, a World Disarmament Conference attended by fifty-nine nations had convened at Geneva. In the following year, Adolf Hitler withdrew Germany from the League of Nations and walked out of the Disarmament Conference, openly defying the restrictions imposed on Germany by the Treaty of Versailles. The lead-up to the war of 1939 can be traced to that point. Neville, perceiving that his careful nurturing of the economy might now be undone, was unrestrained in his comments to his sisters on Germany, 'the bully of Europe', and on Hitler personally, 'a mad dictator'.[52] But he recognised that the time had come to look to the nation's defences and in June 1934 he chaired the Defence Requirements Committee (DRC), which produced the Defence White Paper of March 1935.

Although, as Churchill and others acknowledged, Neville Chamberlain took the lead in advocating rearmament, he acted as a restraining hand on the Service chiefs whom he accused of excessive demands. What he feared was that heavy expenditure on armaments would put an undue strain on the economy and reverse the progress made in the previous years. Consistently he saw the economy as the fourth arm of defence. The strength of the British economy would be a vital factor in war, especially if Britain faced not one but three enemies; Germany, Italy and Japan. He therefore scaled back the increased expenditure recommended by the DRC from £76 million to £50 million and consistently advocated that priority should be given to the RAF and the Navy. Like many of his generation he dreaded a repeat of the land battles and the accompanying slaughter of the 1914–1918 war and believed that this must at all costs be avoided. Some historians have painted Neville as a near-pacifist, pointing to his distress at the loss of Norman Chamberlain in France in 1918, his cousin and close friend and the subject of the only book he ever wrote. It would be truer to say that Neville was paci*fic*: he dreaded war for the loss of life it would cause and the material damage it would wreak and, a supreme rationalist, he found it difficult to understand the mentality of those who contemplated or even sought war.

In the eyes of the Labour Opposition, Chamberlain was chiefly responsible for the decision to re-arm and he was consequently denounced as a warmonger with Herbert Morrison and Arthur Greenwood in the vanguard. Their criticisms received backing from various organisations, notably the Peace Pledge Union (PPU) and the League of Nations Union (LNU). The latter boasted 407,000 members, 3,000 branches and over 4,000 corporate affiliates which included trade unions, Women's Institutes and even Boy Scout troops. Their collective slogan was 'Never Again'. As David Reynolds pointed out, 'in the 1930s, the country nurtured the strongest peace movement in the world'.[53] The strength of this movement was bound to influence Government policy, though Neville Chamberlain was far less influenced than Stanley Baldwin, who replaced Ramsay

MacDonald as PM in June 1935. Baldwin largely shared Austen's view about the 'cranks' who dominated the LNU, but as a politician he had to take due regard of widespread public support for the League of Nations. As his new Government prepared to go to the polls in November 1935, Baldwin, speaking to the Peace Society in Wolverhampton, made his famous pledge: 'I give you my word there will be no great armaments'. Neville, chief draftsman of the Government's manifesto, was keen to make rearmament the central issue, but he too was restrained in his pronouncements: 'we must in the next few years do what is necessary to repair gaps in our defences'.[54] He responded to attacks on him as the chief warmonger by the Labour Party with the epigram, 'Our policy is defence without defiance, their policy is defiance without defence'.

The general election resulted in the expected endorsement of the Government, with Neville Chamberlain's management of the economy surely its strongest card. The Labour Party recovered some seats, returning to Westminster 154 strong, but the result left the Conservatives enjoying a comfortable majority of 255 over the Opposition. In Birmingham, where the economy was buoyant, the Unionists had no difficulty in retaining all twelve seats. On a day of drenching rain turn-out was low, at 63 per cent. Geoffrey Lloyd, private secretary to Baldwin, had a notable triumph in Ladywood where he had been beaten in 1929, enjoying a majority of over 11,000. Patrick Hannon's majority of over 26,000 in Moseley was Birmingham's largest, Simmons' 3,262 in Duddeston the lowest. The newest addition to the ranks of Unionist MPs was Ronald Cartland, brother of the novelist Barbara, returned for King's Norton. Few could have envisaged that the general election of 1935 would be the last for a decade.

Waiting on Baldwin

Baldwin clung on to the office of PM, frustrating the hopes of succession which Neville harboured. To the great relief of its officials, he returned to the Treasury. With the retirement of Ramsay MacDonald, the Chamberlains were at last able to move into No. 11 Downing Street, letting their house in Eaton Place to the German Ambassador Ribbentrop. 'Amusing', he commented to his sisters, 'considering my affection for Germans in general and Ribbentrop in particular'.[55] He continued to manage the nation's finances on the now firmly established lines, though resenting every penny that the growing international tension obliged him to spend on arms, for which, in the 1936 Budget, he imposed an extra 3d on income tax and 2d on tea. However, he was not dissatisfied with the general progress of the economy: 'trade is still expanding marvellously,' he told Ida in August 1936.

No sooner was Baldwin's Government safely installed than it was faced with a crisis in foreign policy, the first of many that would confront the British Government in the ensuing five years. In July 1934, Engelbert Dollfuss, the Austrian Chancellor, was murdered in his Chancellery by Nazis in the course of an attempted *coup d'état*. Mussolini was at that time anxious to maintain Austrian independence and moved troops to the Brenner Pass to deter a German invasion. In April 1935 the leaders of Italy, France and Britain, accompanied by their Foreign Ministers, met at Stresa to discuss a common front against Germany and to issue a formal protest. The Stresa Front proved disappointingly short-lived. On 2 October 1935, Mussolini launched an attack on Abyssinia, which appealed for help to the League of which it was a member. The recent Peace Ballot had demonstrated the strength of public support in Britain for the League of Nations and the British Foreign Secretary Sir Samuel Hoare, with the support of the Cabinet, came out in favour of imposing sanctions on Italy. Among those in favour was Neville Chamberlain, a friend and supporter of Hoare. There existed, however, a current of opinion that argued that Italy's behaviour was none of Britain's concern and that alienating Mussolini for the sake of a ramshackle slave-trading African state would disrupt the Stresa Front and could only accrue to the benefit of Hitler. The Chiefs of Staff reinforced such doubts by advising that Britain had too little strength in the Mediterranean to risk war with Italy, while the Government too was very reluctant to consider coercion. Sanctions were adopted but were half-hearted and therefore ineffective: they included neither an embargo on oil sales nor the closure of the Suez Canal, which would have disrupted the movement of Italian troops and the transport of supplies. Nevertheless, the Government had expressed strong support for the League during the recent election and was therefore severely embarrassed when Sir Samuel Hoare and the French Foreign Minister, Pierre Laval met in Paris in December 1935 and hatched a deal which would have left the greater part of Abyssinia in Mussolini's hands. When news of the Hoare–Laval pact was leaked in the French press there was an outcry in Britain. Hoare, who had left Paris for a holiday in Switzerland, where he broke his nose skating, was obliged to fall on his sword, replaced by the 38-year-old Anthony Eden, identified in the public mind as a firm supporter of the League. Eden informed Geneva that the deal was off, thus saving the Government's, though not Sam Hoare's, battered face.

It was a shabby episode that had an unfortunate sequel. Encouraged by the disarray of the British and French governments, on 7 March 1936 Hitler sent his troops into the de-militarised Rhineland, his first territorial repudiation of the treaties both of Versailles and Locarno. In spite of much to-ing and fro-ing in Geneva, Paris and London, there was no real possibility of any action being mounted. France was once again in a turmoil which led to the creation of a Popular Front Government, while in Britain both press and public were inclined to regard this as no more than German occupation of their own backyard. Neville was disconcerted by the distraction from economic issues, writing to his sisters that 'foreign affairs remain disgusting', and later that 'foreign affairs remain anxious and obscure'.[56] Both because of their salience and from his temperamental need to dictate policy to his colleagues, Neville became thoroughly involved in Cabinet discussions. Austen Chamberlain and Winston Churchill had both been advocating the cancellation of sanctions in order to mend fences with Mussolini and in June 1936, in a speech at a Conservative dining club, Neville took up the theme, describing the sanctions as 'the very midsummer of madness'.[57] Reporting to his sisters on this episode, he wrote 'I have taken after my Pa in committing a blazing indiscretion'.

His call for the end of sanctions was seen as a slight on the League of Nations and he reported a flood of critical letters in his postbag from 'fanatics'. He had concerted his action with Sam Hoare, whom he wished to bring back into government at the earliest opportunity. His desire to maintain good relations with Italy inevitably brought him into conflict with Anthony Eden, but relations at this stage remained amicable.

The fear of Germany which had motivated the demand to call off sanctions on Italy was somewhat abated when, on 11 July 1936, Germany signed an agreement with Austria which seemed to guarantee Austrian independence. Neville saw this as a positive step: 'I do not take Hitler's peace professions at their face value,' he told Ida, but at least it should give Britain 'a little longer space in which to arm'.[58] In November he felt confident enough to tell Hilda, 'the dictators are a bit piano at present'. His attention turned back gratefully to his main concern, the state of the economy and how to finance re-armament. In April 1937 he introduced the last of his five budgets. Calling for 'economy of sacrifice', he proposed a new tax on company profits, the National Defence Contribution. It ignited a storm of protest in the City and in business circles. Neville was shaken by 'the violent abuse of NDC' and feared that 'I have risked the Premiership just when it was about to fall into my hands'.[59] The NDC was quietly dropped from the Finance Bill by his successor, Sir John Simon.

Neville was exaggerating the risk he had run. However unenthusiastic some sections of the party may have been, there seemed to be no other credible successor to Baldwin. For five years he had been the dominant figure in the Coalition, as he frequently boasted to his sisters:

It amuses me to find a new policy for each of my colleagues in turn and though I can't imagine that all my ideas are the best that can be found, most of them seem to be adopted faute de mieux.[60]

Baldwin, he often complained, was lazy and selfish, spending much of his time contemplating the beauty of the hills and vales of Worcestershire or convalescing at Aix-les-Bains. Neville did admit, however, that his quiescent but emollient style of leadership was one that floating voters found congenial. However, 'the King's matter' sparked Baldwin into life for the last time. The death of George V in January 1936 began a sequence of events leading first to the coronation of Edward VIII and then to his abdication when his determination to marry Mrs Simpson proved unacceptable to Baldwin and his Cabinet, to a majority of parliamentarians and to Dominion leaders. Baldwin, although meeting opposition from 'a King's Friends' party, deftly arranged the abdication and the succession of the Duke of York, crowned George VI. Churchill's stance, following his stubborn opposition to the India Act, which gave a degree of devolution to India, increased his isolation from the party mainstream. Amid all this controversy, Neville as a fully paid-up member of the Respectable Tendency was emphatically on the side of the Roundheads. He could not help but admire Baldwin's handling of a complex drama which could have damaged the monarchy much more than it did. In a blaze of public affection Baldwin retired to his country house, Astley, near Bewdley in Worcestershire. Neville kissed hands as his successor on 28 May 1937, a day of rejoicing in the Chamberlain family.

The fateful Premiership

With characteristic energy and self-belief, Neville set about forming his ministry, making it clear to each appointee that he expected their departments to formulate clear plans to cover the next two years. The key appointments were those of Sir John Simon (Exchequer), Anthony Eden (FO), Sir Samuel Hoare (Home Secretary), Leslie Hore-Belisha (War Office), Tom Inskip (Co-ordination of Defence), Lord Halifax (Lord President of the Council) and Alfred Duff Cooper (Admiralty). Neville congratulated himself at having secured the strongest Treasury bench for many years. The country would have need of it because the world was becoming an increasingly dangerous place, especially for the great but declining Empires of Britain and France, under challenge from the 'have-not' powers of Germany, Japan and Italy. Meanwhile, a savage civil war had erupted in Spain in which Germany, Italy and the Soviet Union had become involved. Neville, who might have gone down in history as a great social-reforming Prime Minister, was obliged instead to focus his attention principally on foreign policy and the search for a lasting peace. Although re-armament had been underway since 1935 and was being stepped up year by year, Britain remained deficient in many areas. The advice from the Chiefs of Staff was that Britain could not with any hope of success face a conflict with three potential enemies. No help could be expected from the US. The Soviet Union was a deeply distrusted enigma, France was suffering from high levels of internal turmoil and frequent changes of government and Dominion leaders made it clear that they would not necessarily commit to a war originating in the tangled ethnic politics of Europe. The context in which the British Government operated was indeed a bleak one and must be taken fully into consideration in any judgement of Neville's Government.

Characteristically, and in contrast to his predecessor, Neville had a strategy which can be summarised as appeasement and re-armament. His critics then and later would queue up to say that there was too much of the former and too little of the latter. Although pressing on with re-armament, Neville was always anxious that the levels of expenditure should not damage the economy and reverse the progress of previous years. In 1938–39, there were worrying signs that this was indeed what was happening. The economy, Neville insisted, was the fourth line of defence. And defence was what was uppermost in his mind. The word 'deterrent' was not yet coined, but the role of the RAF was essentially that. Baldwin had warned the nation that 'the bomber would always get through' and the obvious way to counter a threat was to respond in kind. If the Luftwaffe could bomb London, the RAF could bomb the Ruhr. Towards the end of 1937, however, the potential of the new generation of monoplane fighters began to be recognised, their defensive capabilities reinforced by the invention of radar. The Government therefore switched priority from bombers to fighters, an essentially defensive strategy which accorded well with Neville's thinking.

If war should eventuate, Neville was determined that there should be no repetition of the fearful slaughter of the Great War. The Army therefore remained the 'Cinderella' service, the weakness of which would become a major indictment of the Chamberlain Government. The initial plan was to prepare a mere two divisions for operations on the continent, this tiny force to be reinforced in stages by the Territorial Army. Such a force was hardly likely to frighten the Wehrmacht or reassure the French, upon whose shoulders the bulk of the military effort would rest. The shortcomings of the Army, however, cannot be laid entirely at Neville's door. He was constantly worried about the War Office and the obscurantism of the army chiefs, instructing Hore-Belisha 'to stir up the old dry bones'.[61] The latter's dismissal in 1940 was largely the consequence of the resentment he generated among the generals, although it had more than a whiff of anti-semitism about it.

The second prong of Neville's strategy was appeasement, a word with which his name would be forever indelibly associated. As a number of historians have pointed out, it was by no means novel and could be said to have been a feature of British foreign policy for over a century. It had certainly been the consistent stance of British governments since Versailles, reinforced by what Baldwin described as Britain's 'pacific democracy'. Public opinion, largely supportive of the League of Nations and disarmament, tended to blame France rather than Germany for much of the tension existing on the continent between the wars. It was also receptive to the common indictment of the Treaty of Versailles, that it has been too harsh on Germany and therefore accounted for the truculent revisionism of successive German governments. Neville's drive for appeasement, therefore, was assured of general support. The difference between Neville and previous governments, however, was his determination to pursue the policy actively. All the signals going out from Whitehall from influential figures in British society to Berlin indicated that Britain would be sympathetic to Germany's and to a lesser extent Italy's grievances, with the one proviso—that revisions in the status quo should be brought about through negotiation and not by force.

Neville basked in his new-found status. Writing to his sister Hilda in August 1937, he congratulated himself on 'the extraordinary relaxation of tension in Europe', a remark strongly suggesting indifference to events in Spain. Revelling in a sense of power that the Premiership conferred, he wrote:

> As Ch. of the Ex I could hardly have moved a pebble: now I have only to raise a finger and the whole face of Europe is changed.[62]

The first direction in which Neville chose to point his potent digit was towards Rome. Anxious to keep Mussolini out of Hitler's clutches and by-passing the Foreign Office, he sought direct contact with Mussolini through Count Grandi, Italian Ambassador to the Court of St James. A useful go-between was his sister-in-law Ivy, Austen's widow, who was an admirer of Mussolini and a frequent visitor to Italy with access to the Duce. This was done behind the back of Eden, whose objection to Halifax's visit to Germany in late 1937 had also been ignored. Eden rejected the idea of direct talks with Mussolini, which he knew would entail recognition of Italy's conquest of Abyssinia. The breaking point came when Neville rejected a suggestion from Roosevelt to hold an international peace conference. Realistically, as it turned out, Neville judged that the US would play no part in international affairs until Hawaii or Honolulu had been attacked and he feared that Roosevelt would upset his own plans for Europe. Eden, believing that it was essential to bring America into co-operation if at all possible, resigned on 20 February 1938. Although a popular figure in the party and the country, his resignation was not widely understood and had little impact. Gratefully, Neville appointed Lord Halifax in his place. Not only was Halifax a trusted member of his inner circle but, since he was a peer, Neville would now answer for foreign policy in the Commons, reinforcing his control.

Within a month of Eden's resignation, Europe was convulsed by a new crisis. An attack by Germany on Austria had long been on the cards and was precipitated by the Austrian Chancellor's decision to hold a plebiscite on *Anschluss*. Hitler responded by launching the Wehrmacht over the border, the troops being greeted in Vienna by ecstatic crowds. Hitler followed in the wake of his legions amid hysterical scenes. The last remnants of the Stresa Front were shattered, Hitler thanking Mussolini effusively for taking no action. There was little that the British Government could do except remonstrate with Ribbentrop, the German Ambassador in London.

The fate of Czechoslovakia became an immediate concern. As Austen Chamberlain had warned, should Austria fall into German hands Czechoslovakia, notwithstanding its Army of thirty-six divisions, its prepared defence line and possession of the largest armaments works in Europe, would be outflanked and virtually indefensible. Czechoslovakia was a product of Versailles, a polyglot state of Czechs, Slovaks, Hungarians, Poles, Ruthenians and the three-and-a-half million ethnic Germans of the Sudetenland, the prime focus of Hitler's predatory intentions. After the *Anschluss*, reports of German troops massing on the frontiers became an almost daily occurrence. The German propaganda machine went into overdrive, inventing tales of atrocities wreaked on the German population by the Czech Government while the leader of the Sudeten Nazis, Conrad Henlein, was instructed to work up provocations. The annual rally of the Nazi Party at Nuremberg in September, at which Hitler was due to speak, seemed the likely prelude to invasion. It was later learned that the Wehrmacht was under instructions to be ready to act by 1 October. Such an invasion, it was anticipated, would trigger a European war since France was committed by treaty to the defence of Czechoslovakia and the USSR had agreed to support on condition that France acted first.

Chamberlain had no interest in the preservation of Czechoslovakia. To Ida he expressed sympathy for the Sudeten Germans. Drawing a parallel with Joe's War in South Africa at the turn of the century, he wrote 'they want the same things for the Sudetendeutsche as we did for the Uitlanders'.[63] His overriding concern was for the preservation of peace and to this end he applied pressure on the French and Czech governments to accept cession of the Sudetenland to Germany by peaceful means. Churchill was leading a campaign for a 'Grand Alliance' of Britain, France and the USSR to resist Germany. Neville admitted that the idea was superficially seductive but dismissed it as impractical. He had no respect for Churchill's judgement. 'I can't help liking Winston,' he told Hilda, 'although I think him nearly always wrong and impossible as a colleague'.[64] Churchill, having been on the losing end of the arguments over India and the abdication, was no threat to Neville, the band of diehards supporting his attacks on appeasement smaller than he had mustered for his earlier opposition to the India Bill.

Neville was desperate to meet Hitler face to face and on 13 September he sent a telegram to Hitler expressing his willingness to fly to Nuremberg for a meeting. This was Plan Z, an 'idea so unconventional and daring that it took Halifax's breath away'.[65] Unveiled to the Cabinet next day, with one or two exceptions it met with a favourable response.

With Plan Z it has often been suggested that Neville invented summitry. It was, wrote biographer Iain MacLeod, 'a startling and audacious innovation'.[66] Hitler's reply was favourable. 'Hitler was entirely at my disposal,' he told his sisters, 'and would not Mrs Chamberlain come too!'[67] Neville prepared to leave next morning, 15 September, accompanied by his close adviser Sir Horace Wilson and the Foreign Office official Sir William Strang.

If at first you don't concede, fly, fly and fly again

The flight from Heston, in an American-built Super Lockheed Electra, was the first of three Chamberlain would make that September. Even those elements of the press most critical of his foreign policy were impressed by his unconventional initiative. The new polling organisation, Mass Observation, recorded a high level of public approval and he was given a warm reception by the people of Nuremberg as he was driven to the railway station, where a train was waiting to take him to Berchtesgaden. Hitler greeted him cordially on the steps of his famous lair, the Berghof, Neville being somewhat startled by the profusion of nude paintings adorning its walls. He later relayed his first impressions of the Führer to the Cabinet and to his sisters:

> His hair is brown not black, his eyes blue, his expression rather
> disagreeable ... altogether he looks entirely undistinguished. You would

never notice him in a crowd and would take him for the house painter
he once was.[68]

A series of stilted conversations followed. Hitler made clear his intention
of uniting all ethnic Germans in one Reich by force if necessary. Though
provision also had to be made for the Polish and Hungarian minorities, he
disclaimed any desire to include Czechs in his state. For his part, Neville
assured him that the British Government accepted the principle of self-
determination and that he could get all he wanted by peaceful means. It
was agreed that Hitler would refrain from an attack on Czechoslovakia,
while Chamberlain would prepare a plan after due consultation with the
relevant parties.

Neville left Germany radiating self-confidence and plainly enjoying the
limelight. The talks, he told the assembled press corps, were both frank
and friendly. His reports of his experience showed distinct signs of self-
delusion, his head turned by the mysterious charisma exerted by his host.
The man who had told his sisters in May 'how utterly untrustworthy and
dishonest the German government is' now reported, 'I got the impression
that here was a man who could be relied on when he had given his
word'.[69] Encouraged by the flattery of Hitler's subordinates, he convinced
himself that he had made a favourable impression on the Führer as
well as becoming 'the most popular man in Germany'. Blinded by his
overwhelming desire to preserve peace, this sceptical realist was in danger
of being overwhelmed by his own vanity.

Once back in London, Chamberlain began a busy round of consultation
and negotiation. His first task was to ensure the support of his own Cabinet,
in which he encountered criticism from a number of junior ministers
headed by Duff Cooper. He was given heavyweight support, however,
by his inner circle of Halifax, Simon and Hoare and could also report
the emotional endorsement of the King. He next prevailed on Daladier
and Bonnet to retract the French promise to the Czechs, employing the
threat that British support could not be guaranteed if France went to war
with Germany over Czechoslovakia. Shamefaced elements in the French
Government were only too grateful to be led by the nose by Chamberlain.
Benês, the Czech leader, at first resisted, but lulled by the promise of an
Anglo-French guarantee of the reconstituted Czech state, his Government
succumbed to heavy pressure.

On 22 September Neville flew back to Germany and on to Bad
Godesberg, near Cologne and on the banks of the Rhine. His hotel was on
one side of the river, Hitler's—the Dreesen, from which he had launched
the Night of the Long Knives—on the other. Characteristically, Neville
came with a detailed plan for the hand-over of the mainly German districts

and for the necessary arrangements and guarantees. Imperiously Hitler swept all this aside. He intended to occupy the Sudetenland by force on 1 October and to support the demands of Poland and Hungary. In the face of Neville's angry protestations, he tried to soften the blow by an insincere show of flattery towards Neville personally and a declaration that the acquisition of the Sudetenland would mark the full extent of his designs on Europe. The report of one journalist that the two parted on 'cordial terms' was surely one of the most egregious examples of mis-reporting of that century.

Neville had now seen the true face of the Führer, but it did not alter his fundamental strategy. His advice to the Cabinet was to bow to the Godesberg ultimatum. For the first time, however, he met serious resistance, the most crucial of which came from Lord Halifax. Neville was appalled and passed a pencilled note to him:

> Your complete change of view since I saw you last night is a horrible blow to me, but of course you must form your opinions for yourself.[70]

When the news of the Godesberg ultimatum became generally known there was a backlash in the press and in public opinion. The Czechs rejected the terms and mobilised their army. The French followed with a partial mobilisation. Although Maisky had promised Russian support for the Czechs, there were no signs of preparation and Moscow remained an enigma. Chamberlain was obliged to change tack. What seemed like his final effort to preserve peace was to send Wilson to Berlin with a message for Hitler, warning him that if the French went to war in defence of the Czechs, Britain would 'in all probability be drawn in'. Wilson was met with a furious tirade, Hitler re-iterating his intention to smash the Czechs and his indifference to the issue of world war.

On 27 September Wilson returned to report to the Cabinet on his apparently fruitless mission. London was now preparing for an aerial bombardment which was hourly expected. Sandbags were heaped up, trenches dug, gas-masks distributed and the evacuation of children begun. Anti-aircraft batteries were being set up on Horse Guards parade. Without consulting Neville, Duff Cooper had ordered the mobilisation of the fleet. At 8 p.m. that evening the PM broadcast to the nation. Leo Amery described it as 'the utterance of a very weary and heartbroken man'.[71] Neville struck a distinctly false note when he referred to 'a quarrel in a far-away country between people of whom we know nothing'. This reflected his indifference to the fate of small nations and confirmed those critics who perceived him as essentially a provincial, out of his depth in the management of foreign policy.

But Chamberlain had not yet entirely abandoned hope. Telegrams were despatched to Hitler and Mussolini proposing the convening of a Five Power Conference, Neville appealing to Mussolini to intercede with his fellow dictator. Whether it was as a result of Mussolini's intervention or pressure from his generals, the mercurial Führer had an apparent change of mind. He postponed his planned invasion and sent telegrams to Chamberlain and Daladier inviting them to meet him in Munich the next day, the Czechs not included.

Chamberlain was in the middle of a pedestrian recital of recent events to a packed House of Commons when a note from the Foreign Office was passed to him. Interrupting his discourse, he immediately informed the House of Hitler's invitation. It was, Neville told his sisters, 'a piece of drama that no work of fiction ever surpassed.'[72] The moment was witnessed from the galleries by a host of notables including Earl Baldwin, the Archbishop of Canterbury, Queen Mary and a number of ambassadors including Joseph Kennedy, accompanied by his son, John F. Kennedy. Chamberlain asked the Speaker for an adjournment in order for him to prepare for his journey the next day and left the Chamber to an acclamation from the majority of the MPs present, including Labour men. Chamberlain was about to undertake perhaps the most controversial act in British diplomatic history, the enactment of the Munich Treaty, which more than anything else in his long political career would determine his historical reputation.

Leaving next morning for his third flight to Germany and this time at the head of a large delegation, Chamberlain addressed the assembled crowd at Heston airport from the steps of his plane:

> When I was a little boy, I used to repeat: 'If at first you don't succeed, try, try again'. That is what I am doing. When I come back I may be able to say, as Hotspur said in *Henry IV*, 'Out of this nettle, danger, we pluck this flower, safety'.

On reaching Munich the British delegation was driven through streets filled with cheering crowds to the Nazi party headquarters, the *Führerbau*, where the conference was to be held. For such an important meeting it was amazingly informal, even chaotic: 'there was no agenda, no chairman, no-one to take notes and not even any paper or pencils for the leaders to take their own,' wrote David Faber in his graphic account *Munich. The 1938 Appeasement Crisis.*[73]

Hitler opened the discussion in what Neville described as a 'so moderate and reasonable manner', though he later showed his true colours, becoming angry when Chamberlain at one point suggested the need to consult Benês.[74] The basis of discussion was a memorandum, ostensibly the work of Mussolini but in fact prepared for him by the German Chancellery. The final document was ready for signature at 1.30 a.m. Hitler was the first to sign but, as Neville reported later to the Cabinet, 'the inkpot into which Herr Hitler dipped his pen was empty'.[75] This served as an appropriate metaphor for the Munich Agreement itself. Although camouflaged by all the appearance of international agreement—plebiscites in disputed areas, supervision by an international commission—it was a thinly disguised surrender to *force majeure*. Britain and France were to guarantee the independence of 'rump' Czechoslovakia and Germany and Italy were to follow suit once Polish and Hungarian claims, duly submitted on 1 October, had been settled. These terms hardly differed substantially from Godesberg, except that the dissection of Czechoslovakia would be done with a thin veneer of legality and European war for the moment avoided. Neville had no difficulty in accepting what he had been prepared to concede all along. His most unpleasant task was to apprise the Czech delegates of what had been done.

As the conference came to an end, Chamberlain asked Hitler to meet him for a private talk the next morning without the presence of the French. This was the origin of the famous, or infamous, 'piece of paper' which Chamberlain would brandish on his return to Heston and which he seemed to value rather more than the Munich treaty itself. The text read:

> We, the German Führer and Chancellor and the British Prime Minister, have had a further meeting today and are agreed in recognising that the question of Anglo–German relations is of the first importance for the two countries and for Europe.
>
> We regard the agreement signed last night and the Anglo–German naval agreement as symbolic of the desire of our peoples never to go to war again. We are resolved that the method of consultation shall be the method adopted to deal with any other questions that may concern our two countries and we are determined to continue our efforts to remove possible sources of difference and thus to contribute to assure the peace of Europe.

The casualness with which Hitler signed two copies should have betrayed his total insincerity, but Chamberlain regarded the declaration as a personal triumph, a manifestation of Hitler's respect for him.

Neville's return was greeted like a Roman victory. He was cheered through the streets by enormous crowds and from the window of 10 Downing Street he declared that, like Disraeli in 1878, he had brought back from Germany 'peace with honour....I believe it is peace for our time'—words that he would later regret, excusing them by reference to his exhaustion and his emotional state. The press reflected the same jubilation as the crowds. *The Times* proclaimed:

> No conqueror returning from the battlefield has come home with nobler laurels than Mr Chamberlain from Munich yesterday.[76]

The *Birmingham Daily Gazette* acclaimed him as a local hero:

> Birmingham is proud that the peace of Europe when all but lost had been saved by a cool-brained and determined Birmingham man.

Even the *Daily Herald*, the most persistent of his critics, was impressed by his achievement.

After a much needed rest at Chequers, which he and Annie had come to cherish, Neville faced a four-day debate on the Munich Treaty in the House of Commons, beginning on 3 October. The solid Conservative majority ensured that the Commons would reflect the sentiment of the nation, but Neville was thin-skinned enough to resent the criticisms not only of the Labour Opposition but also of the small bands of Churchill's and Eden's followers, 'the glamour boys'. 'All the world seemed to be full of my praises except the House of Commons,' he grumbled to his sisters.[77] He was especially resentful of Churchill, whom he believed to be in a conspiracy with Masaryk, the Czech representative in London. In a hint to his sisters that he was having the phones of his critics tapped, he wrote:

> They of course, are totally unaware of my knowledge of their proceedings. I had continual information of their doings and sayings.[78]

There was more than a hint of paranoia in his final years. His evil genius was Joseph Ball of the Conservative Research Department and formerly an MI5 operative. Ball was the man behind a small circulation weekly paper, *Truth*, which supported appeasement to the hilt, was more than mildly anti-semitic and which historians have considered gives a truer insight into the thinking of Chamberlain's inner circle than Dawson's *The Times*, often regarded as a Government broadsheet.

Neville need not have worried. The debate concluded with a massive endorsement, 344 ayes to 144 nays. True, there were thirty Conservative abstentions, but only one Cabinet resignation, that of Duff Cooper. As Neville's PPS, Alec Dunglass, later the Earl of Home and himself a PM, commented wryly, 'there were many Appeasers in the House that day'.[79] Whatever his critics might say, Neville could find consolation in the endless stream of grateful and congratulatory letters and the numerous umbrellas, fishing rods and other presents delivered daily to Downing Street. His hopes of improving relations with Germany, however, suffered a series of setbacks. The attacks on Jews and Jewish properties in both Germany and Austria on 9 and 10 November, *Kristallnacht*, shocked public opinion and called into question the morality of what had been done at Munich. Would Czech minorities now under Nazi rule meet the same fate? 'I am horrified by the German behaviour to the Jews,' he told his sisters, 'there does seem to be some fatality about Anglo–German relations which invariably blocks every effort to improve them'.[80] He also resented the hostility to Britain and to him personally of the German press, but did not weaken in his resolve to maintain good relations with Germany and not to antagonise Hitler. He found consolation when he and Halifax went on an unofficial visit to France on 23 to 25 November. Its purpose was to strengthen Anglo–French relations and 'to give French people an opportunity of pouring out their pent-up feelings of gratitude and affection'.[81] He received 'a wonderful reception' and managed to include a brief visit to the Duke of Windsor in his Paris flat, but was relieved not to encounter the ex-Mrs Simpson.

Early in the New Year, Neville, once again accompanied by Halifax, went on a three-day visit to Rome. He was again greeted by rapturous crowds and reported to Ida on a 'truly wonderful visit'.[82] Seemingly oblivious to Mussolini's commitment to Hitler and the Axis, Neville still hoped to drive a wedge between the dictators and convinced himself of Mussolini's liking and respect. After audiences with both the King and the Pope, he returned home. Meanwhile, Britain was pressing on with its re-armament programme and Neville was encouraged by the growing figures of aircraft production. Believing that Hitler 'had missed the bus' at Munich—a favourite phrase—he relayed his confidence to Hilda: 'I myself begin to feel at last we are getting on top of the dictators'.[83]

Such complacency was shattered in March 1939. From the time that the ink was dry on the Munich agreement, Hitler had begun the process of disintegrating Czechoslovakia. The final act came when German troops marched into Bohemia and Moravia and entered Prague, shattering any illusions that Hitler's aims were limited to the uniting of all Germans. In the following month Mussolini's troops attacked Albania. Angrily, Neville wrote to Hilda,

> [...] it cannot be denied that Mussolini has behaved to me like a sneak and a cad. He has made not the least effort to preserve my friendly feelings....[84]

When Hitler seized the Baltic port of Memel from Lithuania, it seemed clear that his next target would be Danzig and the Polish Corridor. The brutal two-step of the dictators destroyed any illusions the British public had about the nature of their regimes. Munich, which had occasioned so much euphoria, had failed and many felt regretful and even guilty about the fate of the Czechs, now subsumed in the Greater German Reich. Neville was himself angry and too shrewd a politician not to realise that circumstances had changed, as had the mood of the Cabinet and of the party. On 17 March in a speech in Birmingham, he struck a more defiant note, asking the question,

> Is this the last attack upon a small state or is it to the followed by another? Is this a step in the direction of an attempt to dominate the world by force?[85]

If this was the case, this nation would 'take part to the utmost of its power in resisting such a challenge if ever it were made'. It was no longer possible to deal with Hitler on a basis of trust but this did not mean that Neville had given up his hopes of preserving peace. He still found it impossible to conceive that any leader could possibly contemplate unleashing another Great War and pinned his hopes on pressure for peace coming from the German people. In 1938–39 the British economy suffered a sharp downturn, largely as a result of the high and increasing cost of re-armament. In Germany all available information suggested conditions were far worse. At the end of April Neville wrote to Hilda:

> I believe every month that passes without war makes war unlikely....I can't see Hitler starting a world war for Danzig.[86]

But Hitler now had the port of Danzig and the Polish Corridor in his sights and launched a propaganda war against the Poles, as he had previously done against the Czechs.

On 31 March 1939, Chamberlain startled the House of Commons by announcing a guarantee of assistance to the Poles 'in the event of any action which threatened Polish independence'. This was seen as a step-change in British policy, in Neville's words 'the actual crossing of the stream'. But there was a sub-text to the guarantee. As Dawson in *The Times* and Ball's journal *Truth* pointed out, this was a guarantee of Poland's independence and not of its current borders. This left open the possibility of a Polish–German agreement over Danzig and the Corridor. This was duly noted in Berlin and it is not surprising that Hitler drew the conclusion the British would not fight for Poland and that Neville could be relied on to broker another Munich. The British Government, however, was now intent on building a barrier against Germany in Eastern and South-Eastern Europe. The Polish Guarantee was followed by similar offers to

Romania and Greece and a Declaration of Mutual Solidarity signed with Turkey. Churchill and his followers, the Opposition and even members of the Cabinet now pressed for an alliance with the USSR. Chamberlain was deeply distrustful of the Soviets and took comfort from the fact that the refusal of the Poles and Romanians to entertain any arrangement that entailed the entry of Russian forces on to their territory made an alliance virtually impossible. The Chiefs of Staff encouraged Chamberlain to believe that the Poles were militarily the better option. Negotiations were carried on in a desultory fashion but the Russians chose to respond to offers from Germany to divide up Eastern Europe. The cynical deal, the Nazi-Soviet Non-Aggression Pact, was announced on 2 August 1939.

The pact gave Hitler the green light for his attack on Poland and the refusal of the Polish Foreign Minister, Joseph Beck, to countenance any concessions made war certain. Neville's final effort to save the peace was an appeal to Mussolini to intercede with Hitler as he had done a year before. The German war machine rolled east on 1 September 1939. A flurry of contacts between the British and German governments have led some historians to conclude that Chamberlain still harboured hopes of appeasing Germany up to and even after the point that invasion began. Martin Pugh, for instance, wrote that Chamberlain's inner circle 'remained committed to engineering another Munich-type settlement'.[87] This is a harsh judgement. Both Chamberlain and Halifax bowed to the inevitable. But suspicions were aroused by the delay in declaring war on Germany. When Chamberlain confronted the House of Commons on 2 September MPs were in a sullen, hostile mood. It was on this occasion that Leo Amery wrote himself into the history books, calling out 'Speak for England' as Arthur Greenwood, spokesman for the Opposition, was making his speech. To his sisters, Neville described the Commons as 'torn with suspicions ready ... to believe the Govt guilty of any cowardice and treachery,' with Amery 'the most insulting of all'.[88] He explained the delay by reference to three factors: contact was being made with Göring through the Swedish businessman Dahlerus, it was not yet certain that Hitler would ignore the intercession of Mussolini, whom Neville rightly believed did not want war to begin and the French were demanding more time to mobilise and feared the risk of German air attacks while the process was underway. After 'a short and troubled night' Neville spoke to the nation at 11.15 a.m. the next day. In his speech and the subsequent speech in the House of Commons he was criticised for striking a too personal note:

> You can imagine what a bitter blow it is to me that all my long struggle to win peace has failed. Yet I believe that there is nothing more or anything different that I could have done....[89]

Even his opponents found it difficult not to pity him. Harold Nicolson, a Churchill supporter, noted the 'real moral agony of the PM'.

War Lord

During the struggle to avert war, Neville believed himself to have been the indispensable leader. The position had now changed and he recognised that 'half a dozen people could take my place while war is in progress'.[90] Yet his self-confidence and a strong 'consciousness of moral right' soon re-asserted itself. There was no strong demand from his party for him to step down: the great days of Churchill were yet to come and only his relatively small band of followers saw him as the inevitable war leader. Neville still distrusted Winston's judgement but recognised that he must at last return to government. He became First Lord of the Admiralty in a War Cabinet of nine. Neville ignored growing demands for the dismissal of 'the old gang', principally Simon and Hoare and they remained in post. Eden also returned to government but in a minor post outside the Cabinet.

Neville did not find the role of war leader a congenial one, his whole being revolted against the senseless loss of life and squandering of resources. 'How I do hate and loathe this war,' he admitted to Hilda, 'I was never meant to be a War Minister'.[91] He was shocked and saddened by the heavy loss of life at sea, the sinking of the battleships *Courageous* and *Royal Oak* and even expressed sympathy for the deaths of German submariners. On visits to France—and in contrast to Churchill—he was oppressed by the trenches, the barbed wire, the pill-boxes and all the scenes of preparation for battle.

Always haunted by thoughts of the slaughter of the Great War, it is unsurprising that Neville's strategy was a defensive one.

> You don't need offensive forces to win a smashing victory. What you want are defensive forces sufficiently strong to make it impossible for the other side to win at such a cost as to make it not worthwhile.

He anticipated a three-year war but harboured hopes of a collapse of the German home front:

> My policy continues to be the same. Hold on tight. Keep up the economic pressure, push on with munitions production and military preparations with the utmost energy, take no offensive unless Hitler begins it. I reckon that if we are allowed to carry on this policy we shall have won the war by the spring.[92]

This defensive mentality, shared by the French, produced 'the Phoney War', 'the *Sitzkrieg*'.

This, of course, was cold comfort to the martyred Poles who were left to their tragic fate. On the very eve of the German attack on Denmark and Norway in April 1940, Neville was repeating his belief that Hitler has missed the bus, inferring that he would have had a better chance of victory in 1938 before Britain's re-armament was anywhere near complete.

While the stalemate in France was largely seen as mainly a French concern, interest in the spring of 1940 was turning to Scandinavia. Sweden's Gallivare mines were the main source of German iron ore, which was transported to Germany through Norwegian waters. The Government had shown more sympathy for Finland (attacked by the Soviet Union in 'the Winter War' of 1939–40) than for Poland and an expeditionary force had been prepared to go to the aid of that small but gallant state. The Allies were saved from what could have been a crass error by the refusal of the Swedes to grant passage through their territory. Churchill, impatient for action, urged the mining of Norwegian waters to cut off the supply of iron ore and Hitler promptly responded by launching an attack, occupying Denmark and entering Norway's capital, Oslo, within hours. 'The Phoney War' was about to end and the final agony of the Chamberlain Government about to begin.

Allied troops were landed at several points on the Norwegian coast and there were fierce battles at sea, but the Germans had seized the airfields and the British troops were exposed to aerial attack. They had all been evacuated by the middle of May. Inevitably, disillusionment was considerable and recriminations in Parliament long and loud. Chamberlain was highly critical of the Swedish and Norwegian governments and their troops and, privately rather than publicly, of Churchill, who had proved to be indecisive and had 'changed his mind four times' in the course of the brief campaign. But it was at Neville that criticism was chiefly directed and he confessed to his sisters:

We are not yet strong enough ... we are short of many weapons of offence and defence. Above all we are short of air power.[93]

A debate on the Norwegian campaign took place on 7 to 8 May 1940. Attlee's attack was ineffective but the House was electrified by the appearance of Admiral Keyes, bemedalled and in full uniform and fresh from the conflict. Keyes' attack on the conduct of the campaign was devastating. The heaviest blow was struck by Leo Amery, who famously quoted from Cromwell's speech to the Long Parliament:

You have sat here too long for any good you have been doing. Depart, I say, and let us have done with you. In the name of God, go.[94]

In his own speech Neville struck a false note by calling for support from his friends in the House. This was seized upon by Lloyd George, who attacked Neville with a venom accumulated over twenty years. It was one of his most effective and last major contributions to debate in Parliament before moving to the House of Lords. Neville's supporters were still in a majority and he won the adjournment debate with a majority of 81 votes. But the majority fell well short of the number of Conservative MPs, 41 of whom had voted against the Government while 88 had abstained, through perhaps half of these were absent on war duties. Neville made a second attempt to form a National Government, but Attlee telephoned the Labour Party's refusal from their conference in Bournemouth, with typical laconic bluntness telling Neville 'they won't have you'.[95] At 6 p.m. Neville went to the Palace to tender his resignation. He would have preferred his successor to have been Halifax but the pressure to appoint Churchill proved irresistible. Churchill formed a War Cabinet of five in which Neville was invited to serve as Lord President. Chamberlain still had substantial support in the party of which he remained leader and was therefore essential to Churchill, whom he served loyally. Winston, he told his sisters, had behaved towards him with 'the most unimpeachable loyalty'.

Neville was devastated by his own fall and shortly by the debacle in the Low Countries and France following the German invasion of 10 May. 'All my world has tumbled to bits in a moment,' he confided to his sisters, and 'I frankly envy Austen's peace'. He did his best to carry out his duties, even Attlee confessing that he proved a valuable member of the Cabinet, but he had known for some time that he was a seriously ill man, afflicted by more than just the perennial gout and skin problems from which he habitually suffered. On 20 July he told his sisters that he was suffering from 'considerable trouble with my inside' and was shortly to go into a nursing home for an operation.

In his final days he was oppressed by the venomous attacks being made on him and the calls for him to be ejected from the Government. The most vitriolic was published by Victor Gollancz's Left Wing Book Club on 5 July. This was called *Guilty Men* and proved to be one of the most effective polemics ever written. Its authors, disguised by the pseudonym 'Cato', were three left-wing journalists of whom the best known was Michael Foot. Chamberlain, of course, was guilty man No. 1. He did his best to shrug off the criticisms, which made no attempt at objectivity.

> If I am personally responsible for deficiencies of tanks and AA guns, I must be equally responsible for the efficiency of the Air Force and the Navy.[96]

When history came to be written he felt confident that he would be vindicated. His family would wait a long time after his death for even a plausible defence. *Guilty Men* remained in print for many years, being re-issued as a Penguin classic in 1968. The indictment was powerfully reinforced by Churchill's history of the Second World War, which was long on criticism of Neville but cast a veil over his own shortcomings.

Following the operation Neville made an effort to take up his duties once again. On 17 September he attended the House of Commons for the last time and was gratified to receive an ovation from Conservative MPs. The next day he attended his last Cabinet meeting but, finding the strain of conditions in a London being nightly blitzed too much, he returned to Highfield Park, the Sussex home of his aunt Lilian where he had been convalescing. He was mortally stricken with bowel cancer and recognised that he only had a short time left. Five days later he sent his resignation to Churchill, who, on 9 October, was elected in his place as leader of the Conservative Party.

As Neville lay dying, he reflected on events and remained convinced that his policies had been correct. Responding to a letter from Baldwin on 17 October he wrote:

> Never for one single instant have I doubted the rightness of what I did at Munich, nor can I believe that it was possible for me to do more than I did to prepare the country for war after Munich, given the violent and persistent opposition I had to fight against all the time.[97]

He repeated the same conviction to old colleagues who visited, such as Lord Halifax and Sir John Simon. Also among his visitors were the King and Queen, who drove over from Windsor. He felt the attacks on himself keenly, writing sadly to Baldwin that 'Few men can have known such a tremendous reverse in so short a time'.[98] Churchill was not among his visitors, but his letters reflected his gratitude for Neville's loyalty to him and his firm support in rejecting the desire of Halifax and others to negotiate with Hitler through Mussolini. On 2 October Churchill wrote, 'I look back upon this stern year of comradeship with feelings of deepest respect and regard for you'.[99]

On 9 November 1940 Neville Chamberlain died. He was cremated and on 14 November his remains were carried into Westminster Abbey by pallbearers consisting of Churchill and other Cabinet members and interred next to those of Bonar Law, the PM who had given him his first ministerial post in 1922. There was little publicity and the funeral was thinly attended because of the fear that a couple of well-aimed Luftwaffe bombs could wipe out the whole Government. Two days earlier it had fallen to Churchill to give a memorial address in Parliament and, as he so often did, rose splendidly to the occasion. His speech contained the passage:

> Whatever history may or may not say about these terrible, tremendous years, we can be sure that Neville Chamberlain acted with perfect sincerity.... This alone will stand him in good stead as far as what is called the verdict of history is concerned.[100]

Churchill, of course, powerfully influenced the verdict of history when he came to write his history of the war. In spite of periods of accord between them and his protestations of gratitude to Neville in that final year, in which they had worked closely, Churchill added to the negativity which has since blighted Neville Chamberlain's reputation and which, in spite of efforts at revisionism, has persisted. This role, as Keith Feiling wrote, was as a scapegoat for failure.[101]

Neville's family had chosen Westminster Abbey as his final resting place in preference to placing him next to his father and among his relatives in Birmingham's Key Hill cemetery. His death and the bombs that rained down on the city during the nights immediately following, all served to erode the Chamberlain tradition. In the general election of 1945, the BLP came into its own and won ten of Birmingham's thirteen seats. 'Birmingham exceptionalism' had died with Neville and the Chamberlains persisted only as a myth, which cast Joe in the role of the founder of modern Birmingham but found little room for either of his two sons.

Endnotes

Chapter 1. Joseph Chamberlain

1   Anderton, T., *A Tale of One City. The New Birmingham* (Birmingham: Midland Counties Herald Office, 1900), p. 33.
2   Chamberlain, J., 'Manufacture of Iron Wood Screws' in *Birmingham and the Midland Hardware District* ed. by S. Timmins (1866), pp. 604-609.
3   Marsh, P. T., *Joseph Chamberlain. Entrepreneur in Politics* (Yale: Yale University Press, 1994), pp. 16-17.
4   Garvin, J. L., *The Life of Joseph Chamberlain Vol. 1, 1836–1835* (London: Macmillan, 1932), p. 58.
5   Cash, B., *John Bright. Statesman, Orator, Agitator* (London: I. B. Tauris, 2012), pp. 141-143.
6   Dixon, J., *Out of Birmingham. George Dixon 1820–98. Father of Free Education* (London: Brewin, 2013), p. 74.
7   Jay, R., *Joseph Chamberlain. A Political Study* (Oxford: Oxford University Press, 1981), p. 18.
8   Marsh, p. 100.
9   Lloyd, S. S., *Autobiographical Memoir* (unpublished memoir, with acknowledgements to H. L. Lloyd), p. 7
10 Garvin, p. 202.
11 Ward, R., *City, State and Nation. Birmingham's Political History 1830–1940* (Chichester: Phillimore, 2005), p. 80.
12 Trevelyan, G. M., *The Life of John Bright* (London: Constable, 1913), p. 427.
13 Garvin, pp. 392-407, and Marsh, pp. 165-166.
14 Brown, B. H., *The Tariff Reform Movement in Great Britain 1881–1895* (New York: AMS Press, 1966), p. 9.
15 Fraser, P., *Joseph Chamberlain. Radicalism and Empire 1868–1914*

(London: Cassell, 1966), p. 46.

16 Marsh, pp. 239-241.

17 Joe Chamberlain to Arthur. Hurst, M. C., *Joseph Chamberlain and West Midland Politics 1886–1895* (Birmingham: Dugdale Society, 1962), p. 14.

18 Garvin, pp. 250-251.

19 Garvin, p. 208.

20 Hurst, M. C., *Joseph Chamberlain and Liberal Re-Union. The Round Table Conference of 1887* (London: David & Charles, 1967).

21 Marsh, p. 323.

22 Hurst, *Joseph Chamberlain and West Midland Politics 1886–1895*, p. 64.

23 Jenkins, R., *Gladstone* (London: Macmillan, 1995), p. 601.

24 Joe Chamberlain to Mary on the subject of the Jameson Raid; Marsh, p. 383.

25 Roberts, A., *Salisbury. Victorian Titan* (London: Weidenfeld & Nicolson, 1999), p. 798.

26 Jay, p. 249.

27 Joe Chamberlain to Duke of Devonshire; Marsh, p. 538.

28 Jay, p. 277.

29 Harris, R., *The Conservatives. A History* (London: Bantam Press, 2011), p. 237.

Chapter 2. Joseph Austen Chamberlain

1 Rowland, P., *Lloyd George* (London: Barry & Jenkins, 1975), p. 581.

2 Dangerfield, G., *The Damnable Question* (London: Quartet, 1979), p. 73.

3 Dutton, P., *Austen Chamberlain. Gentleman in Politics* (London: Ross Anderson Publications, 1985), pp. 1-11; and Self, R., *The Austen Chamberlain Diary Letters. The Correspondence of Sir Austen Chamberlain with his Sisters Hilda and Ida 1916–1937* (Cambridge: Cambridge University Press, 1995), pp. 1-21.

4 Amery, L. S., *My Political Life Vol. 1* (London: Hutchinson, 1953), pp. 303-304.

5 Self, p. 9.

6 Macmillan, H., *Winds of Change 1914–1939* (London: Macmillan, 1966), p. 174.

7 Jenkins, R., *The Chancellors* (London: Macmillan, 1998), p. 113.

8 Chamberlain, A., *Down the Years* (London: Constable, 1935), p. 43.

9 Webb, B., *The Diary of Beatrice Webb Vol. 1. 1873–1892* (London:

Virago, 1986), p. 106.

10 Davenport-Hines, R., *Ettie. The Life and World of Lady Desborough* (London: Weidenfeld & Nicholson, 2008), p. 112.

11 Marsh, p. 347.

12 Elletson, D. H., *The Chamberlains* (London: Murray, 1966), p. 114.

13 Dilks, D., *Neville Chamberlain Vol. 1. Pioneering and Reform 1869–1929* (Cambridge: Cambridge University Press, 1984), pp. 83-85.

14 Chamberlain, *Down the Years*, p. 217.

15 *Ibid.*, p. 20.

16 Jenkins, p. 120.

17   Chamberlain, A., *Politics from Inside. An Epistolary Chronicle 1906–1914* (London: Constable, 1936), pp. 22-27.

18 Adams, R. J. Q., *Balfour. The Last Grandee* (London: John Murray, 2007), pp. 191-226.

19 Petrie, C., *The Life and Letters of the Right Honourable Sir Austen Chamberlain Vol. 1* (London: 1939), p. 211.

20 *Ibid.*, pp. 227-228.

21 Dutton, p. 70.

22 Chamberlain, A., *Politics from Inside. An Epistolary Chronicle 1906–1914*, pp. 377-380.

23 Amery, pp. 303-304.

24 Chamberlain, *Politics from Inside. An Epistolary Chronicle 1906–1914*, p. 308.

25 *Ibid.*, p. 580.

26 Dutton, p. 115.

27 *Ibid.*, p. 134.

28 All the following quotations from Austen's letters to his sisters, Hilda and Ida, are drawn from Self.

29 *Daily Mail*, 17 April 1918.

30 Stevenson, F., *Lloyd George. A Diary by Francis Stevenson* (London: Hutchinson, 1971), p. 170.

31 *Ibid.*, p. 326.

32 Morgan, K. O., *Consensus and Disunity. The Lloyd George Coalition 1918–1922* (Oxford: Oxford University Press, 1979), p. 127.

33 Dutton, pp. 100-101.

34 *Ibid.*, p. 115.

35 Steiner, Z., *The Lights that Failed. European International History 1919–1993* (Oxford: Oxford University Press, 2005), p. 387.

36 *Ibid.*, p. 403.

37 Self, pp. 425 and 490.

38 *Ibid.*, p. 502.

39 Dutton, p. 321.

40 Self, pp. 519-520.

Chapter 3. Arthur Neville Chamberlain

1 *Fuchser, L. W., Neville Chamberlain and Appeasement. A Study in the Politics of History* (New York: W. W. Norton, 1982), p. ix.
2 Canadine, D., *Pleasures of the Past* (London: Fontana, 1990), pp. 306-312.
3 Marsh, pp. 140-141. See also Marsh's study of Chamberlain family relationships in *The Chamberlain Litany. Letters within a Governing Family from Empire to Appeasement* (London: Haus, 2010), pp. 3-30.
4 Feiling, K., *The Life of Neville Chamberlain* (London: Macmillan, 1946), p. 8.
5 Marsh, *The Chamberlain Litany. Letters within a Governing Family from Empire to Appeasement*, p. 36.
6 Dilks, *Neville Chamberlain Vol. 1. Pioneering and Reform, 1869–1929*, p. 47.
7 *Ibid.*, p. 70.
8 *Ibid.*, p. 71.
9 Marsh, *The Chamberlain Litany. Letters within a Governing Family from Empire to Appeasement*, p. 57.
10 Feiling, p. 30.
11 Dilks, p. 79.
12 *Ibid.*, p. 83.
13 Ward, R., *City State and Nation. Birmingham's Political History 1830–1940* (Chichester: Phillimore, 2005), p.168.
14 Dilks, pp. 117-122.
15 *Ibid.*, p. 127.
16 Self, *The Neville Chamberlain Diary Letters Vol. 1. The Making of a Politician 1915–1920* (Aldershot: Ashgate, 2000), p. 132.
17 Ward, R., 'Eldred Hallas' (Oxford DNB).
18 Briggs, A., *History of Birmingham Vol. 2. Borough and City 1865–1938* (Oxford: Oxford University Press, 1952), pp. 210-213; and N. Smart, *Neville Chamberlain* (Routledge, 2010), pp. 64-65.
19 Marsh, *The Chamberlain Litany. Letters within a Governing Family from Empire to Appeasement*, p. 133.
20 *Ibid.*, p. 138.
21 Macleod, I., *Neville Chamberlain* (London: Muller, 1961), pp. 73-74.
22 Self, *The Neville Chamberlain Diary Letters Vol. 1. The Making of a Politician 1915–1920*, p. 282.

23 Self, R., *The Austen Chamberlain Diary Letters. The Correspondence of Sir Austen Chamberlain with his Sisters Hilda and Ida 1916–1937*, p. 239.

24 Self, *Neville Chamberlain. A Biography* (Aldershot: Ashgate, 2006), pp. 304 and 351.

25 Self, R., *The Neville Chamberlain Diary Letters Vol. 2. The Reform Years 1921–1927* (Aldershot: Ashgate, 2000), p. 39.

26 Dilks, p. 277.

27 Self, *The Neville Chamberlain Diary Letters Vol. 2. The Reform Years 1921–1927*, p.128

28 Self, *The Austen Chamberlain Diary Letters. The Correspondence of Sir Austen Chamberlain with his Sisters Hilda and Ida 1916–1937*, p. 200.

29 Self, *The Neville Chamberlain Diary Letters Vol. 2. The Reform Years 1921–1927*, p. 151.

30 *Ibid.*, p. 154.

31 *Ibid.*, p. 164.

32 *Ibid.*, p. 207.

33 Self, *The Neville Chamberlain Diary Letters Vol. 2. The Reform Years 1921–1927*, p. 253.

34 Skidelsky, R., *Oswald Mosley* (London: Macmillan, 1981), pp. 171-172.

35 Self, *The Neville Chamberlain Diary Letters Vol. 2. The Reform Years 1921–1927*, p. 257.

36 *Ibid.*, p. 256.

37 *Ibid.*, p. 319.

38 Self, *The Neville Chamberlain Diary Letters Vol. 2. The Reform Years 1921–1927*, p. 412; and Dilks, p. 579.

39 Self, *The Neville Chamberlain Diary Letters Vol. 2. The Reform Years 1921–1927*, p. 344.

40 *Ibid.*, p. 353.

41 R. Self, *The Neville Chamberlain Diaries Vol. 3. The Heir Apparent* (Aldershot: Ashgate, 2002), pp. 8-9; and Dutton, D., *Neville Chamberlain* (London: Routledge, 2001), pp. 33-34.

42 Ward, *City, State and Nation. Birmingham's Political History 1830–1940*, p. 208.

43 Self, *The Neville Chamberlain Diaries Vol. 3. The Heir Apparent*, p. 246.

44 *Ibid.*, p. 269.

45 Marsh, *The Chamberlain Litany. Letters within a Governing Family from Empire to Appeasement*, pp. 247-248.

46 5 Feb 1932.

47 Jenkins, *The Chancellors*, pp. 348-349.

48 Self, *The Neville Chamberlain Diaries Vol. 3. The Heir Apparent*, p. 55; and Macleod, pp. 174-175.
49 Macleod, p. 161; and Marsh, *The Chamberlain Litany. Letters within a Governing Family from Empire to Appeasement*, p. 253.
50 Jenkins, *The Chancellors*, p. 353.
51 Macleod, p. 168.
52 Self, R., *The Neville Chamberlain Diary Letters Vol. 4. The Downing Street Years 1934–1940* (Aldershot: Ashgate, 2005), p. 123.
53 Reynolds, D., *The Long Shadow. The Great War and the Twentieth Century* (London: Simon & Schuster, 2010), pp. 220-223.
54 Macleod, p. 175.
55 Self, *The Neville Chamberlain Diary Letters Vol. 4. The Downing Street Years 1934–1940*, p. 208.
56 *Ibid.*, p. 189.
57 Macleod, p. 194; and Self, *The Neville Chamberlain Diary Letters Vol. 4. The Downing Street Years 1934–1940*, pp.194-195.
58 *Self, The Neville Chamberlain Diary Letters Vol. 4. The Downing Street Years 1934–1940*, p. 201.
59 Macleod, p.192; and Self, *The Neville Chamberlain Diary Letters Vol. 4. The Downing Street Years 1934–1940*, p. 252.
60 Self, *The Neville Chamberlain Diaries Vol. 3. The Heir Apparent*, p. 353; and Self, *The Neville Chamberlain Diary Letters Vol. 4. The Downing Street Years 1934–1940*, p. 257.
61 Self, *The Neville Chamberlain Diary Letters Vol. 4. The Downing Street Years 1934–1940*, p. 263.
62 *Ibid.*, pp. 269-270.
63 *Ibid.*, p. 286.
64 *Ibid.*, p.311
65 Roberts, A., *The Holy Fox: A Biography of Lord Halifax* (London: Weidenfeld & Nicolson, 1991) p. 110.
66 Macleod, p. 234.
67 Self, *The Neville Chamberlain Diary Letters Vol. 4. The Downing Street Years 1934–1940*, p. 346.
68 *Ibid.*
69 Harvey, J., ed., *The Diplomatic Diaries of Oliver Harvey 1937–1940* (London: Collins, 1979), pp. 197-207; and Macleod, p. 239.
70 Roberts, *The Holy Fox: A Biography of Lord Halifax*, pp. 116-118.
71 Faber, D., *Munich. The 1938 Appeasement Crisis* (London: Simon & Schuster, 2008), p. 377.
72 Self, *The Neville Chamberlain Diary Letters Vol. 4. The Downing Street Years 1934–1940*, p. 349.
73 Faber, p. 405.

74 Self, *The Neville Chamberlain Diary Letters Vol. 4. The Downing Street Years 1934–1940*, p. 348.

75 Faber, p. 411.

76 *The Times*, 1 October 1938; and the *Birmingham Daily Gazette*, 1 October 1938.

77 Self, *The Neville Chamberlain Diary Letters Vol. 4. The Downing Street Years 1934–1940*, pp. 366-370.

78 Stewart, G., *Burying Caesar. Churchill, Chamberlain and the Battle for the Tory Party* (London: Phoenix, 1999), p. 368; and Self, *The Neville Chamberlain Diary Letters Vol. 4. The Downing Street Years 1934–1940*, p. 435.

79 Home, Lord, *The Way the Wind Blows* (London: Collins, 1976), p. 65.

80 Self, *The Neville Chamberlain Diary Letters Vol. 4. The Downing Street Years 1934–1940*, p. 363.

81 *Ibid.*, pp. 364-365.

82 *Ibid.*, pp. 372-375.

83 *Ibid.*, p. 377.

84 *Ibid.*, p. 405.

85 *Ibid.*, p. 393.

86 *Ibid.*, p. 413.

87 Pugh, M., *The Making of Modern British Politics 1867–1945* (London: Blackwell, 2002), p. 242.

88 Self, *The Neville Chamberlain Diary Letters Vol. 4. The Downing Street Years 1934–1940*, p. 443.

89 Feiling, p. 416.

90 Self, *The Neville Chamberlain Diary Letters Vol. 4. The Downing Street Years 1934–1940*, p. 445.

91 *Ibid.*, p. 458.

92 *Ibid.*, p. 467.

93 *Ibid.*, p. 526.

94 Churchill, W., *The Second World War Vol. 1. The Gathering Storm* (London: Cassell, 1948), p. 525.

95 Williams, F., *A Prime Minister Remembers: Post-War Memories of the Right Hon. Earl Attlee* (London: Heinemann, 1961), p. 33.

96 Self, *The Neville Chamberlain Diary Letters Vol. 4. The Downing Street Years 1934–1940*, p. 547.

97 *Ibid.*, p. 533 and 553; and Feiling, p. 456.

98 Self, *The Neville Chamberlain Diary Letters Vol. 4. The Downing Street Years 1934–1940*, p. 534.

99 *Ibid., p. 543.*

100 Feiling, p. 457; and Dutton, p. 120.

101 Feiling, p. 443.

Bibliography

Books

Adams, R. J. Q., *Balfour. The Last Grandee* (London: John Murray, 2007)

Amery, L. S., *My Political Life Vol. 1* (London: Hutchinson, 1953)

Anderton, T, *A Tale of One City. The New Birmingham* (Birmingham: Midland Counties Herald Office, 1900)

Briggs, A., *History of Birmingham Vol. 2. Borough and City 1865–1938* (Oxford: Oxford University Press, 1952)

Brown, B. H., *The Tariff Reform Movement in Great Britain 1881–1895* (New York: AMS Press, 1966)

Canadine, D., *Pleasures of the Past* (London: Fontana, 1990)

Cash, B., *John Bright. Statesman, Orator, Agitator* (London: I. B. Tauris, 2012)

Chamberlain, A., *Down the Years* (London: Constable, 1935)

—*Politics from Inside. An Epistolary Chronicle 1906–1914* (London: Constable, 1936) Chamberlain, J., 'Manufacture of Iron Wood Screws' in *Birmingham and the Midland Hardware District* ed. by S. Timmins (1866)

Churchill, W., *The Second World War Vol. 1. The Gathering Storm* (London: Cassell, 1948)

Dangerfield, G., *The Damnable Question* (London: Quartet, 1979)

Davenport-Hines, R., *Ettie. The Life and World of Lady Desborough* (London: Weidenfeld & Nicholson, 2008)

Dilks, D., *Neville Chamberlain Vol. 1. Pioneering and Reform 1869–1929* (Cambridge: Cambridge University Press, 1984)

Dixon, J., *Out of Birmingham. George Dixon 1820–98. Father of Free Education* (London: Brewin, 2013)

Dutton, P., *Austen Chamberlain. Gentleman in Politics* (London: Ross Anderson Publications, 1985)

Elletson, D. H., *The Chamberlains* (London: Murray, 1966)

Faber, D., *Munich. The 1938 Appeasement Crisis* (London: Simon & Schuster, 2008)

Feiling, K., *The Life of Neville Chamberlain* (London: Macmillan, 1946)

Fraser, P., *Joseph Chamberlain. Radicalism and Empire 1868–1914* (London: Cassell, 1966)

Fuchser, L. W., *Neville Chamberlain and Appeasement. A Study in the Politics of History* (New York: W. W. Norton, 1982)

Garvin, J. L., *The Life of Joseph Chamberlain Vol. 1, 1836–1835* (London: Macmillan, 1932)

Harris, R., *The Conservatives. A History* (London: Bantam Press, 2011)

Harvey, J., ed., *The Diplomatic Diaries of Oliver Harvey 1937–1940* (London: Collins, 1979)

Home, Lord, *The Way the Wind Blows* (London: Collins, 1976)

Hurst, M. C., *Joseph Chamberlain and West Midland Politics 1886–1895* (Birmingham: Dugdale Society, 1962)

—*Joseph Chamberlain and Liberal Re-Union. The Round Table Conference of 1887* (London: David & Charles, 1967)

Jay, R., *Joseph Chamberlain. A Political Study* (Oxford: Oxford University Press, 1981)

Jenkins, R., *Gladstone* (London: Macmillan, 1995)

—*The Chancellors* (London: Macmillan, 1998)

Lloyd, S. S., *Autobiographical Memoir* (unpublished memoir, with acknowledgements to H. L. Lloyd)

Macleod, I., *Neville Chamberlain* (London: Muller, 1961)

Macmillan, H., *Winds of Change 1914–1939* (London: Macmillan, 1966)

Marsh, P. T., *Joseph Chamberlain. Entrepreneur in Politics* (Yale: Yale University Press, 1994)

—*The Chamberlain Litany. Letters within a Governing Family from Empire to Appeasement* (London: Haus, 2010)

Morgan, K. O., *Consensus and Disunity. The Lloyd George Coalition 1918–1922* (Oxford: Oxford University Press, 1979)

Petrie, C., *The Life and Letters of the Right Honourable Sir Austen Chamberlain Vol. 1* (London: 1939)

Pugh, M., *The Making of Modern British Politics 1867–1945* (London: Blackwell, 2002)

Reynolds, D., *The Long Shadow. The Great War and the Twentieth Century* (London: Simon & Schuster, 2010)

Roberts, A., *The Holy Fox: A Biography of Lord Halifax* (London: Weidenfeld & Nicolson, 1991)

—*Salisbury. Victorian Titan* (London: Weidenfeld & Nicolson, 1999)

Rowland, P., *Lloyd George* (London: Barry & Jenkins, 1975)

Self, R., *The Austen Chamberlain Diary Letters. The Correspondence of Sir Austen Chamberlain with his Sisters Hilda and Ida 1916–1937* (Cambridge: Cambridge University Press, 1995)

—*The Neville Chamberlain Diary Letters Vol. 1. The Making of a Politician 1915–1920* (Aldershot: Ashgate, 2000)

—*The Neville Chamberlain Diary Letters Vol. 2. The Reform Years 1921–1927* (Aldershot: Ashgate, 2000)

—*The Neville Chamberlain Diaries Vol. 3. The Heir Apparent* (Aldershot: Ashgate, 2002)

—*The Neville Chamberlain Diary Letters Vol. 4. The Downing Street Years 1934–1940* (Aldershot: Ashgate, 2005)

—*Neville Chamberlain. A Biography* (Aldershot: Ashgate, 2006)

Skidelsky, R., *Oswald Mosley* (London: Macmillan, 1981)

Smart, N., *Neville Chamberlain* (London: Routledge, 2010)

Steiner, Z., *The Lights that Failed. European International History 1919–1993* (Oxford: Oxford University Press, 2005)

Stevenson, F., *Lloyd George. A Diary by Francis Stevenson* (London: Hutchinson, 1971)

Stewart, G., *Burying Caesar. Churchill, Chamberlain and the Battle for the Tory Party* (London: Phoenix, 1999)

Trevelyan, G. M., *The Life of John Bright* (London: Constable, 1913)

Ward, R., *City, State and Nation. Birmingham's Political History 1830–1940* (Chichester: Phillimore, 2005)

—'Eldred Hallas' (Oxford DNB)

Webb, B., *The Diary of Beatrice Webb Vol. 1. 1873–1892* (London: Virago, 1986)

Williams, F., *A Prime Minister Remembers: Post-War Memories of the Right Hon. Earl Attlee* (London: Heinemann, 1961)

Newspapers

Birmingham Daily Gazette (BDG)
Birmingham Daily Post (BDP)
Daily Mail
The Times